T0389539

Share Engage Educate

Share Engage Educate

SEEding Change for a Better World

By

Vinesh Chandra

BRILL

SENSE

LEIDEN | BOSTON

Cover image: Drawing by Gwenevieve May Chandra (5 years old)

All chapters in this book have undergone peer review.

Library of Congress Cataloging-in-Publication Data

Names: Chandra, Vinesh, author.
Title: Share engage educate : seeding change for a better world / By Vinesh
  Chandra.
Description: Leiden ; Boston : Brill Sense, [2020] | Includes
  bibliographical references and index.
Identifiers: LCCN 2019028591 (print) | LCCN 2019028592 (ebook) | ISBN
  9789004406865 (hardback) | ISBN 9789004400719 (paperback) | ISBN
  9789004406872 (ebook other)
Subjects: LCSH: Educational technology--Developing countries. | Educational
  equalization--Developing countries. | Critical pedagogy--Developing
  countries. | Computer literacy--Developing countries.
Classification: LCC LB1028.3 .C43 2019 (print) | LCC LB1028.3 (ebook) |
  DDC 371.33--dc23
LC record available at https://lccn.loc.gov/2019028591
LC ebook record available at https://lccn.loc.gov/2019028592

Typeface for the Latin, Greek, and Cyrillic scripts: "Brill". See and download: brill.com/brill-typeface.

ISBN 978-90-04-40071-9 (paperback)
ISBN 978-90-04-40686-5 (hardback)
ISBN 978-90-04-40687-2 (e-book)

Copyright 2020 by Koninklijke Brill NV, Leiden, The Netherlands.
Koninklijke Brill NV incorporates the imprints Brill, Brill Hes & De Graaf, Brill Nijhoff, Brill Rodopi,
Brill Sense, Hotei Publishing, mentis Verlag, Verlag Ferdinand Schöningh and Wilhelm Fink Verlag.
All rights reserved. No part of this publication may be reproduced, translated, stored in a retrieval system,
or transmitted in any form or by any means, electronic, mechanical, photocopying, recording or otherwise,
without prior written permission from the publisher.
Authorization to photocopy items for internal or personal use is granted by Koninklijke Brill NV provided
that the appropriate fees are paid directly to The Copyright Clearance Center, 222 Rosewood Drive, Suite
910, Danvers, MA 01923, USA. Fees are subject to change.

This book is printed on acid-free paper and produced in a sustainable manner.

To my granddaughters
Gwenevieve and Margot,
and all other children of the world

∵

Contents

Foreword

This book is not about technology in education. It is, first, a personal account of how the lives of many people, often impoverished, have been transformed through education. It is also Vinesh's journey to discover with students, teachers, and parents how technology can contribute to that transformation and become a lever for change. To me, reading this book has been a fantastic opportunity to address some of my own personal and professional concerns regarding education, and particularly education in developing contexts.

In Vinesh's work, technology is far less important than what people do with or through it. It is a powerful lesson that this book teaches: in education, technology is part of the landscape even in the most remote rural areas in Sub-Saharan Africa and, yet, we have not reached a consensus on how to maximize this significant opportunity for human development.

Books and reports on technology and education in development contexts are either messianic or pessimistic. Messianic messages insist on narratives of leapfrogging but stop at the point where you would expect to understand how to go to scale and read about specific examples of success. Pessimistic accounts tell the real story about how much resources are being spent on technology without any actual impact on learning outcomes and raise an important question: is the investment in technology in education worth?

Vinesh's perspective is different, fresher and paradoxically purer. He begins by assuming that technology is already there, everywhere in different sizes and looks. Then, he documents how people of all ages, students or teachers, individuals he has met all over the world, absorb the technology they find at their fingertips and actively explore pathways to make it work to address their needs. It can be a basic cellular phone or a donated desktop computer – it does not matter. What Vinesh and his team do, in this exploratory context, is to help people to seize real opportunities for personal and social growth. Sometimes he does so, as you will soon read, in surprising and funny ways. But often, as well, raising questions about social and economic inequalities. And this is where Vinesh's book excels: when he tells us a little story that helps us to discover the beauty of human empowerment through capacity development.

It is in this respect that I would claim that Vinesh's work does not align with messianic or pessimistic views but with a humanistic approach that puts the human being and the social environment at the center of this work in education. And then asks questions about how even the least expensive digital device can provide an opportunity for human empowerment.

Let me add a personal note. I met Vinesh years ago in Paris when he decided to come and join us at UNESCO and became instrumental in our activities in teacher training and technology in developing countries. Now we could not live more distant from one another. When his manuscript reached me, my immediate reaction was to feel that I was, yet again, engaging with him in a very lively conversation about the power of education.

For those readers who, unlike me, have not yet had the chance to meet him in person, this book is an opportunity to discover Vinesh. There is more than the educationalist, the thinker, and the practitioner: an exceptional human being, Vinesh is more than a professor or a researcher: he is someone who cares about whoever happens to be in front of him, and willing to embark on a journey of discovery, empowerment and transformation. I was lucky enough to do that face to face while he worked at UNESCO in Paris but the reader, I am sure, will enjoy the conversation with Vinesh as well through this narrative account of his work. Well, I wrote "work", but one of the things that the reader will realize after the first page is that, for that exceptional educator that Vinesh is, the boundaries between work and life are not blurry – they do not exist.

Vinesh does not work in education – he learns and teaches all the time, with or without technology, but always with people. The pages that follow will tell you how he keeps doing it all over the world, and what he has learned from that. For this reason, I am sure that this book will inspire you to explore by yourself how to use technology as a window of opportunity for human empowerment through education.

Francesc Pedró
UNESCO, Paris, France
February 2019

Acknowledgements

To my mind, having a care and concern for others is the highest of the
human qualities.

FRED HOLLOWS

∴

This is my book. However, it is a book about us. Without the support and commitment of the many good men and women who believe in a socially just world, this book would have never eventuated. It has been a real privilege to know you all. You are indeed a significant part of the SEE Project Family and your actions to tackle issues on social justice will be remembered for a long time yet. I am particularly grateful to those of you who have shared your experiences in this book.

I was moved by the unwavering support of our 5-year-old granddaughter Gwenevieve May Chandra for her commitment to designing the cover of the book. Her drawing depicts a school through the eyes of a child who has just started school. Gwenevieve drew what she considered important in a school. These included the building, play equipment, trees, books, computers, tables and chairs and all under a clear blue sky.

I owe a very special thank you to my colleague and friend Dr Francesc Pedro (UNESCO) for writing such a powerful foreword to the book. I was very flattered by his words! I am also very grateful to Zarina Shahban for allowing me to use some of her photos. Simon Gardiner's editing support with the photos and videos was invaluable.

I would like to thank QUT and others who have donated resources that have found new homes in far-fetched places. They may be second hand, but it is how they are used that makes all the difference. The support of the Deans, Heads of Schools and a handful of other staff at QUT has also been invaluable in this project. Most importantly, without the support of Graeme Baguley, many of initiatives described in the book would not have got off the ground.

I would like to thank Dr Donna Tangen, Dr Siti Suriawati Isa (Universiti Putra Malaysia) and Paul Ogil (Brisbane City Council) for their encouragement and time in giving me feedback on my manuscript. I am also grateful to the editing support provided by Shayla Olsen and Di Sesay. Their input has significantly sharpened the quality of this book.

Last but not the least I would like to thank my wife Ramila, my family and friends who spent countless hours to make things happen in various ways.

Thank you for your efforts. I am looking forward to continuing to work with you all by seeding changes for a better world.

Illustrations

Figures

Table

Where Is the Library?

> Educating the mind without educating the heart is no education at all.
> ARISTOTLE

 The video accompanying this chapter is freely available online at https://doi.org/10.6084/m9.figshare.10305047

I followed the head teacher on a tour of my old primary school, revelling in the nostalgia of returning after so many years. There were classrooms where I learned to read; there was the playground where I played with my friends and the flashbacks went on and on. So much had changed for me since I was a student here. Whilst on this tour, impulsively I asked, 'Where is the library?' and he led me to the same room I remembered from my childhood. An empty room, devoid of books, and I realised nothing had changed at all. All this happened in November 2009 when I went to Fiji for a few days to sign off on the paperwork for the sale of our home where four generations of my extended family had once lived. It was like flying into another world. Little did I know that this trip and a visit to my primary school would be a tipping point in my life that would interrogate my "critical consciousness" in a way that I had never experienced before (Freire, 2000). This school was significant because my illiterate and oppressed ancestors were instrumental in laying its foundations. All this was done in the hope that their descendants could get an education and as consequence have a passport to a better life. My education enabled me to move on, yet the world that I had come from seemed to have changed little in terms of educational opportunities.

I was born in Fiji but now I am a very proud Australian citizen. I have lived in this country for more than half my life. Back in 1987, I was very fortunate to have been given an opportunity by the Department of Education in our state of

© KONINKLIJKE BRILL NV, LEIDEN, 2020 | DOI:10.1163/9789004406872_001

Queensland to teach mathematics and science in high schools. This was how I was able to migrate to Australia with my wife Ramila and our son Ravi. The family has grown since – we now have another son Ronesh, two daughter-in laws Jo and Emily and two lovely granddaughters Gwenevieve and Margot. Throughout my teaching, I have been very passionate about using all sorts of different technologies in my classrooms. Quite rightly, technology is only a tool, but like all other tools, when used appropriately, it can deliver highly meaningful outcomes. Technologies are enablers and they can empower users. I took this interest further in my doctoral thesis by investigating the impact of a web-based environment on physics and science students in high schools. The findings of my study reaffirmed my beliefs about the usefulness of digital technologies in classrooms. Upon the completion of this study, I gained employment at the Queensland University of Technology (QUT) in Brisbane. My work is primarily focussed on teacher training and research.

I have always been very passionate about creating educational opportunities for the underprivileged and the marginalised. One can never predict what a chance in life can lead to. Take for example the legendary Black American Actor Sidney Poitier. He was illiterate and came from the Bahamas to work as a kitchen hand in restaurants in New York. In his late teens, a workmate with a big heart took him under his wings and taught him how to read and write. This opportunity propelled him to new heights and his name will be forever etched in the history books of Hollywood. One of my heroes who has created remarkable opportunities for the often forgotten is the late Professor Fred Hollows. He specialised in ophthalmology and strongly believed in a world where no person should be unnecessarily blind. To fulfil this vision, Professor Hollows broke off from the shackles of his privileged work environment and stepped into the world of the poor and the underprivileged. He developed ingenious and creative low-cost solutions to tackle the problem of blindness. The work that he started nearly five decades ago has continued and to-date has restored vision in more than two and half million people in 25 countries. While not all of us can be like Professor Hollows, we can certainly extend a helping hand to make the world a better place for all its citizens. All that the underprivileged and the marginalised sometimes need is an opportunity, a chance and you never know what they can become.

I believe that things happen for a reason. Little did I know that the question "Where is the library?" would start a chain reaction. Books are technologies from yesterday and as Dr Seuss rightly said: "The more that you read, the more things you will know. The more that you learn, the more places you'll go". But not everyone has a passport to access books. Why are many children in developing countries still deprived of this opportunity? How do we create opportunities and make the world an even playing field for all children who are born into it? What can we do so that all children get a chance to use not only the technologies of yesterday but also the technologies of today?

This book is an autoethnography (Wall, 2008) and presents some of the real-world outcomes of the chain reaction that followed after my visit to my former primary school. It provides accounts of the initiatives that I have undertaken with the assistance of a few good men and women, and my students, to create opportunities for teachers and their students in eight developing countries. Nearly all these schools were in rural and remote areas who catered for children from low socio-economic backgrounds. Throughout this book I draw upon the works of Freire, Giroux and others who have made significant impact in the field of critical pedagogy. Freire viewed pedagogies as the "knowledge, skills and social relations" (Giroux, 2010, p. 715) one needed to be a critical citizen. He viewed critical thinking as a tool for self-determination and civic engagement by weaving the future with the past, and the present. Critical pedagogy takes this one step further by strongly focussing on empowering citizens "to seek justice" and "to seek emancipation" (Burbules & Berk, 1999, p. 51). More importantly, the emphasis is on bringing about changes through collective actions that work towards creating a more socially just world. Paulo Freire is one of the pioneers in this field. He is best known for his work that was focussed on promoting adult literacy amongst Brazilian peasants (Freire, 2000). He reasoned that being literate not only opened doors to read and write but it also had a positive impact on confidence and self-esteem (Burbules & Berk, 1999). In the 21st century one also needs to be digitally literate. Our initiatives in underprivileged schools targeted both the language and the digital literacy agenda. This book highlights experiential episodes that show how critical reflection and interpretation of situations led to actions that seeded changes and, in the process, unveiled opportunities of hope (Burbules & Berk, 1999; Giroux, 1988). The flow on benefits of our actions were bi-directional. The schools benefitted and so did we in some unique and unseen ways.

1   A Trip down Memory Lane

To understand the thread which led to these connections, shedding some light on where I grew up and some memories of my schooling experiences is important. Our home was in a rural settlement called Cuvu (pronounced *thu-vu*) near the town of Sigatoka on the southern coast of Viti Levu; the main island in the Fiji Group. Attached to our dwelling was a small store. In terms of business, the store had seen some good and some very bad days. There have always been eight or so other stores that serve the community. When I lived there, the population at most would have been a few hundred. The majority of the people lived in very simple dwellings. A prominent feature in many homes was a framed coloured photo of Queen Elizabeth II. These were hung with "pride" because Fiji was a British colony. The government provided the free coloured prints of the Queen and the people had them framed. There were few utilities. There was no town water and most people had to rely on water drawn from wells either with a bucket or a water pump. The close proximity of the village to the ocean affected the water table which impacted on the salinity of the well water. Consequently, most of us relied on rainwater tanks for drinking. Electricity came to our village when I was nine years old. Apart from newspapers, radio was the sole source of information and entertainment. Radio broadcast from the two stations was transmitted in three languages at set times – English, Fijian and Hindi. They started transmission at about 6 o'clock in the morning and concluded at 11 o'clock each night.

There were very few places for adults or children to 'hang out'. The famous Cuvu beach was a place that people would visit every now and then. The western beach culture was almost non-existent. Many people could not swim. There were no opportunities to learn swimming anywhere because no one was qualified to provide lessons. There were no swimming pools. Some learnt to swim the hard way. I learnt to swim when I was just about to drown. This incident happened as I was trying to cross a fast-moving current between the mainland and a small island. I now know what the idiom 'sink or swim' literally means. Apart from the beach, there were no playgrounds for children, or libraries, or outside school activities. We had to find our own strategies to keep ourselves occupied with some traditional games that did not require any specialist hardware. All we needed was some creativity. We could not afford expensive toys either. However, we were creative and made our own toys with coconut fronds, old car tyres, and used metal containers. In the process we unknowingly developed our knowledge of gears, pulleys, levers, and other STEM concepts. We often learnt some of the tricks of making these gadgets from our more able peers. Each gadget became a hands-on project that was connected to the real world and facilitated learning by doing. Thus, I understood the fundamentals of John Dewey's idea of project-based learning long before I learnt about it at university (Maida, 2011). Unsurprisingly none of these rich learning experiences were promoted in school.

When I was growing up in Cuvu, the people were mainly of Fijian and Indian origin. On the timeline of human habitation, the indigenous Fijian people (also known as the *itaukei*) have lived in the Fiji Islands for thousands of years. The

National Genographic Project (https://genographic.nationalgeographic.com/ human-journey/), has used advanced DNA analysis to understand the origins and migratory patterns of the human race. Their findings provide credence to the "Out of Africa" model which proposes that humans began their journeys to the rest of the world as one race (and presumably with one or no religion!) more than 60,000 years ago. Like many of us, the Fijians left the Great Rift Valley in Western Africa and made their way to the Fiji Islands via Asia and South Asia. On this time scale, the Indians are relatively newcomers. After Fiji became a British colony in 1874, more than 60,000 Indians were brought into this colony as indentured labourers. They brought their diverse religions and culture with them. Most chose to call Fiji their home and never returned to India – even for a visit to see their families and friends. As a descendent of these indentured labourers, this is how my life began in Cuvu.

Going back to my village made me feel like Paulo Freire (Freire, 1983) when he went back to his home in Brazil. Like Freire, "I stepped on the same ground on which I first stood up, on which I had first walked, run, began to talk, and learned to read" (p. 8). I was back in the home that I had come from. I had fond memories of this world which first "presented itself to my understanding to reading it" (p. 8). Through this time, my reading went a lot deeper and included many messages. While Freire left his home after his visit "feeling the joy of someone who has re-encountered loved ones" (p. 8), I felt sad that I was also saying my final good bye, not just to my home and my village, but my country as well. As I signed on the dotted line to seal the deal for the sale of our home, it was like severing the umbilical cord with my country of birth. Despite many challenges and obstacles, Fiji played a significant role in shaping my destiny. In my mind I was convinced that on my next visit I would be a real tourist. And like all other tourists, I too would be sitting on a beach, gazing over the pristine waters of the Pacific Ocean and sipping a glass (or two) of overpriced imported red wine! Once I signed off on the paperwork in the lawyer's office in town, I went back home to congratulate the new owners. Like us, they too were descendants of indentured labourers. It was a moment of joy because another family had moved in. They were going to write new chapters of their lives as we did. In fact, what was even more satisfying was that it was an extended family with members from four generations. It was very much like our family as we were many years earlier. The new owners were once sugarcane farmers in a neighbouring village called *Ulusila*. They had leased 'their farming land' from the local Fijian landowners. After many years of toiling, their land was 'reserved'. Almost 90% of the land is owned by the indigenous Fijians (Naidu & Reddy, 2002). This land can never be bought or sold – it can only be leased. Most of the leaseholders are Indians. Depending on the type of the arrangements, leases can last from 5 to 99 years. When the land is reserved, families have to move on and the land reverts to the Fijian landowners. There is no compensation for any capital improvements that the tenants have made on the land. Unless they have saved up and made alternative arrangements for this 'rainy day', families can become landless. For many families this is the case and over the years there has been a steady rise in squatter settlements on the outskirts of the urban centres (Barr, 2012). Luckily, the future trajectory for the family that bought our home was going to be a different one and I was happy for them.

Before I left my place of birth, I had an urge to go visit my primary school for one last time. It was almost like concluding the final chapter on this stage of my life. This is how I met the school head teacher. In our village, the school played a very important role because it was one of the few places where children had a chance to 'catch up' during school hours. The school grounds were out of bounds except for the teachers and their families. Both the primary and the secondary schools were a stone's throw away from my home. They were adjacent to each other, sharing facilities like the oval. I completed my eight years of primary and four years of secondary schooling here. I always felt that I had a stronger connection with the primary school because my ancestors played a pivotal role in the conception and the construction of the school.

As I made my way to the school, walking on the side of the old Queens Road (Figure 1.1), which had deteriorated to a state of disrepair, my journey of recollection and reflection began. Most of the children who went to school with me were from families where one or both parents were either farmers, service industry workers, labourers, or unemployed. Some of the children were fortunate – their parents worked in either the local five-star Fijian resort or for the Fiji Sugar Corporation. While they were not employed in executive or senior positions, their low-prestige jobs ensured regular income for their dependents. My dad was employed as a storeman at the resort for a few years in the mid 1960's and his starting hourly wage was 35 cents an hour (about 0.17 USD). After a couple of years, there was much reason to celebrate when the hourly wage went up to 50 cents. Many families could not afford to buy cars, so the local buses were the best option for transport. Short distance travel was covered either on horseback, bicycles, or on foot. Almost all children from the neighbouring farming communities walked bare feet, up to 5 km each way, on unsealed feeder roads to get to school. Thus, most people in and around Cuvu were not highly educated. The level of parental education, their incomes, and occupations are three common measures of socioeconomic status (SES) (Hattie, 2008). These three measures collectively and individually impact on students' achievement. When I was growing up, I had no realisation of my low

FIGURE 1.1   Small stores along the old Queens Road

SES status. Now I do, and without doubt my parents and their attitudes towards education had a lot to do with where I have got to in my life.

I was not a big fan of school and I cannot say that I liked most of my teachers. Nonetheless, even today I value the significance of their input in my life. Whenever I saw one of my teachers, I always crossed the road to say hello to them. On this visit, I was particularly keen to take photos of some of the memorable moments of my time in my primary school. It was going to be memorabilia that I would leave behind for my grandchildren and future generations. As I entered the head teacher's office, he welcomed me with open arms. On the wall behind his desk was a photo of the founding members of the school management committee (Figure 1.2). In some ways, the photo depicts how they needed to dress up in order to fit in with the ruling class. Even today, hardly anyone dresses up like this unless they really have to. The absence of women in the committee speaks volumes about the patriarchal social order that existed at that time. Regrettably this trend has continued in rural and remote areas.

For as long as I can remember, this photo has always had a place in the head teacher's office. It was particularly significant to me this time as a grown up because two of the founding fathers of the school were my ancestors. They were my great grandfather (*aajua*) and my grandfather (*aaja*). My great grandfather was the president and my grandfather was the treasurer of the founding school committee. My great grandfather arrived in Fiji as an indentured

FIGURE 1.2   The founding members of the school management committee Seated (L–R): Ram Jiwan Sharma, Bechan (*aajua*), Raghunandan Singh, Sarju Prasad Standing (L–R): Ram Charitra Sharma (head teacher), Shri Ram (*aaja*), Ram Prasad

labourer with my great grandmother from Northern India while my grandfather was born in Fiji. Next to this photo was a list of the people who initially donated money to set up the school. This is how many schools in Fiji were set up and as a consequence more than 95% are community owned and run. Religious groups and organisations manage a significant number of schools. While the people in the photo in the head teacher's office may not have been literate, they believed in the value of education for their future generations. Many from that era had lived a life of oppression (Freire, 2000) and they perceived education as a passport to a better life. This mantra was also drilled and instilled in all of us. So, the way forward for future generations was through the building of schools. The photo in the head teacher's office of the founding school committee has always made me feel very proud.

School had ended for the day and as I walked around with the head teacher, many memories flooded my headspace. When I was growing up there were no kindergartens or early learning centres in my village. Most of the learning occurred at home or in the community. My mum was my first teacher. Her educational opportunities ended in primary school. While my mum had the ambition of becoming a nurse, her parents who were illiterate farmers did not allow her to pursue this career path because they strongly believed that a woman's place was in the home. She would tell my sister and I, stories that she heard from her days in school. For example, Mum told us the story of emu *chidiya* (bird) – it could not fly and was the second largest bird in the world. We did not have any images of this weird sounding creature. The only birds that I saw regularly were Indian mynas and doves. My imagination did not help either to visualise this strange bird. I cannot recall what it looked like in my mind. Mum also used the back of an old shop signboard, painted in a dark turquoise colour, as our 'blackboard' for learning to write numbers and recite basic spelling. In the evening after she finished her household chores, we would sit next to a *dhiberi batti* (kerosene lantern) for our lessons. One of the lessons that she taught me was to never put my foot on books because it was disrespectful. Every now and then she would remind us that, "If you do not respect a book you will not get *vidiya* (knowledge)". I have carried on this philosophy all my life – I have never knowingly stepped on a book or written text. While I may not have understood the value of my mum's lessons, sub-consciously she was teaching me about importance of education. Home is after all the first learning environment and parents are the first teachers in any child's life.

At the age of about six, most children started Class 1 – it was the start of their formal education. When I was five, the head teacher of the school at the time who was a good friend of my grandfather stretched his friendship by letting me join Class 1 on an ad-hoc basis. It was meant to be a transition from home to school. I believed that the experience did not add any value to my education and I saw it as a waste of time, so I eventually found a good reason for not attending school – at least in the short term. A rumour had started in the village that an old man drove around in a black car and kidnapped little children. Apparently, this old man then took the children home, extracted their liver, and made medicines out of it. At the age of five, I did not quite understand why my body needed a liver. I did not have the inclination to ask questions about it or what happened to children after their livers were removed. Neither did I have the intelligence to query the motives or interests of the people who were spreading these rumours. Young children take rumours as the truth. They think as objectivists rather than constructivists (Richardson, Best & Bromley, 1991) and I was no different. Nonetheless, the liver sounded like something that was important and not worth losing. Fortunately, I managed to convince my parents that school attendance was not important if my liver was on the line. I stopped my 'work experience' in school and my life got back to normal in the short term.

As we went past my Class 1 room, I recalled the enrolment figures. In Class 1 there were two classes with 92 students in total. In Class 2, this number dropped to 84. Students had to pass internal assessments to proceed to the next level. In Class 1, if you could read a few words in Hindi, you were good to move to Class 2.

So, some of my contemporaries who failed Class 1 obviously could not read the words. A handful may have left because their parents could not afford the school fees. They had to either repeat Class 1 or ended up leaving school altogether. The Hindi we learnt was different to what we were used to. The spoken and the written text taught in schools was based on the Hindi from mainland India. The "Fiji" Hindi had no place in the curriculum. For example a question such as "How many men were there?" would translate to *Kitna admi raha* in Fiji Hindi. The mainland Indian equivalent would be; *Kitne admi the*. Some of the vocabulary was India-centric and quite foreign to us. Being a British colony at the time, schools had no choice but to embrace Western intellectual models, which were academic in content and orientation. Likewise, the cultural capital that was embodied amongst the locals in the form of traditional knowledge and skills learnt at home and from community elders had no significance in the classrooms (Bourdieu, 1973). Some of the boys in my class who were dropouts in primary school would have begun their apprenticeships on their family farms. Others would wander around aimlessly until they reached an age where they could find some employment. Girls on the other hand who left school early would be trained in household chores by their mothers, elder female siblings, and relatives until they were old enough to be married. For some of the girls, their roles and purpose in life as married women would be to fulfil the needs of their male-chauvinistic husbands, produce children, and be obedient daughters-in-law in their extended families. Like previous generations, these boys and girls had also become a part of a cycle of poverty and despair.

I had an interesting bullying experience in Class 1 which I have never forgotten. Even though our family was financially challenged, my parents always went out of their way to ensure that I had all the basic resources for schoolwork. I always had chalk which I carried in a small tin container. These tins once contained tobacco that was imported from the UK and by today's standards had very high levels of nicotine and tar (Russell, 1976). My maternal grandmother used to roll them into cigarettes and have a puff every now and then with no understanding of first, second, or third hand smoke. But I always looked forward to receiving the empty containers from her for carrying chalk and for making toys. At school, I was pretty nifty in the chalk department because I also had coloured chalk. Thus, I became a target of two bullies. One of them had failed Class 1 the previous year and consequently he had a good understanding of how the establishment ran. The other one was his sidekick. They would take me into a corner and snatch the coloured chalk from me and this action posited for some time. The bullying ended when I whinged to the assistant head teacher. Both the bullies did not complete primary education. In adulthood, one became a handyman while the other ended up working as a kitchen-hand at the local resort. Research has shown that one of the reasons why children become bullies is to show off to their mates (Thomson & Arora, 1991). They probably do not have any other skills and talents that they can feel good about. Consequently, they fall back on "aggression and a carefully controlled level of violence to demonstrate their dominance over another child who is not a member of the bully's social group" (p. 11). In hindsight, the bullies I dealt with may also have been victims of their circumstances. Their parents could not provide them with coloured chalk and I became their soft target. I have met them both a few times since and we communicate as though there was no yesterday. But before it is too late, I will have a man to man chat about the time they stole my chalk.

My walk around the school also reminded me of corporal punishment – it was rife in those days. Teachers got away with it because they were always held in high esteem. Unlike the West, teachers in Fiji and many other developing countries are highly respected and never questioned. This is the case even today. In many instances, they may also be one of the few in rural and remote communities who are educated. With their guaranteed respect comes their unauthorised power for abuse which is sometimes unleashed physically on the children. These powerless children do not have a voice. If they complained to their parents, they were quite likely to get into more trouble. Parents often perceive teachers' actions as quite legitimate, that they are undertaken for a good reason and for the good of the children. Even if parents chose to pursue a matter, they would not know where to start and who would listen to them? Even if someone listened to them, would they be heard? If they stirred the pot too much, it was most likely to negatively impact on the educational future of their children. So, the most logical stance for most parents was to act like ostriches and bury their heads in the sand in the hope that their child gets a different teacher the following year. More recently, the Fijian government has advocated 'zero tolerance' on corporal punishment. But there are grey areas within the existing laws. For example, Article 41 in the Fijian constitution protects children from "abuse, neglect, harmful cultural practices, any form of violence, inhumane treatment and punishment, and hazardous or exploitative labour", while Article 11 only prohibits "severe punishment" (Republic of Fiji, n.d.). However, one might ask: When does punishment became severe? But Fiji is not alone. Child maltreatment is a complex global issue and it largely stems from the fact that internationally there is "a lack of common definitions" and inconsistencies in "the way in which child maltreatment is classified, reported, recorded and managed" (Brown, Lei, & Strydom, 2017, p. 247). As a side, I was quite surprised that in non-government schools in our state of Queensland (which is in a developed country), teachers can legally use "a reasonable force towards a child by way of correction, discipline, management or control" (Section 280 of the Crimes Act, 1899) (Matthews, 2017, para. 2). Thus, even in developed countries like Australia, corporal punishment is still an option that teachers can pursue to manage students.

Whenever I encountered 'sticky' situations in school I always opted to take the corporal punishment rather than go home and complain. It was shameful enough to be at the centre of this heinous act in front of peers but I also knew that if I complained to my parents, the punishment that my mum would dish out would be far worse. My dad was a lot cooler when it came to things like this. We understood each other a lot better. Even though I am a Hindu, I was unknowingly following the teachings from the bible which states that; "I tell you not to resist an evil person. If someone slaps you on your right cheek, turn to him the other also" (Matthew 5:39). As a consequence, my mantra was that whatever happened in school stayed in school unless it was something to brag about at home. I was quite happy to take any punishment that was dished out to me. Some of my peers suffered quite badly at the hands of their teachers. They too adopted a similar attitude to corporal punishment.

There is one personal experience of corporal punishment that I will never forget. When I was in Class 2, there were two classes. I was in Class 2B and I had a licenced teacher. She was not formally trained. Their educational experience would be three or four years in high school. The leading teacher taught the other class. I will call him Osama because he was known for terrifying his students. Every morning Osama would bring both classes together and rave about something that he must have felt was important. Most times, like others, I could not work out what Osama was saying but we all pretended that we did. It was possibly the content of his slurred speech, that many of us could not connect with, that forced us into this zombie state. Halfway through Class 2 we started writing in books. We had big fat pencils and we would practise our writing skills in books that had lines drawn which to me appeared miles apart. Apparently, these exercise books were developed in a way to help students with their writing skills. To this day I do not know how they worked and what was the logic behind how these special exercise books and pencils were meant to work in tandem. I remember the time when I first wrote in this special book with the big fat pencil. The next morning, we turned up for our morning briefing and listened obediently as Osama delivered his morning sermon. Most times at these briefings I was there in body but not in the mind – I was half asleep. On this particular morning Osama called my name and he asked me to step forward. I felt quite good. For once I thought that I had done something right. As I marched forward with possibly 84 pairs of big brown googly-eyed students watching me, I did not realise that I was a dead man walking. As I got closer, Osama assumed his terrorist stance and slapped me so hard that to this day I can see his ugly look and his black hand approaching my face. Apparently, I had done something wrong but that was not all. He ripped the first page that I had ever written in my life and threw the book away. Years later when I had the courage, I approached Osama to explain his actions. He did not even recall the incident. Perhaps he had hit so many children in his career that he had lost track. I did not tell my mum about this incident until I was in my 40's. This was an example of how the oppressed-oppressor scenario plays out in the real world (Freire, 2000). It still operates in many education systems where teachers have absolute power and children have no voice. I assume Osama was providing me with some feedback through physical force. There is no doubt that feedback is one of the most powerful influences on student achievement (Hattie, 2008). However, the feedback needs to inform the learner on what he has demonstrated and what else he needs to do to fulfil the needs of the task (Sadler, 1989). In this instance, I realised that my response to the task was inadequate, but I did not know what I had done wrong nor what I could do to improve my effort. As has been shown time and time again, the deliberate use of pain does not necessarily bring about behavioural change. Even to this day, my handwriting is quite bad. I do not have words to express my gratitude to the inventor of computer word-processors.

I began my journey of rote learning in Class 3. Upon reflection, I can now see how the "banking model" proposed by Paulo Freire (2000) played out in my life when I was a student. In this model, education is,

> an act of depositing, in which the students are the depositories and the teacher is the depositor. Instead of communicating, the teacher issues communiques and makes deposits which the students patiently receive, memorise, and repeat. This is the "banking" concept of education, in which the scope of action allowed to the students extends only as far as receiving, filing, and storing the deposits. (p. 72)

To implement such an approach, the teacher played the role of "a narrating subject" and the student a "listening object". From time to time, the narration occurred in the form of notes that were written on the board which we were expected to very neatly copy into our exercise books. The content of the narration that had to be memorised often conveyed little meaning to us:

> The outstanding characteristic of this narrative education, then, is the sonority of words, not their transforming power. "Four times four is sixteen; the capital of Para is Belem". The student records, memorises, and

repeats these phrases without perceiving what four times four really means, or realising the true significance of "capital" in the affirmation "the capital of Para is Belem", that is, what Belem means for Para and what Para means for Brazil. (Freire, 2000, p. 71)

To illustrate this point, by the end of term 1 in Class 3, I had memorised the times tables up to 12. My Chinese friend, who lived next door to us, and I were the first in class to achieve this life-changing feat. Without any understanding, I could easily regurgitate $3 \times 4=12$, $11 \times 2=22$ etc. It was many years later that I realised what three times four really meant. Quite a number of my peers who struggled with memorising were labelled as 'no good' in mathematics. I wonder what would have happened to these children if the teacher had taken the initiative to demonstrate what the times tables meant in real life. No sophisticated teaching aids would have been needed – just some pebbles from the garden would have done the job. By putting four lots of four pebbles would have not only demonstrated the answer, but also bridged a connection to real life. Drill sessions led by the teacher to memorise the times tables were very common in the classroom. Little did I know that I must have been a 'good container' for storing and re-extracting the content that was being drilled by the teacher:

> Narration (with the teacher as narrator) leads the students to memorise mechanically the narrated content. Worse yet, it turns them into "containers", into "receptacles" to be "filled" by the teacher. The more completely she fills the receptacles, the better a teacher she is. The more meekly the receptacles permit themselves to be filled, the better students they are. (Freire, 2000, p. 72)

While I was very proficient with the times tables, I struggled with division even though multiplication and division are opposite operations. I could not understand how nine divided by two equalled four with a remainder of one. I am sure that part of the problem was that I did not understand what the terms "division" and "remainder" meant. I remember the first time we were 'taught' how to do division in class 3. We went straight to division with remainders. At the end of this first lesson we were given a formative test that had seven questions on basic division. I only got one question correct. I wonder how it would have impacted on the outcome if the teacher had explained division using the pebbles from the garden. "Okay children, what happens when nine pebbles are put in groups of two?" The underlying problem here was that I did not understand the syntax of multiplication and division and how they connected with each other.

I must have also been good at regurgitating the content because from Class 4 onwards my academic fortunes changed. Twice a year, we were assessed through verbal and written assessments. Most of the tests relied on our ability to recall content. The marks we achieved in each subject were aggregated to generate a total. All students in the class were then ranked on the basis of these totals. I came either first or second from Class 4 onwards until I got into senior secondary classes. At the end of Class 5, I came first, and I was promoted straight into Class 7. Once again, I was the top of the class and came first. In Class 8 my report card read – *Character – Good, Attendance – Good, Class teacher's comments – Obedient, cheerful, intelligent, responsible. Has done very good work throughout the year.* Class 8 was also the final year of my primary schooling and about half who had started together in Class 1 progressed to Class 8. We all had to do the Fiji Secondary Entrance Exam. It was our first external exam that was set centrally, and we had to complete four subject tests – Mathematics, English Composition and Letter Writing, English Comprehension and Grammar, and General Studies. Each was marked out of 100 and to pass the exam we had to achieve at least 200 out of 400 marks to qualify for secondary school. Primary schools and teachers were judged by the percentage of students who passed this Secondary Entrance exam. Teachers would prepare their students for months through trial tests. For some children, their education career ended when they failed and chose not to repeat Class 8. For those who passed, they had a chance to continue their education. I applied to go to a selective government school. While this school was about three hours on the bus from home, it was far better resourced with well qualified teachers. It also had boarding facilities and for this reason I was prepared to go to this school. There were only five government boarding schools in the country and three were exclusively built for indigenous Fijian students. The other two schools were more multicultural in composition and open to enrol pupils from all ethnic backgrounds including indigenous Fijians. However, the Fijian Ministry of Education botched up my Secondary Entrance Exam results. In General Studies, I scored 84% but my mark was recorded as 48%. This impacted on my chances to enrol at the boarding school because it took the education department more than five months to rectify the problem. By the time this was done, there was no room for me at the boarding school. Years later I realised that if you had some special connections with the principal, spaces were magically created in the school. This lack of transparency was a common issue. The working class were voiceless and did not have the power to question the actions of those in higher echelons of society. Even in the twentieth century not much has changed but Fiji is not alone. This is rife throughout the world – it is almost ingrained in human DNA (Olken & Pande, 2012). I was left with no choice but to complete my next phase of education from Form 3 to Form 6 at the secondary school across the oval from my primary school.

The walk around the school brought back the past in a way that I had not anticipated. It could have also been a coincidence, but the stars appeared to have lined up as well. The head teacher told me that there was going to be a school management committee meeting and he invited me to stay on. While my initial intention was to spend a few minutes at the school and leave, something was forcing me to stay. I agreed to join the people and it was the first time I would attend such a meeting in Fiji. It was held in my Class 4 room (Figure 1.3).

FIGURE 1.3   My class 4 room

This was the room where my fortunes changed, and I catapulted from an average performer to the top of the class. The room had changed very little. All the desks were front-facing towards the blackboard with the teacher's table in the right hand corner of the room. There was little evidence of any quality resources and the room was in need of a makeover. There were no computers, interactive whiteboards, or data projectors that I have become so accustomed to. I could visualise myself sitting in the room as a Class 4 student. As I pursued this nostalgic path, I recalled the names of some of my mates and wondered what had happened to them. I knew some of them had passed away and others had left the area to work in urban centres. The committee members slowly drifted in and I was pleasantly surprised to meet them. Some of them were my friends from my school days. Within this group were farmers, taxi drivers, shopkeepers, labourers, and some who were unemployed. They were the ones who were left behind because they did not have the qualifications, wealth, or the opportunities to move to greener pastures. But like my ancestors, they too had a good heart and a belief that education can have a positive impact on future generations. As the meeting got underway, the agenda items were discussed, and I had an opportunity to fathom the challenges that the school committee was facing. One of the items discussed was the annual prize-giving day. It has been a part of the school tradition for generations. The students who came first, second, and third in their classes (on the basis of their aggregate totals) are awarded books as prizes. I received some of these prizes in my time. However, a major conundrum for the committee was how to raise funds to buy books for the prize winners. One of the ideas was to seek donations for some groceries that could be used to cook food that would be sold at a food stall. The members of the committee debated for some time on the selling price of the plates of food. Some members believed that levying a price of two dollars (about 1 USD) to feed a family of four to be quite unaffordable. I put my hand up and offered a donation to help them offset the cost of buying books as prizes for the annual school event. By the time the meeting was over, I had a good appreciation of how difficult things were in terms of running a school in this part of the world.

Perhaps the most baffling, confronting, and mind-blowing part of my visit was the empty space that I saw when I asked the head teacher, "Where is the library?" This empty space used to be my library when I was student. Wow! I did not have the privilege of going into a library to browse, and to borrow books as a student because there were no books to borrow. I thought that the world had moved on. The empty space was not a sight that I had anticipated. School libraries in the West have existed for almost 200 years. But in the 21st century, we have a significant number of children who have yet to step in a library to browse and borrow books that take them beyond the school curriculum. These are the children who live in another world! Albert Einstein correctly pointed out that "the only thing you have to know absolutely, is the location of the library". I then asked the head teacher about computers and digital technologies. Both print and digital resources can facilitate a heightened level of learning. His body language and his response said it all. "Yes, we would like some technologies but for us it is no more than a dream".

2   **Lesson Learnt – Sometimes Things Happen for a Reason**

The visit to the school jogged many memories. My observations together with the chat that I had with the head teacher and the school committee members made me realise that the school had changed little since I was a student here. There was no comparison between this school and the Australian schools I knew. As I left the school, I kept thinking about the vision of my ancestors and the many other illiterate commoners in my village who were instrumental in setting up this school. A string of questions kept popping up in my mind. How do I add value to this institution that my ancestors worked so hard to set up? What can I do to improve the quality of education at this school? What sustainable strategies will lead to new teaching and learning opportunities for teachers and students? I felt quite challenged because I considered myself as an experienced educator. What is the real value of my education if I cannot make a difference in a school that gave me the chance to be educated? Questions like this kept pushing me towards a tipping point and interrogated my "critical consciousness" where I was "reading" this world by reflecting on my past and on the current situation (Freire, 2000). I was in my own state of 'praxis' where my reflections continuously challenged me on what actions I could take to remedy the situation. It was a case of social justice that I could not walk away from.

The Vision of the Oppressed

> It is indeed a desirable thing to be well-descended, but the glory belongs
> to our ancestors.
>
> PLUTARCH (c.46–c.120)

The video accompanying this chapter is freely available online
at https://doi.org/10.6084/m9.figshare.10305080

Schools, especially in the developed world, are taken for granted because governments play a significant role in setting them up. They inject a lot of money in capital works. But in the developing world, establishing and sustaining such an entity is a ginormous challenge because the local communities have to contribute financially. Given the situation of many people in such contexts, making financial contributions to schools is a big call. As a consequence, in some rural and remote areas, there are no schools. This probably explains why more than 100 million primary school-aged children are deprived of education in these countries (Ricci, 2015). Band-Aid solutions to improving the quality of education in poorer communities can be problematic without an understanding of the context. In this chapter, I present the historical background to why my ancestors established the primary school in our village. This is an important step in critical thinking (Giroux, 2010). It highlights the value that these illiterate people placed on education, which has enabled many of their descendants to lead a life less impacted by oppression (Freire, 2000). As indentured labourers who were brought to Fiji by the British, under-educated, bereft of control of their own destinies, they had their share of burdens and barriers. Despite never being given this same opportunity, they selflessly prioritised their children's and future descendants' chances of getting an education. The indentured labourers probably also perceived education as the single most important asset that

© KONINKLIJKE BRILL NV, LEIDEN, 2020 | DOI:10.1163/9789004406872_002

one could have for an oppression-free life. Nearly a hundred years since their arrival, my visit to the world they left behind in India demonstrated the opportunities that education can create in people's lives. For many in my village, it all began with the setting up of a primary school. This chapter presents the string of events, mostly unintended that foreshadowed the setting up of the school.

1   The Indian Indenture System

Between 1879 and 1916, a recorded 60,965 Indians, predominately from the poorer states of India, left for Fiji as indentured labourers to work on sugar cane plantations. They 'signed' an agreement, which was written in English and drawn by their British rulers, with their thumbprints to serve their labour contracts for a period of five years. As history states, these illiterate Indians could not say the word 'agreement', and they coined the term *girmit* to describe it. Thus, anyone who signed this agreement became a *girmiteer*. The majority opted to stay in Fiji once their indenture agreements expired. They called Fiji home and catalysed a change that transformed the country forever. Many went one step further and put their paltry savings towards the building of schools. My ancestors built Naidovi Indian School – the primary school that I attended as a child.

The seeds of the indenture system were sown in the early 1600s when the British East India Company arrived in India. They successfully convinced the Moguls, who were the rulers at that time, that they had the capacity to positively influence the country's economy. Fifteen years later, they set up factories and started to trade with the outside world (Tharoor, 2017). As the company spread its tentacles, it set up its own army, which fought in several wars during this era. In the 1700s, as the Mogul Empire began to crumble, control opportunities emerged for the British, and they stepped in. While there was significant interest from various countries in Europe to rule India, the British knew how to play their cards. Through their game of divide and conquer, they got the local movers and shakers on their side to take control of the country piece by piece. They fought with the French to take control of South India (Tharoor, 2017). Amongst the string of British-motivated events in the 1700s was the setting up of businesses and political transactions. Some of these were highly contentious and questionable. The establishment of the British capital in Calcutta and wars with various Mogul rulers were notable events which, signaled that a change was in the air. Strategic alliances with the maharajahs also paid dividends. The start of the 1800s was marked by the British capture of Delhi and large parts of India, and by 1835, English was made the official language and western education was introduced (Tharoor, 2017). Other new changes also started to take shape. A 'doctrine of lapse' was also introduced that enabled the British to take over a state when a ruler died without an heir apparent. By the mid-1850s, the Great Indian Peninsula Railway Company, with its economic and engineering roots in Britain, began building railways to connect Bombay (Mumbai) with other parts of the country including Madras (Chennai) and Calcutta (Kolkata). The trains facilitated the transport of goods such as cotton, silk, opium, sugar, and spices to the main ports for export. By this stage, the British East India Company was seriously taking charge of the country.

The Indian Rebellion of 1857, or the Sepoy Mutiny, was a turning point for both Britain and India. This mutiny was an uprising of the locals against British rule. This event is believed to have generated more discussion and debate than any other single event in the history of the country (Brodkin, 1972). Marshall (2017) described it as an age of ill-considered reform that was followed by the age of iron conservatism. The latter provoked a "reaction" and a form of "nationalism out of which modern India was to be born" (para. 5). Britain was able to draw on its military might from home to quell the local uprising. This outcome buoyed the empire's confidence. A year later, Britain assumed full control and India became one of its many colonies. It was yet another addition to the empire's collection of countries. India was a good catch because it had the potential to enhance the economic and political prosperity of the empire. It has been suggested Britain either invaded or had a conflict with more than 90% of all countries in the world at some point in its history. So the empire was a well-oiled machine – it had the experience and knew how to play its cards of conflict and domination.

As all this was happening in India, a new model for the labour market was emerging in some of the British colonies as an alternative to the slave trade that was abolished in the Empire in 1833. Like slavery, it involved uprooting the poor, the desperate, and the least literate people to send them to far-flung destinations like Fiji. At the end of their reluctant journeys, the *girmiteers* were assigned to jobs that involved hard labour in conditions that at the very least can be described as harsh and inhumane. However, unlike slavery, indentured labourers 'signed' up to a contract with a defined timeframe. A lot has been written about the dodgy practices that were used to enlist the prospective labourers. However, to understand the indenture system, it is essential to revisit the origins of slavery. Despite the bitterness and the sourness of the slave trade, it was the sweetness of sugar that started it all.

Sugar has always been a valuable commodity in Britain. Dating back to the time of Napoleon in the past to Brexit negotiations in the present, this sweetener has influenced how political and economic decisions are made (Roberts, 2017). According to the National Archives (n.d.) in the UK, in the early days, Dutch merchants introduced the growing and processing of sugarcane to planters in Barbados. They brought the knowledge and skills from their experiences in Brazilian plantations which they apparently "seized from the Portuguese in 1630" (National Archives, n.d.). The Dutch played a pivotal role in setting up Barbadian plantation slavery through the supply of African slaves who, through their blood, sweat and tears, helped produce sugar that was sold in Holland. The planters realized that the model that would work best to achieve optimal outcomes was through huge farm holdings.

By the mid-1850's, settlers from various European countries began setting up farms in Fiji. Like Barbados, these settlers were setting up plantations where crops such as cotton were grown. However, the lack of reliable labourers was quickly realised as a critical issue. Plantation owners with the support of the local Fijian chiefs approached Indian officials to supply labourers (Lal, 2000). However, without a stable government in Fiji, the authorities in British India turned down the idea. At about the same time, moves to have Fiji annexed to Britain failed, mainly on the grounds of uncertainty in terms of its political and economic viability as a colony. It was also a time of metaphorical rough sailing for Fiji, with a number of changes and challenges facing its people simultaneously. When I was in school, we learned about Maafu – a Tongan Chief who was threatening to take over the country with the support of his tribe just before Fiji became a colony. While this did not eventuate, Fiji and the rest of the Pacific was primarily an unchartered and untouched territory, and there were challenges of dominance posed by other European countries such as France. It was also a time when the number of Europeans, predominantly of British origin, settling in the country was on the rise (Lal, 2000). While their numbers in comparison to the local population were small, their actions were noticeable. Some planters had resorted to unpalatable strategies of importing labourers from other countries. Factors such as these influenced Britain to formally accept the offer of unconditional cession on 10 October 1874. According to the Fiji Times published on 3 October 1874, the formalities of the signing commenced on 30 September 1874 in Fiji (Fiji Times, 1874). The Fijian contingent was led by Ratu Seru Cakobau and 11 paramount chiefs from various tribes in Fiji. *Ratu* is a title that is bestowed on a Fijian chief and is only acquired through birth. Queen Victoria was represented by the Governor of New South Wales, Sir Hercules Robinson. Once the memorandum of cession was signed, the Governor was presented with five turtles and a canoe as a gift to the Queen. While a western style of government was a new concept to the locals, it brought new hope of engaging with a country that was predominantly white. The signing of the deed of cession also answered calls from plantation owners who had for some time tried to import labourers from India to work on their plantations. The setting up of a western-type government by Britain made this dream a reality. It also safeguarded the native Fijians from labour lines – a policy that was put in place by the incumbent government. The rationale here was to cause minimum interruption to the Fijian way of life. In addition, the laid-back lifestyle of the natives would not have sustained the rigid timetabled work culture that the plantation owners imposed to ensure the viability of their new farms.

Sugar production was seen as a viable industry. Like Barbados, companies such as the Colonial Sugar Refining (CSR) Company from Australia began setting up large farming operations and sugar mills in Fiji. However, for businesses to prosper in the new colony, there was a need for cheap and reliable labour. Britain had found a solution to this problem. From their past experiences in other colonies, they knew that India was a source of cheap and reliable labour. It was a British colony, so the rulers could do whatever they wanted. This strategy had worked in other British colonies such as Mauritius, Trinidad, Jamaica, and South Africa. Thus, it was likely to succeed in Fiji as well. The colonial masters acted quickly. In 1879, five years after exerting their power in Fiji, the first shipment of Indians arrived to serve their 5-year indenture or *girmit*. If the labourers worked to the satisfaction of their masters, they were given a further five-year extension. After ten years, they had the option of either repatriation at the expense of the government or settling permanently in Fiji. *Girmit* enticed more than a million Indians to walk into the unknown in the hope of a better life – 5.2% who pursued this option were destined for Fiji. They served the CSR company with diligence. Today there is no mention of CSR's overseas operations from the past on its website!

A lot has been written about the indenture system by the descendants of the labourers (e.g. Lal, 2000). However, there is almost nothing written by those who experienced *girmit* firsthand. I was quite fascinated to learn from a BBC documentary that the British Museum holds more than 100,000 manuscripts with personal records such as wills, diaries, and letters from the East India Company era (Snow, 2014). These records fill nine miles of shelving for future generations to access and ponder about the lived lives of their British ancestors. Regrettably, the descendants of the indentured labourers do not have this privilege. According to Gillion (1958), "Indian emigration to Fiji was both a selective and an individual process; the emigrants were mostly illiterate villagers and were not integrated institutionally" (p. 431). Thus, they had to demonstrate the potential to be moulded in ways that would suit the needs of their future employers. If a resumé were to be written for these labourers, it would read as follows: Education: *Nil*, Experience: *Nil*, Leadership skills: *Nil*, Communication skills: *A good listener who never asks any questions*. In this way, the labourers were purposely selected so that they offered the least resistance and headache to their colonial masters.

One *girmiteer* who slipped this net and did not fit the mould was Totaram Sanadhya. He seemed to have been the only one capable of writing his account of the indenture system in Hindi. It is also plausible to suggest that some of the earlier writings may also have been lost or destroyed. Sanadhya's book *My twenty-one years in the Fiji Islands* (1914) was translated into several South Asian languages soon after it was published. However, it was only translated into English in 1991 by Kelly and Singh. Sanadhya was born in 1876 in a province that is now known as Uttar Pradesh. All my ancestors were also from this state. Sanadhya arrived in 1893, and he soon became a prominent voice raising issues that were pertinent to the labourers. He even wrote to Mahatma Gandhi to express the plight of his Hindustani brothers (Sanadhya, 1914/1991). Unlike many who opted to call Fiji home, Sanadhya returned to India in 1914 and played a significant role in bringing an end to the indenture system. His book gives an idea of the life on the inside and helps decipher some of the drivers that led people like my ancestors to leave their homeland and walk into the unknown. It helps understand the context and the factors that led to this mass migration. Gillion (1958) described Sanadhya's intellect as follows:

> His writings in Hindi (for he knew no English) show a perception, idealism, tolerance, wit, balance and shrewd practicality seldom matched by any of his European or Indian contemporaries. (p. 438)

The factors that compelled Sanadhya to sign up for *girmit* mirror that of other *girmiteers*. At the age of 17 and after his father's death, Sanadhya left his home on foot in search of work. His family was facing financial hardship and Sanadhya could not withstand the suffering his mother endured to sustain the household. After walking for 16 days, he arrived in a township called Prayag with seven *annas* (Indian coin) in his pocket. To put this money in perspective, and based on today's currency exchange, Sanadhya began his journey with less than one US cent to his name. He was in a hopeless situation because there were no opportunities for work. Sanadhya did not want to go back home and be a burden on his mother who was already facing financial hardship. However, one day when he was aimlessly wandering in a market, a stranger approached him and asked, "Do you want employment?" (Sanadhya, 1914/1991, p. 33). Understandably, he replied in the affirmative. The man responded, "Good, I can get you a very good job. It's the sort of work which will make your heart joyful" (p. 33). The man convinced Sanadhya. "When you wish, then quit working. Nothing will happen". The man that Sanadhya met was an Indian local and a recruiter. "This *arkati*, fooled me and brought me to his house" (p. 33). The labourers called these recruiters *arkatis* because they were their own brothers who could not be trusted. They were like sweet-talking shonky salesman full of hot air that the ordinary villagers could not see through. For every labourer they signed up, the *arkatis* were paid a few rupees in commission (Lal, 2000). Once Sanadhya was inside the *arkatis's* house, he realised that it was like a holding yard. He saw 100 men sitting in one line and 60 women in another while others were busy cooking to keep this camp going (Sanadhya, 1914/1991). He was quite confused to see the women and he was not allowed to talk to them either. Those who were on the inside were now trapped – they were not allowed to leave, and they could not communicate with anyone outside. Information about their proposed work was filtered to them in small packages. The recruiter explained, "Look brothers, the place where you will work you will never have to suffer any sorrows. There will never be any kind of problems there. You will eat a lot of bananas and a stomach full of sugarcane and play flute in relaxation" (p. 34). According to Andrews and Pearson (as cited in Gillion, 1958), the marketing strategy that was used to entice potential labourers was as follows:

> It is the ordinary villager's cupidity which is the lever most frequently used. If he is of the stupid, ignorant type, then Fiji is referred to as a district near to Calcutta where high wages are to be paid ... If the villager, on the other hand, is of the more intelligent type, then the full details of the indenture are revealed. But the work is made out to be very light indeed, and the most glowing prospects are offered. Nothing is said about the penal laws, or the hard conditions of compulsory labour. (p. 91)

After spending three days at the recruiter's house, Sanadhya and all the other men and women were loaded in cars and driven to face the local magistrate. Sanadhya (1914/1991) recalled that the recruiter told them to say "yes" to any questions that the magistrate asked. The magistrate must have been Indian to ask them questions that would make sense to them. If they replied in the nega-tive, chances were that they would be jailed. At the courthouse, the magistrate asked each one of them if they had agreed to go to Fiji. He did not tell the prospective labourers where Fiji was or what they would be doing. According to Sanadhya, some 165 men and women were registered in 20 minutes. From here, Sanadhya and his fellow countrymen were "loaded on rail cars" (p. 34) and transported more than 2,000 kilometres to the depot in Calcutta. It was a direct train which did not stop anywhere to pick up other passengers. The travellers were not allowed to talk to anyone. However, "if someone wanted to talk to himself it was allowed" (p. 34). Once they arrived at the depot, the immigration officer spelt out more details about the work. They were told that they would be going to Fiji and work in fields for five years. If they returned home before the contract was over, they would have to pay their fares. If they returned after ten years, the government would meet their transportation expenses. They were also told that they would earn 12 *annas* a day or about 1 US cent (1 rupee = 16 annas, 1 rupee = 0.015 USD). The agent added that Fiji was like Heaven, and "you will live with great bliss there" (p. 34). After listening to the *saheb's* (white man) "slippery talk" (p. 35), Sanadhya became confused. He did not understand what chores this hard work would really entail. As a consequence, he refused to go to Fiji. He said, "I have never done any field labour. Look at my hands. They can never do field work. I won't go to Fiji" (p. 35). The *saheb* was not going to tolerate such nonsense from an unequal human being. He asked two of his trusted Bengali elders to "explain things to this one and fix it up" (p. 35). Sanadhya was locked up in a room for one whole day with no food or water. Eventually, he caved in and agreed to make the trip.

In preparation for their trip, they were taken to a river nearby for bathing. They were given a cake of soap. Many had never seen soap before – they thought it was *barfi* (sweet which tastes like fudge) and they started eating it. They learnt quickly. Medical examinations followed, which were conducted by male doctors. It was signed off by the depot surgeon and countersigned by the surgeon superintendent on the emigration pass of the indentured labourers. They were fit to travel if the labourer was "free from all bodily and mental disease and that he/she has been vaccinated since engaging to emigrate" (see emigration pass – Figure 2.1). Once the examination was finished, in readiness for the journey, they were given "prisoners shirts, caps, and pants to wear" (Sanadhya, 1914/1991, p. 36), a tin jar for water, a tin plate for food and a small sack for their belongings. Many had nothing because the *arkati* recruiters stole all their possessions.

2 The Coming of My Ancestors to Fiji

Like Sanadhya (1914), all my ancestors were leading uncomplicated lives and were surviving on very little. Even their names were little – most had just one name, unlike the first, middle, surname that many of us have today. Some even changed their names to pursue their perceived adventurous journey. On the whole, they were very insignificant people in a vast country with many states, further subdivided into districts. Dotted throughout the districts are *thanas* (police stations) which maintain peace and order in the surrounding communities. Most people in these communities live in hamlets; smaller than villages with a population of a couple of hundred at most. This is where all my ancestors

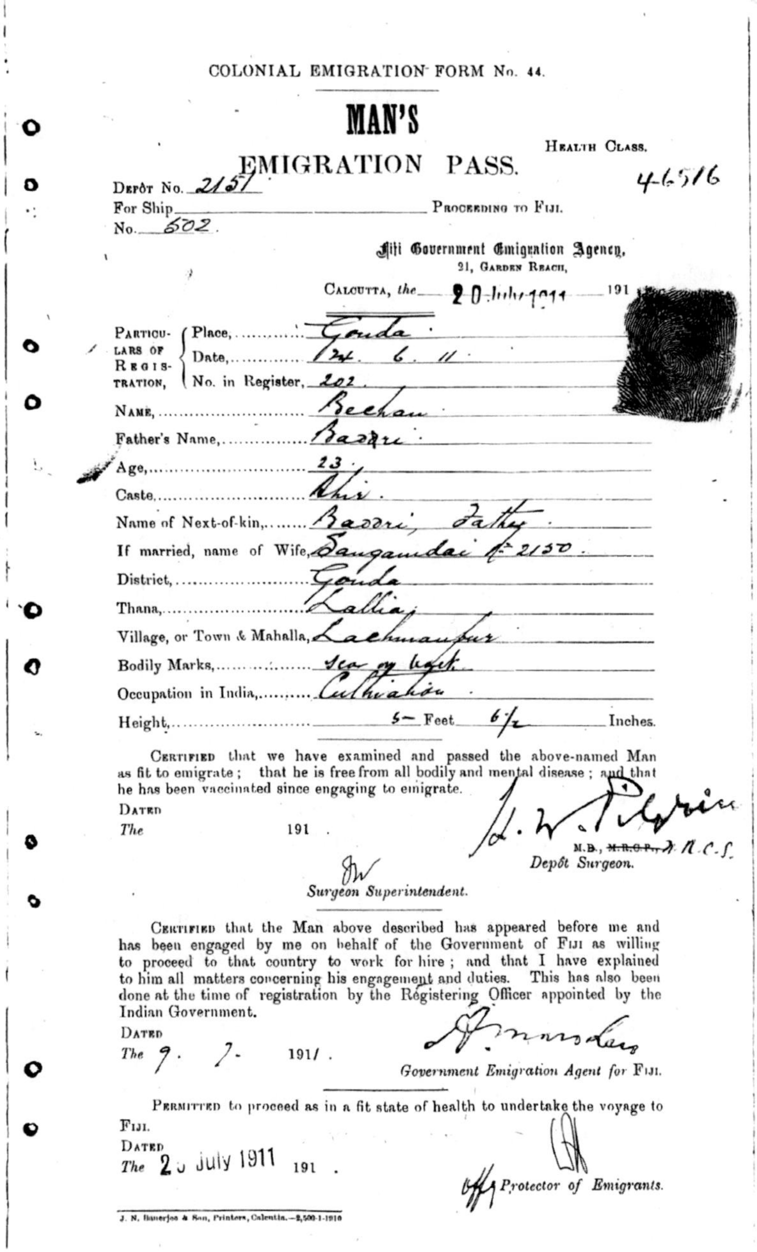

COLONIAL EMIGRATION FORM No. 44.

MAN'S

HEALTH CLASS.

EMIGRATION PASS.

46516

Depôt No. _2151_

For Ship _____ Proceeding to Fiji.

No. _502_ .

Fiji Government Emigration Agency,
21, GARDEN REACH,

CALCUTTA, the _20 July 1911_ 191

PARTICU-LARS OF REGIS-TRATION,	Place,	_Gonda_
	Date,	_24. 6. 11_
	No. in Register,	_202_

NAME, _Reehan_

Father's Name, _Bazru_

Age, _23_

Caste, _Ahir_

Name of Next-of-kin, _Bazru, Father_

If married, name of Wife, _Sangaudai No 2150_

District, _Gonda_

Thana, _Lalia_

Village, or Town & Mahalla, _Lachmanpur_

Bodily Marks, _Scar on left_

Occupation in India, _Cultivation_

Height, _5_ Feet _6½_ Inches.

CERTIFIED that we have examined and passed the above-named Man as fit to emigrate ; that he is free from all bodily and mental disease ; and that he has been vaccinated since engaging to emigrate.

DATED

The   191 .

M.B., M.R.C.P., L.R.C.S.

Depôt Surgeon.

Surgeon Superintendent.

CERTIFIED that the Man above described has appeared before me and has been engaged by me on behalf of the Government of Fiji as willing to proceed to that country to work for hire ; and that I have explained to him all matters concerning his engagement and duties. This has also been done at the time of registration by the Registering Officer appointed by the Indian Government.

DATED

The _9 . 7 ._ 191/ .

Government Emigration Agent for Fiji.

PERMITTED to proceed as in a fit state of health to undertake the voyage to Fiji.

DATED

The _2ᴜ July 1911_ 191 .

Protector of Emigrants.

J. N. Banerjee & Son, Printers, Calcutta.—2,500-1-1916

FIGURE 2.1   Emigration passes of my aajua

came from. My paternal ancestors (*aajua* and *aajiya*) lived in a hamlet called Luxsmanpur Dhrampur (stated as 'Lachmanpur' in the emigration pass) in the *thana* of Lalia, in the district of Balrampur. My dad's maternal grandparents,

Tulshi and Rajpali, were from a hamlet called Do in the *thana* of Kalwari in the district of Basti. My mum's paternal grandparents, Jaina and Mangal, came from a hamlet in the Bansi *thana* in the Basti District. They all left their villages in search of work as married couples. My mum's maternal grandparents were different – they both came as singles. Her maternal grandmother arrived as a spinster. She was from a village called Rajaipur Sarai from a *thana* called Pura Kalandur which is in the district of Faizabad. She met her husband Prabhu who arrived in Fiji as a bachelor on an earlier voyage. A search on Google Maps shows that all these hamlets were relatively close to each other in the State of Uttar Pradesh. Most of the labourers came from the areas that my ancestors once called home (Lal, 2000). These were some of poorest parts of the country.

Of all my great grand-parents, *aajua* and *aajiya's* sacrifices have been the most significant in my life. In the Hindu custom, we do not take the names of our elders. They all have a specific title, such as *aaja* for paternal grand-dad and *aaji* for paternal grandmother. There are no specific titles for great-grandparents. Some used to call them *par aaja* and *par aaji*. Titles were created by families in whatever way it suited them. To make the distinction, we called our grandparents *aaja* and *aaji*, and great-grandparents *aajua* and *aajiya*. As I grew older, and long after they were gone, I began researching on my *aajua* and *aajiya* who had influenced my life in so many different ways. I felt very grateful to the British and the successive Fijian Governments for preserving the Emigration passes of these labourers in the archives and making copies available to various national libraries around the world. These one-page documents mean so much to us, the descendants – it is the only straw that we can cling onto to build a story of our ancestors. It is disappointing yet fascinating to think that this one page of 'data' can lead to so many connections. I once approached the Australian National Library in Canberra to create a database of the *girmiteers*. I was willing to assist them in developing this invaluable digital resource. They were not interested, and I was told by one of the staff members that "it was not Australian enough". The ignorance of the staff member was evident in this instance, but it was not worth questioning her response. She was probably not aware of the amount of wealth that was generated by the CSR company in Fiji which was channelled back into the Australia economy. I am still pondering with this question – when does a migrant become Australian enough so that his or her history becomes relevant to a country of their sworn allegiance?

From the emigration passes (Figure 2.1), I established that my great paternal grandparents – *aajua* and *aajiya* – began their journeys to Fiji in Gonda on 24 June 1911. This is where they were registered with details such as father's

THE VISION OF THE OPPRESSED

name, age, caste, spouse's name (if married), address (in terms of the district, *thana* and so on), height, and occupation. Interestingly 'bodily marks' such as birth marks, scars, and tattoos were also recorded. All my ancestors had a scar on some part of their bodies. The next stage of their processing occurred two weeks later at the Fiji Government Emigration Agency at 61, Garden Reach, Calcutta. They would have possibly made a similar trip by rail to Calcutta as Sanadhya (1914/1991), which covered some distance of 2,000 kilometres. In Calcutta, the next three levels of clearances were obtained almost two weeks later. The Depot Surgeon signed without bothering to date their fitness to emigrate. The text in their emigration passes stated that their colonial rulers had "explained ... all matters concerning" their "engagement and duties"; the *girmiteers* were not given the option to agree to all the conditions of their "hire". Like *aajua* and *aajiya*, many *girmiteers* were illiterate. A thumbprint from an ink pad was all they could provide to confirm that they agreed to all conditions of their *girmit* in Fiji.

I have always been fascinated to find more about the steamers that transported them. I came across a page on the *Wikipedia* for Norse Line – a shipping company that was used to transport the *girmiteers* to their destinations. Before the 1900's, the company used sailing ships for these trips. Post-1900, they began using steamers which were built by the Charles Connell Company Limited in Glasgow, Scotland that were capable of cruising at 11.5 knots. At this speed most of the steamers were able to cover the journey from Calcutta to Fiji in about a month. Travelling on the high seas in a steamer would have presented a new set of experiences. Our ancestors not only saw the ocean for the first time – but they also experienced a new mode of transport. However, these steamers were not cruise liners, and they were not paying passengers. This was a harsh experience, and some did not even make the journey. If they died at sea they were thrown overboard (Lal, 2000). In the present day, this action is synonymous with live sheep and cattle trade that operates out of Australia. When the animals die on the trip, they too are thrown overboard (Worthington, 2018).

Aajua and *aajiya* boarded *Mutlah II* on 20 July 1911 for their onward journey to Fiji. This was the steamer's second voyage to the country. Hence, it was identified by the number 2. *Mutlah* was a 3,393-ton steamship which was built in 1906 and carried about 900 passengers. As *aajua* and *aajiya* set foot on this steamer for the first time, they could not have known that their feet were never going to touch their homeland again. On this voyage, there was a total of 863 *girmiteers*. Men and women were kept in separate compartments. Life on board the steamer was tough. Each passenger was allocated a floor space measuring one and half feet wide and six feet long or about two by half a metre (Sanadhya, 1914/1991). This was their cabin space for their journey. There was no sympathy for those who complained about these confined spaces. Their white masters and their loyal Indian sidekicks who were in charge yelled to ensure any voices of discontent was quelled and quietened: "Son of a bitch, you have to stay here" (Sanadhya, 1914/1991, p. 37). The image that comes to my mind is of livestock on cattle trains, trapped in confined spaces with no real understanding of their destinies. There was nothing too fancy about the food, both in terms of the quality and quantity. There was also a ration for water – each passenger was assigned two bottles of water daily (Sanadhya, 1914/1991). Life on the high seas was a harrowing experience for most of the illiterate Indians. Later in their lives, many recalled the treacherous waters as the dark waters or the *"kaala paani"* (Lal, 1998). At times, they would go up and down huge waves and this would have been like riding a roller coaster. They were both travelling on a steamer and experiencing the ocean for the first time. "In the four directions, there was nothing to be seen but blue sky. At that time, many emotions were born in our hearts. In just the way a free bird is imprisoned in a cage, we were all locked in" (Sanadhya, 1914/1991, p. 37).

After travelling nearly 12,770 km on the high seas, *aajua* and *aajiya* arrived in Fiji – almost a month later on 18 August 1911. This was their first and last overseas trip. Like all other *girmiteers*, after the ships docked at the Suva Port, they were put on barges that were towed to Nukulau – a small island off the island of Viti Levu and not far from the City of Suva (Gounder, 2011). This was used as a quarantine station for the emigrating indentured labourers. Like the trade of slaves, the *girmiteers* were bought by the plantation owners on the basis of their needs. Sanadhya (1914/1991) noted that while slavery may have been abolished in civilised countries, in this part of the world, a modified model was thriving. As they were assigned to different plantations, they were reminded that for the next five years they would be servants of the white man or *saheb* (Sanadhya, 1914/1991).

Our *aajua* and *aajiya* went to a plantation owner in Olosara near Sigatoka where they served their five-year *girmit*. They were provided accommodation in 'coolie lanes'. Their British masters used the term *coolie* to describe the Indian labourers. The coolie lanes were large rectangular wooden buildings with six to eight poorly ventilated rooms. Some of them measured no more than 3 by 2 metres. These rooms were multi-purpose spaces used for sleeping, cooking, dining, and everything else. In many homes in the West, this would equate to the size of a walk-in robe or a bathroom! Gillion (1958) described the coolie lanes aptly as follows:

> To assist ventilation, the partitions [between the rooms] were not carried to the ceiling but were topped with wire netting; privacy did not exist ...

There were no floors, although it was usual for Immigrants to make one out of cow-dung and clay, as in India. Inside there were three bunks, and with firewood, field tools, cooking utensils and wet clothes cluttered about, there was very little room to move ... With smoke, soot, spilt food, and flies and mosquitoes, living conditions were uncomfortable. Some-times fowls or a dog were kept in the room, too, adding to the already unsanitary conditions, but affording a precaution against theft. The mud and straw houses the immigrants had come from in India had often been miserable hovels, but they had at least been detached and had blended into the surrounding earth. The lanes were not just crowded and dirty; they were ugly. (pp. 328–329)

For the first few months on their indenture, the *girmiteers* received weekly food rations. As a former mathematics teacher, I found the unit of measure-ment that were used at that time to be very interesting. Some of the items they were given comprised sharp flour (10 *chatank* = 583 grams), cowpeas (2 *chatank* = 116 grams) and ghee (0.5 *chatank* = 29 grams) (Sanadhya, 1914/1991). Two shillings and four pence were deducted from the weekly wages for the supply of these rations. They were also given two three-legged cast iron pots for outdoor cooking with firewood (Gounder, 2011). These food ingredients and the pot would have set them up to make curries. They would have possibly also received a flat iron plate (*tawa*) to cook their *rotis* (flatbread). Each day when they arrived at the plantations, they would be assigned to daily tasks such as "draining 200–300 cubic feet [of dirt]; holing 150–200 holes; weeding and trashing 10–15 chains, 6 feet wide; cutting, 3 tons per day; loading, 36 cwt. of cane; shovel-ploughing, 7–10 chains" (Gillion, 1962, p. 109). Most of them worked nine-hour days on the plantations from Monday to Friday with 3 a.m. starts. On Saturdays, they would knock off at around lunchtime, and Sunday was their day off. For all emigrants aged over 15 years, the daily wages were one shilling, or 12 pennies, for males and nine pennies for a woman. On aver-age, the *girmiteers* had the potential to earn about one pound each month (20 shillings = 1 pound). To the *girmiteers*, a penny was roughly equivalent to an *anna* in Indian currency (Lal, 1998). As Sanadhya (1914/1991) mentioned in his book, when he left his home, all he had in his pocket were seven *annas* with no hope of work or earning any money. While the life in Fiji was terrible, it was at least generating some income for them and giving them a sense of pride.

Like many others, *aajua* and *aajiya* opted not to return to India. Their inden-ture experience would have taught them so much. They were illiterate, but this did not mean that they were unintelligent. Episodes of experiential learning embedded in the fabric of their daily lives would have influenced their feelings, thinking, reflections, and actions (Kolb, 1984). After weighing the options, they would have concluded that Fiji offered them some hope as opposed to their villages in India where they had perceived no future for themselves. I have always wondered about how much psychological pain and suffering they must have endured in making this decision. How much they would have grieved in silence, and with each other. This decision meant that they would NEVER step on their home soil again. They would NEVER see or physically embrace their loved ones. For me, today, it is like saying I will get on a spacecraft and go to Mars. I will stay there forever and never return home to see my families and friends on Earth. While from Mars, I may be able to communicate in some way with my loved ones, my ancestors did not have this opportunity because they could neither read nor write. Any communication was confined to handwritten letters by a knowledgeable person in their village whom they knew and could trust. But in such situations when correspondence occurs via a third person, the expression of personal feelings and emotions are pushed to the side. In the world-acclaimed movie *Lion*, the main character, young Saroo, gets lost on the streets of Calcutta, is adopted, and ends up growing up in Australia. In the film, Dev Patel plays the role of Saroo and eloquently expresses the feeling and the pains that he goes through for being away from his family. In my view these feelings parallel what *aajua, aajiya* and their contemporaries must have experienced. *Lion* has a happy ending. Saroo is reunited with his family. *Aajua* and *aajiya* never had such a positive outcome – they died without ever re-connecting with their families and friends back in their little hamlets. In my view, this is the ultimate sacrifice any human being can make for their future generations. They were trailblazers and opted to call a foreign country their home. An important point of note here is that, even today, only 3% of the world's population live outside their country of birth (Goodhart, 2017).

With the support of the Colonial Sugar Refining (CSR) Company, most Indians who chose to stay in Fiji were able to lease land from the native Fijian landowners (Australian National University, n.d.; Gillion, 1958). The process was described as follows:

> After securing his land, which had to be accurately surveyed, the Indian put up a house, usually a Fijian-style bure or a shanty, built of old packing-cases, kerosene and biscuit tins and old corrugated iron on a wooden frame. Sometimes more substantial houses were built, but these usually waited upon prosperity. (p. 401)

Keeping Indians on the land was also in the best interests of the company. They understood the work ethic of the Indians. Once they secured a farming plot, the company could sign up sugarcane contracts with them. It was a win-win situation. Hardworking farmers would cultivate good sugarcane. This would ensure the continued supply of raw materials to the CSR company's sugar mills. Collectively these outcomes would also add to the prosperity of this young colony and at the same time deliver handsome rewards to the company and its shareholders in Australia.

After completing their *girmit*, *aajua* and *aajiya* moved from Olosara to a place called Yandua that was about 20 kilometres away. They started growing sugar cane, and even today the crop is still grown by some of our extended family members who live there. It has been one of the most productive farms in the area. I am assuming their initial contract, which ended in 1916, would have been extended for a further five years. As a consequence, they would have moved to their new home in 1921. Gillion (1958) noted that the Indians "settled not in clustered villages as in India, but in homesteads" (p. 403). The settlement was dependent upon wherever they could find suitable land, and the focus was on the family unit. While *aajua* and *aajiya's* homestead was only accessible via bush tracks, the land was relatively fertile, close to a creek and railway tracks. The latter ensured easy access for the transport of sugarcane which they grew on their leased land.

Aajua and *aajiya* and many of their *girmiteer* contemporaries seem to have never shied away from hard work. Like *aajua* and *aajiya*, many were still in their twenties, and for the first time in their lives, they had the freedom to toil on the land in the way they wanted. For once, they got a chance to think for themselves and were no longer under the complete grip of their colonial masters. Over time, the hard work of the new settlers began paying off as the once virgin land was slowly being transformed to productive farms (Lal, 1992). This was evident throughout the colony and this what the rulers had hoped for. Overtime it became evident that "the Indian settlers were much more prosperous than they had been in India, as indicated by the figures of bank deposits and fixed assets" (Gillion,1958, p. 405). At last self-autonomy appeared to facilitate some changes in the lives of the *girmiteers*.

3   Educational Opportunities for Indians

One of the main sticking points for the Indians in the new colony was a lack of educational opportunities for their children. While the *girmiteers* were illiterate, they were smart enough to see education as the key to a more prosperous life that extended beyond the farms. The legislative assembly in Fiji at that time was predominantly European, and they did everything within their reach to maintain their superiority. For example, to maintain a white look in the government, the European members of the assembly pushed for the "introduction of a literacy test in the English language, in elections to the Municipal Council" (Gillion, 1958, p. 448). This legislation led to a decrease in the number of non-European voters and eliminated the possibility of non-European candidates from being elected. Thus, for people to vote and run for office, they had to demonstrate their proficiency in the English language by passing this test. According to the 1911 census (cited in Gillion, 1958), 86.5% of Europeans, 52.8% of Fijians and 9.4% of Indians were recorded as proficient in English literacy. This difference was wholly due to the lack of educational opportunities for Indians. The literate amongst the Indians together with members of other minority groups protested this legislation. The British Government in India conceded that while there were good reasons to promulgate this legislation, it also pointed out that the European-dominated "government of Fiji was disfranchising Indians who did not know English but, at the same time, was not providing them with the facilities to learn it" (Gillion, 1958, p. 448). While there were some noises within the ranks of the ruling class about educating Indians, the colonial Government of Fiji showed no real interest in taking proactive steps to deal with the issue. In 1909 an Education Commission emphasised that Indian education "compared most unfavourably with those offered for any other class of the community" (Government of Fiji, 1926, para. 4). Special government laws banned non-European children from attending the best-equipped government schools that were reserved for Europeans (White, 2001). Opportunities to educate Indians was largely a no-no for the ruling class. There was widespread belief that the "Indians had been introduced primarily as an unskilled labour force, and it was believed that general education would spoil them for this purpose, for they would develop new aspirations" (Gillion, 1958, p. 453). Similar views were also held in other parts of the world as well. Gillespie (2014) pointed out that educating the masses is a relatively new phenomenon in the world. The rationale of the ruling classes was that "A farmer's child did not need to know how to read or write in order to keep a pig fed or a field ploughed" (p. 7). The industrial revolution in the late 1700's was the trigger for change. The masses needed to be educated so that they could operate the machinery.

Like the rest of the world, the education of the masses was left to the church. Missionaries affiliated with the Marist Brothers, the Methodist Church, and the Anglican mission offered opportunities to those who lived close to large townships, but some Indians were reluctant to send their children to these schools because of the fear that they may be converted to Christianity (Gillion, 1958). According to Tavola (1990):

> By 1900, due to the efforts of the missions, there were schools in most
> Fijian villages offering up to four years of education and school attendance
> had become a normal part of Fijian childhood. There was consequently a
> high literacy rate in the vernacular. Compared to Indians who at that time
> had very limited participation in schools, Fijians were significantly ahead
> in terms of literacy, access to and attendance at schools. (p. 94)

For the *girmiteers,* education was the only vehicle that would enable future generations to break out of the cycle of oppression and hopelessness. This belief was
entrenched in the psyche of other free Indian settlers as well, as they "looked for
means of advancing themselves and education appeared to be the obvious route
for upward mobility" (Tavola, 1990, p. 98). In 1916, the government introduced a
model that had a significant and lasting impact on the education system in Fiji
(Tavola, 1990). It was known as the grant-in-aid scheme and was common in
other British Colonies. Under this scheme, communities were responsible for
the building and maintenance of their schools. The government paid the salary
to "certificated teachers whose training had been in English" (p. 97). The government also paid annual efficiency grants, and these were vaguely defined. There
were building grants which the government subsidised on a one-on-one basis.
Consequently, the government matched every dollar that was raised by the local
community to build a school building (Tavola, 1990). Many Indian communities
and organisations took advantage of this opportunity.

By 1917, there were 12 schools established by Indians themselves in which
untrained teachers taught in Hindi. In places where there were no such opportunities, parents were finding other means to educating their children. A*ajua*
and *aajiya* were very pro-education. However, there were no schools in the
village where they had settled. My grandfather (*aaja*) was sent to board with
another family and be schooled by a Hindu priest more than 150 km away
near the town of Tavua. He hated this and used to hide in the bushes. I would
have done the same! While there was a growing body of a self-help movement
amongst the Indians themselves to build schools, in rural areas there were
significant issues associated with "the shortage of teachers, the multiplicity
of languages, and the indifference of the parents and their opposition to the
education of girls" (Gillion, 1958, p. 455).

The year 1926 was the tipping point on the issue of education for my family
and others in the village. It was five years after *aajua* and *aajiya's girmit* was
over. It became evident to them that the government was not going to build
a school in their village which was in a rural and remote part of the country.
There were no whites living in this village. Thus, from the perspectives of the
ruling class, there was no need for a school. So *aajua* teamed up with a few

other good Indian men in the village to take advantage of the government's grant-in-aid scheme for building schools. They started collecting donations and the board I mentioned in the first chapter in the head teacher's office lists the names of the donors. In total, there were 55 donors – all were Indians. The names are listed in the amounts they donated and this ranged from 15 to 40 pounds (Figure 2.2). I would imagine that there may have been others who donated smaller amounts. While women may have equally contributed to the donations, the board only lists the names of men. *Aajua* (and *aajiya*) donated

FIGURE 2.2   School donor board in the headmaster's office

30 pounds. These donations collectively raised 1155 pounds and marked the start of Naidovi Indian School. While I have seen this donation board many times, it meant very little to me as a child. After all, my ancestors had only donated 30 pounds – no big deal. However, it was in the writing of this chapter and the research that I undertook that made me think deeper about their contribution. Gillion (1958) made references to money saved by the returning indentured labourers and noted:

> Most repatriates had no savings whatever. The average savings declared by those who returned to Calcutta from Fiji in the five years 1892–1896, were £10.7.0. But, following improvements in the condition of Indian in Fiji, they rose considerably; in 1904, they were £20, and in 1913, £24. These sums seem small when it is remembered that most had been away for ten years .... (p. 386)

Each time I saw the donor board, I interpreted them as paltry sums of money. Based on the data reported by Gillion, it is highly likely that most of the 55 donors who contributed to building the school gave a significant donation, if not most of their savings. Each person had an average monthly income of one pound (Lal, 1998). So *aajua* and *aajiya* would have had a combined income of about 20–25 pounds a year. Their donation of 30 pounds would have been equivalent to more than a year's wage. When it came to education, *aajua* was an activist who wanted to bring about a change to the status quo. *Aajiya* was very intelligent and possibly the "brains trust" amongst the duo. She was always there to stand behind her husband on education related matters. The donations were made in good faith – not just to create educational opportunities for their children but others in the community as well. It was done in the spirit of comradery and good will. In these modern times, how many of us can contribute more than a year's salary for a school building fund? *Aajua* was not just a donor but in the early days he was also the president (*Sabha Pati*) of the school committee (see Figure 1.2). My *aaja* (grandfather) served alongside him as the treasurer. Except for the school head teacher, all other committee members were illiterate like my *aajua* and *aaja*. Amongst the many achievements of this committee was the construction of a school building with concrete and Besser blocks (built on site) – it was the first of its kind in the Western Division of the country. This building also boasted many remarkable design features that included resistance to adverse weather conditions. The latter has stood the test of time. Even with all my experiences and educational qualifications, I would feel quite challenged to match their achievements. I always felt so proud of them because they achieved so much with so little.

Naidovi Indian School was the launch pad for most Indian and some Fijian children in Cuvu, Yandua, Ulusila, Navovo and some of the surrounding villages. After graduating from Naidovi, two of *aajua* and *aajiya's* children, younger brothers of my *aaja,* left the village for further education. One of them attended a high school that was more than 60 kilometres from their home. Both went on further to attain tertiary qualifications. One of them joined the local teachers' college while the other went overseas and enrolled at the University of Auckland in New Zealand. He graduated with a Bachelor of Arts degree – thus becoming one of the first in Fiji to possess this qualification. This was a remarkable feat. It is hard to fathom the courage of my *aajua* and *aajiya* to send their son to a country that they had no knowledge or understanding about. How they supported him financially is admirable given that they had seven other children to look after. Even in countries with well-established education systems in the 21st century, the percentage of students who are the first in the family to attend university is relatively high (e.g. Spiegler & Bednarek, 2013). Thus, there are still many families in developed countries where no member has attended a university. In terms of education, my *aaja's* brothers became trailblazers – not just in the family but to others in the village and in the country.

Over the years, Naidovi Indian School gave many children in the village the opportunity to complete primary education. Some went on to secondary education and either proceeded to universities or joined the workforce. All my first cousins, from my *aaja's* side who attended Naidovi, completed their university studies. Some of us ended up with masters or doctoral qualifications. The change in educational opportunities for many children happened because of the beliefs and values that my *aajua* and *aajiya* and their illiterate contemporaries, held about the value of education. Their vision and determination has enabled us to live this life which is not only free of oppression but presents good opportunities from time to time. Their proactive actions led to building a school, which was just the beginning for those of us who came after. This story is not uncommon. Many Indians and Fijians walked similar paths and strived very hard to give their descendants a chance at an education in Fiji.

4　　Taking Their Spirits Back

I made visiting my *aajua* and *aajiya's* hamlet as one of my life's quests. In hindsight, I felt a bit like the main character, Saroo in the movie *Lion*. He wanted to re-connect with his parents. I had no other choice but to just visit where my ancestors had come from. They had passed on and were no longer with us, but symbolically I wanted to take their spirits back to their home. I was fortunate in getting copies of their emigration passes from the Fiji Archives. One of my *aaja's* brothers also told me that my *aajua* was the eldest in the family and had two other brothers. Their names were Murli and Nepal. Apparently, another brother of my *aaja* used to write to the family in India at some point. When I approached him, he knew "nothing". I had no other clues and tracing my roots in India looked like an insurmountable task. I knew of some other individuals who had made contact with the families of their ancestors. But the families of these individuals in Fiji had maintained some contact with their folks in India over the years. No such connections were maintained by my family. I had to develop my own strategies to make contact with my past. How could I find these people in a country which has a population of more than a billion people? It was going to be like finding a needle in the most colossal haystack – India.

All my searches in libraries and on the Internet ended up in vain. It demonstrated that despite all the affordances of digital technologies, conventional approaches to finding information on the Internet does not always work. Then one Tuesday in 2007, there was a lightbulb moment. I decided to conduct some searches on members of the Indian *Lok Sabha* (Parliament). I was able to find the phone contact of the elected member who represented the people in Balrampur – the district that my ancestors have come from. I called the number and explained my intentions of locating my family roots to the staffer who had answered the phone. It was my lucky day. The member of parliament was also in the office. My call was transferred to him. I relayed my intentions once again. He was very excited to hear that even after almost 100 years of my ancestors leaving India, I was still so motivated to trace my ancestral history. He promised to undertake some enquiries on my behalf and asked me to email him the emigration passes and any other information that I had in my possession. The conversation that I had with the member of Parliament also demonstrated the power of the Internet. The Internet is a tool. Like all other tools, the quality of the outcomes depends on how the tool is used. My research and my experiences of teaching with technologies is a testament to this claim. Without the Internet, phonebooks would have been the only option to find phone numbers. I would have had to take a chance and fly to India to put my hands on the phonebook. But due to my work and family commitments, this would have never happened and more importantly, I would not have known where to start!

I exchanged emails and had a few phone chats with the member of parliament. He had arranged one of his staffers to visit the hamlet and make some inquiries. The gesture and the kindness of this parliamentarian cannot be put into words. There are very few human beings who would go out of their way to assist another for no apparent gain or reward. Coincidently, we had also planned a trip to India at the end of that year. It was our first trip, and at the back of my mind, given the time that had elapsed, I was not so sure if finding connections with my *aajua* and *aajiya's* families would indeed be possible. Nonetheless, in our itinerary, we planned to make a trip to Gonda. This was the city where *aajua* and *aajiya's* emigration passes were registered. We booked to fly into the capital of Uttar Pradesh, Lucknow, from New Delhi. From Lucknow, we booked hire cars for an overnight round trip to Gonda and Balrampur.

Our trip to India was for about four weeks. We visited some different places of interest – as visitors do! On the day of our flight into Lucknow, I had a call from the member of parliament. He informed me that his staffer who had visited the hamlet met an elderly lady who had claimed to be a daughter-in-law of *aajua's* brothers. He had arranged his staffer to meet us at our hotel in Balrampur the next day and take us to the lady in the hamlet. It would be an understatement to say that I was over the moon to hear the news. As we boarded our flight in Delhi to Lucknow, news came that the former Pakistani President Benazir Bhutto had been shot during the election campaign in her country. The flight took off, and I felt perplexed. There were all sorts of mixed messages and doubts going through my mind. I did not know where we were going and who we were meeting. How would they respond to our presence? Will there be a miracle? Will we meet our relatives?

We made an early start the next morning. On the trip to my ancestral village, I was accompanied by my mum, Ramila, our sons Ravi and Ronesh and our daughter-in-law Jo. We were possibly travelling on the same road that *aajua* and *aajiya* had travelled for the last time almost a century ago. Little would they have known that one day members of their own family would follow the same road and pass through the same landmarks in search of their beginnings. I wondered what was going through their minds as they travelled on this road. Did the thoughts of their future generations cross their minds? It was a special moment, it had to be felt and cannot be described in words. The choices and the sacrifices that *aajua* and *aajiya* made, gave us this life where we could travel together as a family in search of them.

Our journey took us through the districts of Barabanki and Gonda and we passed many miles of fields that were cultivated with sugarcane, millet, mustard, and wheat. Along the way, we also passed many overloaded trucks with produce, grubby looking buses and utes filled to beyond-capacity with people. The mud houses and shacks gave more clues about the socioeconomic status of the people who lived here. As we drove further away from Lucknow, it became increasingly evident that we were entering a part of India that was in dire need of infrastructure development. The distance from Lucknow to *aajua* and *aajiya's* hamlet was about 200 km, which took about seven hours. It was past midday when we met the parliamentarian's staffer at the Heritage Hotel Mahamaya. The hotel was built in 1860 by the Maharaja of Balrampur as a European Guest House to accommodate dignitaries and government officials. Prime Ministers like Jawahar Lal Nehru, Indira Gandhi and Rajiv Gandhi also spent a few nights on this property. I am sure some of the agents who went to recruit indentured labourers may have also stayed here. More recently it has become the only hotel in the district that can boast a three-star rating. Many worshippers of Buddha stay here to visit the neighbouring town of Sravasti which is famous for the Buddhist stupas and ruins. Lord Buddha spent part of his life here and demonstrated his supernatural powers.

As we made our way to Luxmanpur Dharampur, *aajua* and *aajiya's* hamlet, we did not know what to expect. It was about an hour's drive from the hotel. Once we were off the main highway, we drove on a short track, through fields of mustard, pigeon peas, and other assorted vegetable crops to reach the hamlet. Word must have been passed around about our arrival. More than 50 men and children from the hamlet had gathered and were waiting for our appearance. Most men had stopped work on their farms to come and see us. We were warmly welcomed and invited to sit in an area that was set up with chairs and rope beds. The absence of women in this crowd was evident. We saw glimpses of women peeping through windows – all were covered in *ghoongat* (a veil covering the head and face). These veils are traditionally worn by Hindu women who are married. Evidence of patriarchy was on show before my eyes. One by one we were introduced to our extended family. They were all males who were dressed in their traditional outfits comprising a *turban* (*cloth wound around the head*), shirt and *dhoti* (*long loin cloth worn around the waist*). As they embraced me, they also touched my feet. The latter is a prevalent practice in India. It is a way to show respect to an elder – I despise this practice because I believe that all of us are equal. No one person is more important than another. Personally, I show respect and love by either shaking hands, nodding my head, or hugging people in such contexts. But this is still their way.

Conversations started once we all sat on chairs and beds in a grassed area in the hamlet. Tea and some sweets were served. As an Australian family, we were very conscious of hygiene, and we went easy on what was served. We had done our research on some of the health risks associated with food and water in rural areas. They did not look too impressed when we politely refused what was being served or did not finish drinking the tea or eating the sweet that we had accepted. I would have felt that same if my guests responded in the same vein. But there was no way in which I could explain our behaviour. I did not think that there was anyone in this audience who have understood the rationale of our actions.

Understandably, those that had gathered were very keen to know more about *aajua* and *aajiya's* lives and their descendants. While none of their brothers or their wives were alive, the story of an elder brother and his wife who had left their village to go to a *taapu* (island) was told and re-told through the generations that followed. Being fluent in Hindi was a real asset. We were able to tailor the Fiji Hindi to suit the local audience. They were surprised and pleased that even after nearly 100 years, our language was relatively intact. We learnt that *aajua* and *aajiya* left the village because there were no opportunities for work. As far as they knew, no one else from the hamlet and surrounding villages had left for the *taapu* (meaning Fiji Islands). I was surprised to hear that even in 100 years since, no one from the generations that followed left this hamlet to work in other parts of India.

The conversations reaffirmed that *aajua* was the eldest, with two brothers, Murli and Nepal. Murli had three sons – Chedi Ram, Sukhai and Munnu. Chedi Ram's son was Ram Dhiraj who had three sons – Saankchit, Ravi, Parmod, and Lognath (who had deceased). Sukhai had a son – Racha Ram. Munnu had a son – Ram Surat. Nepal had two daughters – one in Lalpur, and one in Luxmanpur Dharampur. According to the old and challengeable traditional Hindu customs, once daughters are married, they leave their homes forever. Thus, none of Nepal's descendants lived in this hamlet. *Aajiya* was from Kunwa that was a neighbouring village.

The people of Luxmanpur Dharampur who had gathered also wanted to know more about our religious beliefs and the caste system in Fiji. We are Hindus and Hinduism is our religion. The caste system is ingrained in the fabric of this religion. Much like royalty, it is a closed system and a person's social status is determined by the caste they are born into. As a consequence, the system also places boundaries and imposes protocols on how people of different castes interact with each other (Deshpande, 2010). High caste Hindus would often look down upon those who were identified as low caste and kept their distance – both socially and physically. The caste system also dictated where people lived. In some instances, resources such as well-water would not be shared by people of different castes. High caste Hindus would also not accept food that was prepared by someone of a lower caste. Weddings were also arranged between members of the same caste. While the Indian constitution prohibits discrimination on the basis of caste, I could sense from the conversations that in this hamlet, the caste system was alive and well. I am not sure what they would have construed from my comment that the caste system was long gone amongst most Hindus in Fiji.

As the conversation rolled on, I still had some doubts about whether these people were really the members of my extended family. However, everything changed once I was introduced to *Masterji*, an elderly gentleman who was once a teacher of Sanskrit in the local college. *Masterji* had a special place in the family. He was one of the few in the village who was educated. Thus, on behalf of the family, he was the person who used to respond to the letters that the family received from *aajua* and *aajiya* in Fiji. One of their sons used to write these letters on behalf of them. The older members of the family and *Masterji* shared some of the stories that they gathered from the letters. They were all correct – it was information that I had not shared with the member of parliament when I emailed him the details. One of the highlights, mainly for my children, was when I recited a lullaby with *Masterji* which I learnt from my *aaja*. He had learnt this lullaby from my *aajua* and *aajiya*. *Masterji* said that it was an old *lori* (lullaby) that parents would sing to their children to help them sleep in olden times. Apparently, *Masterji* was probably the only one in the hamlet who knew this *lori*. The others looked a bit stunned as we recited it. My sons also learnt this from me and hearing it from *Masterji* was an experience that they could not put in words. It is a lullaby that defines my family and me in some way. It is unique and will hopefully be passed on through the generations still to come as it has through the generations that have already passed. Our granddaughter Gwenevieve has been reciting parts of this *lori* since the age of three. Meeting *Masterji,* learning about the letters, and the recital of the lullaby reaffirmed that we were indeed in the right hamlet.

For all the time during the conversation, we were sitting in front of a house which looked in very good shape. Built in concrete, it was about the size of a three-bedroom home. I thought it was the home of our family. About 45 minutes into the chit-chat, I requested if I could go inside the family home and meet the female members of the family. We were told that the house that we were sitting in front of belonged to the local *tahsildar* (government official responsible for revenue and land matters). We appreciated his hospitality but were surprised to learn that our family like others lived behind *tahsildar's* house. We were not invited to go into his house. We were not introduced to the female members of his family either even though we noticed a few heads covered in *ghoongat* bob up and down from the balcony.

As we got up to go to head in the direction where our relatives lived, the whole crowd followed us through a track that went past the *tahsildar's* house and through the farm. It opened into a narrow dirt lane with houses on either side. These dwellings were very different to the *tahsildar's* house. A range of materials was used in the construction of these houses, and some looked no more than shacks. There was no evidence of electrical power poles or water taps. We also went past cow paddocks. My family by caste are *aahirs* and by occupation they are cow herders and farmers. The presence of cows suggested that many residents in the hamlet were *aahirs* (Figure 2.3).

The original family home was divided into two sections. We entered one of the sections and were led through a dark room (presumably the central part of the house) with mud floors and no windows or significant furniture, to a much smaller adjoining room. We were told that this was the room where *aajua* was born. Connecting the two rooms was a corridor, and this is where we met the female members of the family. All were in *ghoongat*, and some of them looked quite young. They embraced my mum, Ramila, and Jo but kept their distance from us, the males. This behaviour is deeply rooted in the traditional Hindu culture. However, they all touched my feet. As all this was happening, the neighbours were trying to have a look as well to see what was going on and for some the roof served as an excellent viewing platform. We were then taken to the other part of the house where they rolled out a rope bed in a small court-yard. I had seen these beds in Bollywood movies many times. It just felt so good because at last I was sitting on one of these beds with my own people in rural India. As we went through the houses, it became very evident why we were seated outside the tahsildar's home. There was no suitable place or furniture in their homes for us to sit and have a chat.

Our tour of *aajua* and *aajiya's* hamlet lasted for a little over two hours and it was getting late in the afternoon. Apparently, *daakus* (bandits) still roamed in the area, and we were told that generally after dark the area became a bit unsafe. I was thoroughly touched by the old and the young of my extended

FIGURE 2.3   A view of the hamlet

family who held our hands and did not want to let go. They seemed to have nothing, but they kept saying, "please do not go, stay here". A couple of others wanted to come with us. For most of them, us coming from Australia in an aeroplane did not seem to make much sense. Our trip was a surreal experience and one of my life's moments that I will take to my grave. At last, we were able to take my ancestors' spirits back to their homes. It was an indescribable emotional experience. The words of Sir Issac Newton ring in my ears each time I think of this visit: "If I have seen further than others, it is by standing upon the shoulders of giants". This quote resonates with me because by standing on the shoulders of my *girmiteer ancestors,* we were able to see beyond the boundaries of Luxmanpur Dharampur.

5   Lesson Learnt – Education Is a Passport to a Better Life, But Getting This Privilege Is Not Always Easy

These *girmiteers* had the courage to take risks and open the world in unseen ways for those who came after. Despite living oppressed lives, they never whinged or whined. They just got on with it and faced the challenges head-on. In the process, they were able to create unseen opportunities for descendants like myself. On my visit to my ancestral hamlet, I felt that my extended family in India were trapped in time and little seemed to have changed since my *aajua* and *aajiya* left for Fiji nearly a century ago. There was a stark contrast in terms of the education levels and the living standards of those who grew up in this hamlet and those of us who were born in Fiji and Australia. The visit showed the transformation that education makes in people's lives. The visit confirmed that education is one of the few ways that gaps between the oppressors and the oppressed can be eliminated. My ancestors did just that by setting up Naidovi Primary School which has enabled us to carve our lives in unseen and unique ways. They never got a chance to get out of their oppressed lives through education. However, while they were illiterate, they also smart enough to collectively recognise their place within the oppressive system (Burbules & Berk, 1999). They would have become increasingly more conscious of their situations. They also had the courage not to accept the *status quo* and over time this belief would have triggered the start of their own reflections and actions or "liberatory praxis" (p. 52). One of their concrete actions that followed was the building of the primary school. Without any education, the girmiteers seemed to know a lot about critical pedagogies! For them, education was a leveler and the only way to break away from the oppressive cycle of hopelessness and despair. And they were right. Their vision, hard work, and sacrifices has paid off and made a huge difference to our lives.

Going Back to Naidovi

We can change the world and make it a better place. It is in your hands to make a difference.

NELSON MANDELA

The video accompanying this chapter is freely available online at https://doi.org/10.6084/m9.figshare.10305089

My visit to my ancestral village in 2007, followed by a brief stop at my primary school in 2009 and then my return to my home in Australia, set me on a journey of critical thinking about education in the developing world. My in-depth reflections and recollections led me on a path of temporality where I was connecting the dots between yesterday, today, and tomorrow (Freire & Macedo, 2005). The reflections interrogated my critical consciousness because I was problematising the context. In this process, I was critically analysing the reality by not only feeling connected with it but also by thinking of strategies that could be implemented to address the issues through dynamic social interactions with the school community. In the words of Martin Luther King, Jr., the "function of education is to teach one to think intensively and to think critically". It was my time to put my education to the test by not just thinking intensively and critically but also by acting accordingly. For me the big question was – What value can I add to the work that was started by my illiterate ancestors at my primary school? This chapter highlights the initiatives that were taken to tackle some of the issues that the school was facing.

© KONINKLIJKE BRILL NV, LEIDEN, 2020 | DOI:10.1163/9789004406872_003

1   An Initial Way Forward

In many systems, the issues that are visible on the surface are the effects of
underlying causes. These issues can vary in terms of complexities. However,
specifically targeted investigations can sometimes lead to an understanding of
the mechanics of the causal factors. The research focussed on the Fijian Education System suggests that factors such as a lack of strategic teacher professional development and resources have significantly impacted on the quality
of education, especially in rural and remote schools (e.g. Bessell, 2009; Mohan,
Lingam, & Chand, 2017; Tavola, 1990). Both these issues stem from the fact
that there is inadequate funding for education. The government supports all
schools in Fiji through per-capita and fee-free grants (Lingam & Lingam, 2013).
The fee-free grant option was set up in 1994, and despite inflation, government
subsidy remained at approximately $30 per pupil per year (about 15 USD) for
more than 20 years for most children in primary schools. In many instances, this
would be the only funds that primary school head teachers would have to buy
resources. More than 99% of the schools in the country are managed by either
locally elected school committees or religious organisations because they are
all grant-in-aid schools. The system set up in 1916 to support non-government
schools has stood the test of time, but it has not been a fair and equitable model
(Tavola, 1990). As explained previously, it is a system which is underpinned by
a partnership between the government and local communities. Through this
arrangement, the schools have to meet their running expenses by contributing
towards their capital and recurrent expenditure. Understandably, schools in
more prosperous neighbourhoods tend to do a lot better under this arrangement because parents are wealthier and generally better educated. Of significance is the fact that more than a third of the rural population (37.6%) live
below the poverty line (Fiji Bureau of Statistics, 2015). The bureau estimates
adults who can afford weekly living expenses of $55.12 (urban) (about 27 USD),
and $49.50 (rural) (about 25 USD) live above the poverty line. The International
Labour Organisation (2016) noted that rural workers earned less than half of
their urban counterparts which has led to higher levels of poverty. Given this
state of affairs, for a significant proportion of rural dwellers their day to day
survival would be a priority over channelling their meagre incomes to support
schools. My interactions with those that I met during my visit to the school
made it abundantly clear that many in the community were struggling. For
these reasons, there was a compelling case to support Naidovi Primary School.
    Upon my return from Fiji, I had numerous conversations with my wife and
children, family members, work colleagues, and friends about the situation in
my primary school. These conversations enabled me to brainstorm and identify

what was realistically doable as a way forward. Based on my observations and discussions with the school's head teacher and members of the school committee, it became abundantly clear that there were two areas that we could support and provide our expertise. Our first priority was resources. Ramila, my wife, has extensive experience as a librarian. Her focus was on gathering library books. I started my hunt for new and second-hand digital technologies such as laptops, cameras, data projectors and robotic kits. With no funding for our initiatives, we relied on donations to beef up our personal contributions. Our idea was to set up a learning centre where both print and digital resources could co-exist and be used productively. Our second priority was to provide professional development so that the teachers could use the resources with confidence. We planned to deliver these activities through co-teaching by working with the teachers on the ground (Cook & Friend, 1995). Accordingly, our idea was to volunteer and spend up to three weeks with the teachers. This can be an effective strategy to understand the dynamics of a school. But our first priority was to source and ship some resources that could be used in the classrooms.

To get this initiative underway, we needed library books so that every child could borrow at least one book on a weekly basis. We called this our 'one book per child' strategy. The primary purpose was to introduce students to a range of materials to promote the enjoyment of books through reading and researching. Ultimately this could enhance their literacy and facilitate lifelong learning skills. But more importantly, Carlos Maria Dominguez's famous quote sums it all, "to build up a library is to create a life. It's never just a random collection of books". The strategy was to source second-hand library books that were suitable for primary school students. However, a key criterion was that the book had to be in good condition. Just because we were donating resources did not mean that we could give junk. It had to be resources that we would willingly use ourselves. One of the colleges in the local area was weeding out its collection in its library – we were able to buy some of the books from here at low cost. Friends and relatives donated some books from their collections. Students at Kedron High School in Brisbane also donated some books. We also bought some to make the numbers up to 400. We drove and collected the books ourselves and stored them in our garage. The next phase involved preparing the books for the library shelves. This meant putting labels and stickers to identify their appropriateness for lower, middle and upper primary school students. Ramila created a spreadsheet so that the library had a digital record of its collection. Entering the data in the spreadsheet also took a while.

Gathering a suite of useful technologies was our next focus. We opted for laptops because they do not need a permanent room in a school. They are also lighter – therefore transportation costs are lower. Our strategy here was to secure a class set of 12 second-hand laptops. For a while, we did not know where to source these devices. A month before our proposed trip to Fiji, I had a call from a member of the university staff. It must have been about 9 am in the morning. "Mate, this is Kevin from the Faculty of Science and Engineering. We have second-hand laptops to give away. Are you interested?" For a moment, I thought I was talking to God. It was such an excellent gesture especially from a colleague in another faculty from within our university. Kevin was a logistics officer and after this initial connection, he has been very supportive of our initiatives. The laptops were different models and as the saying goes, beggars cannot be choosers. I accepted them all and was truly thankful to Kevin. We were still short, and my head of school generously donated two of her laptops to make the numbers to 12. The support provided by Professor Kar-Tin (Head of my School), Professor Wendy Patton (Former Dean of our Faculty) and Professor Martin Betts (Former Dean of the Faculty of Science and Engineering) was invaluable in getting this initiative underway.

Then we had another hurdle. Most of the laptops did not have an operating system because they were erased from the hard drive at the time of handover. To buy a brand-new Windows XP system would have set me back a few hundred dollars for each laptop. Luckily, Issac Pursehouse, one of our students who was a member of Engineers Without Borders (EWB) came to my rescue. Through his efforts, we were able to install the Windows XP operating systems legally at a relatively low cost. Once the operating systems were in place, the next challenge followed. Finding the right drivers for the computers was not an easy task. Almost all the laptops were different – therefore we had to hunt for the drivers. My colleague Dr Andy Yeh who has an excellent background in digital technologies gave me hand. Eventually, we got there – all operating systems were loaded on the laptops and they were ready for the next step.

Once the systems and drivers were installed, we had to find software that was suitable for primary school children. The logic here was to install software that could run offline and were free. We found a range of applications. *Libre Open Office* is a powerful suite that includes a range of options: *Writer* (word processing), *Calc* (spreadsheets), *Impress* (multimedia), *Draw* (vector graphics and flowcharts), *Base* (databases), and *Math* (formula editing). Other applications which we installed included *Microsoft Photo Story 3 for Windows, Audacity, Google SketchUp, Jing, Freemind, TuxPaint, TuxMath*, and *Scratch*. Getting some of these to download and work after installation was also challenging. To download these applications, we had to be connected to the Internet – luckily this task became a lot easier once the drivers were installed. We also explored ways to ensure that Internet could be wirelessly picked up by the laptops in Fiji. This was based on the assumption that the school had an Internet connection. A wireless router was the best option to do this. We also managed to get a second-hand data projector, digital cameras and some brand new external hard drives. We were most grateful to a friend in Hong Kong who was very generous with his donation of a class set of LEGO robotic kits for our project which was shipped directly to the school.

Packing the books and the digital resources into suitable cartons was the next hurdle. It is amazing how heavy books can be. As a consequence, we sourced cartons that could be lifted by one person when packed with books. On the other hand, digital technologies are a lot lighter but are more fragile. Finding cartons of appropriate size with packaging materials was very difficult. After much searching and creative thinking, we managed to package all the books and all the digital resources. Our next challenge was to find a freight forwarder whose charges were affordable. We did notice that there were some significant differences between the quoted prices. One of the companies initially quoted an inflated price and then gave us a discount to show their commitment toward supporting our work. Eventually we found a reliable freight forwarder and we able to transport all the resources and documentation to the freight forwarding company a week before our departure. Brian our neighbour was kind enough to lend his ute to transport all the cartons. We paid for the shipment from Australia to Fiji ourselves. We left the clearance expenses and on the ground transportation costs in Fiji to the school. It was all a part of a learning process – it had to be lived. Figure 3.1 summarises some of the key steps that were undertaken to facilitate the deployment of the resources package to Naidovi Primary School.

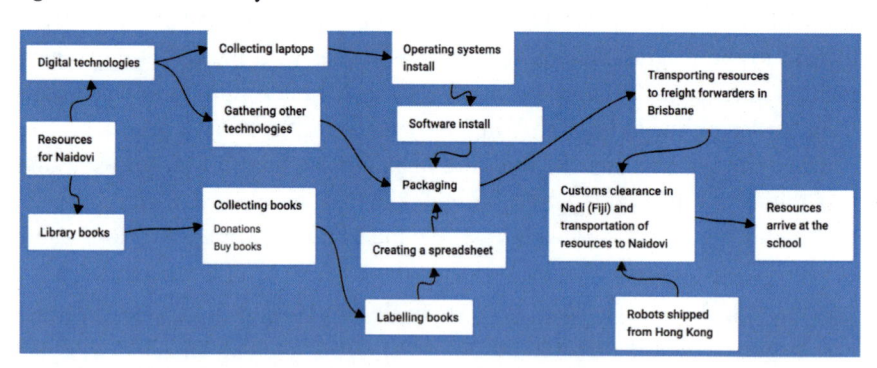

FIGURE 3.1   Deployment of resources to Naidovi Primary School

2   Three Weeks at Naidovi

In October 2011, we arrived at Naidovi Primary School. We were going to work alongside teachers and students at the school. Since my last visit in 2009, a new library block had been built. This building was funded by the Japanese

Government and included some tables, benches and shelving. To my knowledge, this would probably be the first time that foreign aid was given to this school for capital works. The Pacific Islands are "one of the most aid-dependent regions in the world" with $178 billion handed out in 2014 (Dornan & Pryke, 2017, p. 386). However, how this aid manifests on the ground is anyone's guess. I have not been able to work it out – neither as a citizen in a recipient country (Fiji) or as a citizen of a donor country (Australia). Thus, for many of us understanding the ins and outs of foreign aid is a real puzzle. Citizens of donor countries, the real tax payers, never get to know the nuts and bolts of how the money is spent. Many Australians think that foreign aid is a handout with money that is given holus bolus to the recipients. This is far from the truth. Citing a report prepared by a Bristol-based group Development Initiatives, Provost (2013) pointed out that at least 20% of the aid never leaves the shores of the donor counties. In 2012, Julie Bishop (then Shadow Minister for Foreign Affairs), claimed that Australia was the third largest recipient (after Indonesia and Papua New Guinea) of its own foreign aid (Vasek, 2012). While large headlines are presented as if "aid is entirely a cash lump sum", a lot of the money gets used up in the hire of consultants and staff who provide "advice" and "training" (para. 4). Political parties like "One Nation" which is anti-foreign aid, take a worryingly uneducated view of the "golden money flow out of Australia" (One Nation, 2014) at the expense of potentially benefitting the unfortunate and the elderly in the recipient countries. There is also limited will amongst the politicians of major parties to fully explain the mechanics of foreign aid to the wider community. For example, in Australia, we hardly hear any good stories about what foreign aid has achieved in a developing country. The real impact of this funding on the ground is barely shared with the citizens. As a consequence, it fuels perceptions and speculations that foreign aid does not deliver any real outcomes in the recipient countries. Many taxpayers conclude that it is money which is poured down the drain.

On this occasion, seeing the library building made me feel very grateful to the people of Japan. This 8-metre by 8-metre library block will make a real difference to the children at this school, both in the present and for many years to come. The Japanese support would be one of the most effective forms of foreign aid. It was a tangible outcome that the Japanese taxpayers could be proud of. Under their government's Grant Assistance for Grassroots Human Security Projects program, 256 projects were undertaken to address basic human needs that directly impacted on education, sanitation and water supplies. This project cost $90,000 (about 43,000 USD). Without this support, the community would not have been able to raise the money. Under the grant-in-aid scheme, they would have needed to raise at least $45,000 before they could seek government contribution. This would have been a formidable task and probably explains why the last time a building was built at this school was in 1972. It was the year when I finished primary school. Since then the school has not been in a position to undertake any major capital works. Apart from the new library block, all other buildings looked very tired, and it was evident that no significant renovations had occurred either.

The laptops and other technologies which we had shipped from Brisbane coincided with our arrival at the school. They arrived on the day we met the teachers for the first time. The boxes were intact. The Government of Fiji ought to be commended because it did not charge any duty on the second-hand resources that we had shipped. The computers were stored in the library and I was quite fascinated to see that the school had arranged a watchman because the security grills had not been installed on the windows in this building. A few members of the school community joined in for a few hours in the evening outside the library to give the watchman company. I also joined in to catch up on the stories and the latest village gossip. Fiji and the Pacific Islands' national drink, *Kava* (explained in detail in Chapter 5), was also on offer and I sculled a few bowls. It was after a very long time that I joined such a social gathering. These sessions create opportunities to share the knowledge and information at the grassroots level. Regrettably, in many instances, membership is open to men only whilst women are chained to their homes and vested with the responsibilities of dealing with all sort of chores that go beyond the management of households. Education may change all this one day!

Before our travel, we had discussed our plans with the head teacher, and the staff were well-versed regarding our intentions. However, we still had many doubts about what we would do with the teachers. Prior to our travel, it was difficult to ascertain what they would be doing as there were no annual or term teaching programs that we could put our hands on. The first time we met the teachers, we explained our objectives. A quick survey showed that in this group, about 75% of the teachers had their own computers which were at least one year old. They had intermittent access to the Internet, and all were using their computers for school work which included the creation of test papers for the new classroom-based assessments (CBA). We started a conversation with the teachers to understand more about their interests and the work they were doing with their students. Our mantra was to assure the teachers that we were at their school to work with them and not impose anything on them (Freire, 2000). Our primary objective was to ascertain what was happening in schools and then formulate a plan that would not only blend in but enrich the classroom landscape. Understandably there were some reservations, but a couple of points came through as we chatted with the teachers.

When I was a student here, it was predominantly an Indian school. This was clearly stated in its name – Naidovi Indian School. Thankfully, a government initiative was encouraging school committees to do away with racial affiliations in their names. Polarising communities through schools in this way was a divide-and-rule formula that was implemented by the British during the colonial era. There was no place for such divisions in a multi-cultural society of modern-day Fiji. During my time, there were hardly any indigenous Fijian students even though the school was a stone's throw away from their homes. The parents opted to send their children to a Fijian school which was at least a 30-minute walk from their homes. With a name change to Naidovi Primary School, the school's diversity of ethnicity also changed. Now, almost over half of the children at the school were Fijians. We did not have any Fijian teachers during my time either. But this also changed because the school had both Indian and Fijian teachers. It was a very pleasing and positive change to see.

Another change was that teachers now had to complete a Fiji Island Primary School Learning record for each student. This document listed the content and achievement indicators as dot points under units in each subject. The expected outcomes and benchmark statements were also listed for each unit. In Class 1, there were seven subjects: English, Literature, Mathematics, Science, Social Studies, Health Sciences, Physical Education, Art and Craft, and Music. Fijian, Hindi, Urdu and Rotuman were optional language subjects. Teachers had to state the assessment methods (formative or summative) that were used to assess the identified learning outcomes and also report on students' achievement levels as 'basic', 'proficient' or 'advanced' against each achievement indicator. From my point of view, the text in the student learning record booklets had all the hallmarks of the 'traditional' Outcomes-Based Education. It was strongly aligned with "established disciplines" that had "a strong focus on content and year level organisation" with limited explicit and meaningful connections to the real world (Spady, as cited in Donnelly, 2007). This approach also mandated teachers to design classroom-based assessments (CBA) so that they could report on student progress for each of the listed achievement indicators. The overall achievement levels were determined by taking into consideration students' knowledge and understanding, skills and attitudes demonstrated in the classroom-based assessment.

Both these approaches were very new to the education system in Fiji. As a consequence, teachers' anxieties and lack of knowledge regarding how to proceed were evident. I remember when outcomes-based education was introduced in Science in Queensland Secondary Schools in 1999. At the time, I was teaching at a high school and was in charge of the Science Department. In this role, I had to not only develop unit plans with pedagogies and assessment tasks, I also had to sell the idea to my colleagues. It was a nightmare! Two teachers reading an outcome would interpret it in different ways and from where they were standing, both would be correct. At times it was like being on a rudderless ship – we knew we were going somewhere but the destination was unclear. We were not alone. Teachers throughout Australia were struggling with the implementation of outcomes-based education (Dawson & Venville, 2006). We were expected to interpret the achievement indicators and then design appropriate assessment tasks. However, we also struggled to shift away from marks to terminologies such as 'Not yet competent', 'Progressing', 'Very good' and so on to describe students' performance. The complexity of this change increased as the outcomes approach was introduced in other subjects. The terminologies used to describe performance varied across subject areas which complicated the picture for all stakeholders – teachers, students, and parents. For many parents, the terminologies that were used in grading the students did not make much sense. In the case of the teachers at Naidovi, I understood their problems – too much was impinging on them simultaneously. They had to adapt to designing classroom tasks where the assessment was neither based on exams nor on marks. Also, they had to figure out how to distinguish between students' work and grade them as 'basic', 'proficient' or 'advanced'. To demonstrate such capabilities teachers needed to be skilled so that they could conduct moderations between student responses.

From my observations, the content and achievement indicators that were given to teachers at Naidovi were very vague with limited details. They were far too open-ended. For one of the themes in Class 1 Science, students were expected to conduct investigations to understand the characteristics of animals. For example, something as mundane as "Identify places where hair grows in people" was simple, yet it became complicated when there were no guidelines regarding what types of responses would be considered as 'basic', 'proficient' or 'advanced'. Some of the indicators were quite confusing. In the theme on animals, there were achievement indicators such as "State that insects have four legs" (Really? An insect is supposed to have *six* legs!) and "State that insects have three body parts". There were no supporting strategies on how these concepts should be taught. How would a student be rated if he said an insect had four body parts? Some of the indicators specifically needed students to use specialist materials such as hand lens, propeller, syringe, mirrors, and magnets. This would have been an issue for poorer schools like Naidovi. Some indicators listed the use of ice. Twenty-five percent of remote and rural schools in Fiji did not have electricity (World Bank, 2017). How would these schools deliver this outcome? Narayan (2014) investigated the challenges of the internal assessment system in Fijian schools by interviewing 57 teachers. Amongst the findings, the researchers noted that in some of the achievement indicators, parents had to provide their children with resources, such as research tasks that were Internet dependent. Some of the parents were unable to provide their children with this technology support because of financial and connectivity barriers. As a consequence, the curriculum expectations had the potential to negatively impact on the performance of many students.

In order to develop a deeper understanding of the context, it was important for me to understand the drivers and some of the reported impact of this new change in Fijian classrooms. According to Narayan (2014), the adoption of outcomes-based education model was fuelled by the Fiji Education Sector Program (FESP). This was a $28 million AusAID project that spanned six years from 2003 to 2009 (Pennington, Ireland, & Narsey, 2010). It was delivered by Cardno ACIL, in conjunction with the Western Australia Department of Education and Training, and the Curtin University of Technology. The Ministry of Education in Fiji was the implementing partner. The goal of this program was to assist the Fijian Ministry of Education (MoE) to implement strategic reforms, thereby improving the quality of educational services in Fiji, "especially to disadvantaged and remote children" (p. 15). An independent assessment of the program by Pennington et al. (2010, p. 29) reported that it was "unclear whether anything" had actually changed in the classroom. The assessment team also noted that "indicators such as student enrolment, retention and academic performance" were not influenced by "changes in management practice, new curriculum and assessment approaches or improvements in teacher capacity" (p. 30). Many of the benefits that were introduced by the program never made it to the classrooms. Amongst other findings, the reviewers also noted little evidence of "school-based planning" that influenced the design of classroom activities, provision of resources, and monitoring of management practices. Many of these points were evident as I made my observations at the grassroots level at Naidovi.

It was baffling to comprehend that an outcomes-based approach that was known to be so problematic in developed countries with far more resources (e.g. Australia, UK, and the US) was adopted for the Fijian system as a way forward. In a review of outcomes-based education, Donnelly (2007) argued that such an approach was "conceptually flawed, difficult to implement and superficial in its approach to detailing essential learning" (p. 183). The emphasis on attitudes, dispositions, and competencies diverged from the essential learnings that are associated with the structure of the disciplines. Even the Western Australian Department of Education Services (2001) pointed out that the introduction of outcomes-based education was a major change that all entities within the system, from education offices to schools, were not well-equipped to deal with. Within the Fijian context, teachers identified the lack of resources, increased workloads, over-assessment, lack of professional development opportunities, and student absenteeism as factors that were directly associated with the introduction of the outcomes-based education model (Narayan, 2014).

The issues and challenges faced by schools in Fiji were not novel. Education systems throughout the world are like machines and whenever there subjected to changes, they take time to recalibrate and readjust. Almost fifty years ago, when the education system in Queensland was undergoing major changes, the late Les Winkle, Executive Officer of the Board of Secondary School Studies acknowledged the impact as follows; "I am well aware that sometimes this rather large machine has creaked and rumbled, lurched and faltered, and this I regret" (Board of Secondary School Studies Information Bulletin as cited in Clarke, 1987, p. 26). It takes a strong leader of change to acknowledge such challenges. Curriculum implementation in Fiji follows a top-down model. Teachers do not have a strong voice because apparently "the ministry knows" what they are doing. However, after having made all these observations, we had to work with what was in front of us. My role here was neither to critique nor whine about the system but to work with it. We had to internalise US President Roosevelt's profound advice, "do what you can, with what you have, where you are", and run with it.

3   Designing and Implementing Technology-Driven Classroom Activities

No matter what the education system, my experiences have led me to the belief that technologies can cause a disruption in classrooms. It is a tool and when it is used thoughtfully, it can change the classroom dynamics in terms of teaching and learning. My research in schools has demonstrated that technologies can have a positive impact on students' perceptions and attitudes (Chandra & Fisher, 2009). It can have a positive influence on their learning outcomes (Chandra & Lloyd, 2008; Chandra & Briskey, 2012; Chandra & Watters, 2012), and facilitate changes in teachers' pedagogies which can ultimately influence the core business of teaching and learning in classrooms (Chandra & Mills, 2014). However, teachers need to have an understanding of the why, how, and what of using technologies in their classes. Given our limited time at Naidovi Primary, our approach was to explain why technology should be used and then showcase how it could be implemented to enable students to demonstrate the achievement indicators listed in their 'Student Learning Record' booklets. We had group meetings with teachers in their cohort groups; junior, middle, and upper years. The idea was to ascertain what was going to be taught in the immediate future, and how they proposed to teach it. These conversations eventually meandered to brainstorming ideas that would enable teachers to embed technology into some of their existing classroom activities. Through such an approach, we did not impose our own ideas but worked with the teachers to explore possibilities for varying their pedagogies to deliver the content using technologies. As a consequence, we agreed that LEGO robotic kits would be a lunchtime activity for older children. Three of the computer applications – *LibreOffice Impress, Microsoft Windows Moviemaker,* and *Microsoft Photo Story 3 for Windows* would be used in classroom activities that aligned with the achievement indicators in the 'Student Learning Record' booklets. Teachers were highly responsive to the ideas. However, we acknowledged that there was a need for strategic planning, given that we only had access to 12 laptops, two digital cameras, two web cameras, and no access to the Internet. Many of the children would also be using computers for the first time, thus familiarising them with this new technology was also viewed as a significant challenge. Nonetheless, we began our engagement with the teachers and their students in earnest.

3.1   *Class 1 and 2 (6–7 Year Olds)*

In Class 1 and 2, the unit that the children were studying in social studies was called "A local Festival". Suitable achievement indicators for the activity were, 1. Name a local festival and 2. Identify events that occur during the festival. As part of this activity, the teachers talked to the students about a festival that they had been to and what they had done. From their recollections, they were asked to draw a sketch of their experiences. Understandably their interpretations on the sketches varied. Within the room there was scarcity of sheets of paper that were uniform in size. A lot depended on what the teacher could provide. The papers ranged from pieces of A4 sheets to ruled pages from exercise books. The students did some fantastic drawings for their presentations of a local festival. Of note was that they all saw different things that were of interest to them at the festivals (Figure 3.2). Every sketch seemed to focus on a different aspect – 100 points for creativity! We took digital images of these sketches and created a multimedia presentation using *LibreOffice Impress.* This activity enabled students to showcase their work and explain what they had drawn to their peers. This was a first-time experience and all children in the class were excited about this new engagement approach to sharing their work.

FIGURE 3.2   A sketch of a festival from a student

3.2   *Class 3 and 4 (8–9 Year Olds)*

Class 3 and 4's were studying a unit called "Life in an Indian rural settlement", though the teachers had decided to focus their attention to include the Fijian rural context, too, given that the school was in close proximity of both these settlements. There were a couple of Fijian villages in the vicinity and many Indian families also lived in the neighbourhood. All were within walking distance. We set them a challenge of creating a multimedia presentation using *Windows Photo Story 3*. The students had to create a digital story comprising 10 images on either an Indian or Fijian settlement. For the task, students were divided into groups as they headed off to either a Fijian village or an Indian settlement. I joined the groups as well. The first group went to *Voua* village which is about 300 metres from the school entrance. Most of the indigenous population in rural areas have always lived in villages. Even though we did not have enough cameras, the students willingly shared them and took lots of photos. The children were very well behaved. One of the village elders, the late Lepani, showed a lot of interest in our work at the school. He visited us at the school almost daily. When I lived in this neighbourhood, Lepani used to be our neighbour – his family lived around the corner from our home. Like some of the villagers who were very close to my family, Lepani also was always there to lend us a hand in need. Playing the guitar was one of his passions and he always enjoyed Indian music. As Lepani took us around, I also got a chance to meet a number of villagers – some I had not seen for decades.

One thing that struck me was the design and construction of the houses. *Bure* houses seem to have long gone. Traditional *bure* houses were made from materials that could be sourced locally such as straws and bamboo for walls and roof, and timber poles for framing. Nowadays, houses are made of brick, timber, and corrugated iron. It makes sense to make houses this way given that cyclones are very frequent in this part of the world. While on the one hand it was pleasing to see the changes that have occurred, on the other hand it would have also been good to capture some of the images and videos of the village as it changed over time. But this could not have been done because in the past, cameras were a technology that was in the hands of the rich and the professionals. These days with increasing affordability and capability of these technologies, many can engage and participate in telling a story of the changing times. The visit prompted me to think about how digital stories can capture the evolution of the world and its people over time. Most of us can participate in this journey. Engaging students in the craft of digital storytelling at the school level is probably the starting point. Such an opportunity can also extend and enhance the school curriculum in unseen and remarkable ways.

I joined the next group which headed to *Hanahana* village. This village is directly across the road from the school. The last time when I lived here, this village did not exist. It used to be Sakiusa's sugarcane farm. He was a Fijian landowner and often due to a lack of drive and motivation, the land was left barren and uncultivated. I do not know what the arrangements were, but the farm became a village. Most of the people who now lived here came from other parts of the country and work at the local five-star resort. Lepani was once again our guide. To an outsider like myself, there was nothing special about the homes or the surroundings but the villagers were very proud of what they had. The construction was basic with evidence of ingenuity and improvisation scattered throughout the village. The walls and the roofs of the homes were made of corrugated iron, with concrete flooring. Like many homes in rural areas, cooking was done in a small makeshift shed adjacent to homes. The design of the stoves was basic. Three besser blocks were positioned at right angles to each other leaving an opening for the firewood. Metal rods or steel mesh was placed on top of the blocks to support cooking pots. Like many houses in developing countries, there were vegetable gardens and fruits within close proximity. For the students, this little excursion was exciting. It was a rare opportunity to walk around with their classmates and take photos.

Lepani returned to the school with us bringing his guitar and sang some songs. I have always admired his talent, and more so as a native Fijian who sang Hindi songs. Almost all people who live in rural and remote parts of Fiji have developed their musical talents through their own efforts and persistence. Opportunities for developing these skills at school or with a specialist tutor outside school are non-existent. However, in some instances there is a chance for the locals to develop their skills through observation and coaching from a village elder. This is how traditional learning has occurred outside the school for generations in the developing world. It is a good example of cognitive apprenticeship where novices are initiated into a community of expert practitioners (Berryman, n.d.; Collins, Brown, & Newman, 1989). Learners are exposed to a variety of methods that systematically encourages them to explore and become independent. The village elder scaffolds the learning by breaking the content into parts and, over time, hands the control of the learning process to the student. Despite the depth of knowledge and skills (e.g. playing musical instruments) that exists in these locals, they are kept at bay and out of schools. They are not encouraged to participate in schools because their real-world talents and skills are undervalued. More importantly, and regrettably, their knowledge did not have a place in the curriculum!

The third group went on an excursion to the Indian community that has lived behind the school buildings for generations. Here again, students took lots of photos and thoroughly enjoyed the outing. Even though they probably did not go any further than 500 metres from the school, the fact that they went as a class made the experience enjoyable. Some of them probably walked on the same path and road to get to school every day. Now they were seeing their village through a 'different lens'. On this occasion they were walking in the company of their classmates and they also found opportunities to play the role of tour guides, pointing out areas of interest for the photos. The teachers also said that such excursions were rare and that they too were able to see the value in this experience. It was pleasing to see what a small shift from their usual chalk-and-talk classrooms could achieve. I too was excited because I was bumping into some of the old folks after many decades.

After these excursions, the photos were downloaded from the camera to the laptops and made available for the students to create their Photo Stories. Working in groups of three to four students, they embraced this task and worked towards creating their presentations to showcase the aspects of life that they thought were important. *Windows Photo Story 3* was a versatile application that enabled students to create their audio-visual presentations. It allowed simple edits to images (e.g. cropping, rotation) and the addition of captions, titles, narration, sound effects, and background music. The files were able to be saved in the versatile WMV format, making them viewable on other devices. With some help, many students were able to go to the respective folders, identify, and import up to 10 photos for their photo stories. However, some students felt quite challenged to insert captions, due to their literacy skills. Their keyboarding skills were still evolving, and this tended to slow them down and cause some frustration.

3.3 Class 5 and 6 (10–11 Year Olds)

In classes 5 and 6, students were studying a unit focussed on "Sharing responsibilities" in their Health Science subject. In the achievement indicators, they had to demonstrate how they could "accept assigned duties, and share responsibilities at home, school, and community". Students created and acted out the scenarios in groups which demonstrated these outcomes. Their performances were videoed and shared with other classes. Through this exchange, students were challenged to decipher the messages that were being presented in the videos. More importantly, the videos were shot without any re-takes or special props. The students improvised to fill the gaps and all presentations had very clear messages which were aligned with the achievement indicator. The assigned duties and sharing of responsibilities that were focussed in the presentations ranged from those associated with ordinary citizens, to students, teachers, and policemen. It was pleasing to see that the teachers were able to embrace the activity with ease. They were able to get their students to brainstorm an idea with a "sharing responsibilities" theme, write a script, and put up a performance for the camera. All this was achieved in a relatively short time. And for the students, this was the first time that they had demonstrated an achievement outcome through role play and in front of a video camera.

I was very impressed to see the impact that these technologies had on teachers and their students. It does not take much to motivate the teachers to venture beyond their comfort zones and adopt new approaches in their teaching. However, if these technologies were simply donated to the school, without any support for the teachers in terms of how they can be integrated in their teaching, then the outcomes would have been very different. Without the infrastructure, resources and support; things do not just happen. More importantly the professional learning of the teachers needs to go hand in hand with any new initiatives that are implemented in schools.

4 Setting up of the School's Library

As Ramila took charge of setting the books, my focus was on setting up the digital technologies in the library. The head teacher decided that all technologies would be stored and used in the library. As the laptops were unpackaged, new issues started to emerge. Some of the laptops did not have the software installed on them. This hitch wasted a lot of time. The batteries in a couple of laptops were not holding charge. While this is expected of second-hand laptops, in this part of the world it can be a real issue. Schools do not have money to either access the services of computer technicians or replace defunct components. The design of the room was also an issue. There were two power points on opposite walls. With only one power outlet in each, the challenge of connecting 12 laptops was difficult. I did not want to overload the existing electrical circuit. The only option was to use multiple extension cables that powered the laptops on an intermittent basis. In doing this, there was a workplace health and safety concern as well. However, we did our best to hold the cords as close the floor as possible to prevent students from tripping over. There were problems with the Internet. The library was more than 50m from the school office. The router, which was hardwired to the modem, was kept in the school office, making a wireless connection to the library problematic. These teething problems highlighted the challenges schools faced when computers were donated to them from overseas. At least in this instance, I had some knowledge on how to deal with them.

Our understanding prior to our arrival was that the school did not have any library resources. But to our surprise some of the shelves in the library appeared reasonably filled. However, it turned out that many of these books were old textbooks and class sets that had been hiding on classroom shelves. According to the head teacher, in trying to save face, the staff had put some books on the shelves ahead of the official opening of the new library. It was held at the school a few weeks prior to our arrival. That was a special moment for the school with the Japanese Ambassador and other dignitaries in attendance. A green chalkboard was also donated – it was a first and a transition from the good old blackboard. We started to weed through their collection and my eyes were caught by three particular class sets of textbooks – *Fiji: The Land and Its People*, *Stories of Famous People*, and *World History*. I had used these books when I was a student here in classes 5 and 7. When I was in class 7, *World History* as a textbook became obsolete because in 1971, we became one of the trial schools for Social Studies – so history was no longer taught. While these books may still have had some aspects of the content that remained relevant, they were showing critical signs of aging. Many had gone past their use-by date. I was amazed that even after more than 40 years, many of these books were still in the school. There was no place for them in the curriculum either. I reasoned that the old books were not thrown away because they would leave gaps in the shelves. The school did not have financial resources to fill the shelves.

No one in the school had any significant knowledge about cataloguing and management of a library. Ramila worked with some of the staff to develop these skills. The 400-plus books that we had brought with us comprised a range of fiction, non-fiction, and reference books. A simplified library system was used to classify the collection into four major categories: fiction, non-fiction, reference books, and teacher reference resources. There was also a special collection which included language, student texts, and class sets of readers. The fiction collection was divided into three levels: beginner (Classes 1 & 2), intermediate (Classes 3 & 4) and advanced (Classes 5 & 6). For the ease of distinction for both teachers and students, the books were colour coded and given spine labels with call numbers denoting collection and author initials for ease of cataloguing. Once the cataloguing was finalised, the books were placed strategically on the shelves. Books for the lower grades were placed on the shelves closer to the floor to be easily reached. Colour codes help students select books that are appropriate to their age level. Uploading the details about books into a spreadsheet under headings such as book number, author, title, and spine label enables the school to find out exactly how many books they have of a particular type. This is a good way to stocktake and make decisions in terms of what other books are needed in a library collection. This is also practical information for donors who may be interested in donating books. Such documentation is also useful in terms of resource accountability and transparency of their use. Apart from showing the school staff how books are catalogued, Ramila also demonstrated how the details about books are entered and accessed from the spreadsheet. She created a library guide as a reference for the teachers where she provided information about strategies for cataloguing and shelfing books, suggested rules for library use, proposed ideas for creating a borrowing record, and pedagogies for conducting library classes. We also suggested to the headmaster that he appoint at least two teachers who would be directly responsible for managing the library.

Towards the end of our stay at the school, the library was open for business (Figure 3.3). The joy in eyes of the students and teachers was evident. For the first time, they had a chance to walk into a library and put their hands on books that they could actually take home for reading. One part of our strategy was to ensure that every child had a chance to borrow a book to read each week. Hence, our 'one book per child' idea could only succeed if we provided this library with more books. We had started them with 400 books. They needed another 300 to make this strategy work. This was our challenge for the following year. Until we got these books, students could only borrow every second week.

FIGURE 3.3   School library – Open for business

5   The Professional Learning of Teachers

Normal teaching occurred simultaneously with our activities. We ran professional development sessions after school for the teachers. Ideally it would have
been good if blocks of time were allocated for us to work with them, allowing
us to get stuck into some serious learning. However, the most feasible option
was for us to interact with the teachers after hours. Each of the sessions lasted
up to an hour and they willingly gave up their time to participate. Their enthusiasm created a very positive working environment and demonstrated their
interest in furthering their knowledge. In fact, for almost all teachers, this was
the first time that they were given an opportunity to participate in professional
development associated with digital technologies together with the management and use of libraries. We focussed on a range of topics. These included
the three software applications (*LibreOffice Impress, Windows Photo Story 3,
Windows Moviemaker*) that we had used in the different classes, giving all staff
a global understanding of what the children in the whole school were using.
We ran sessions on building and programming robots. The library sessions
presented ideas on how to catalogue and loan books, add data to the library
records spreadsheet, run library sessions for students, and design rich activities
using library resources.

    One of the senior education officers from the Education Office in Sigatoka
visited us. He was interested in our work. He told us that at the beginning of

each term, there was a meeting for head teachers and school principals in his district. The idea of this meeting was to inform these school leaders about the key issues that needed to be dealt with during the term. This meeting was scheduled to be held at another location. However, after seeing the work that we had started at Naidovi, he decided to shift the meeting to the school. He invited us to address the principals and head teachers. He also wanted us to showcase some of the work that we had started in the areas of library management, technology integration, and robotics. We were very pleased to see his level of interest and the fact that he rescheduled this meeting meant that the work that we were doing was adding value to the quality of education in the local context. More importantly, we would get the opportunity to address more than 60 school principals and head teachers in the district.

The presentation was held in the main building of the school that was built through the efforts of my ancestors and their colleagues. There are no school halls. Each time the school needs space for a special function with a large audience, the dividing walls between the three classrooms are removed and the building becomes a school hall. It is not a fancy hall like schools have in the West, but this setup does do the job. I have always been amazed by this design and the vision of designers in the 1920's. Standing in the room that was once my Class 4 room, I presented to the school leaders. They also toured the learning centre to see how the library was set up with the digital resources. The feedback we received from the participants made it obvious that our initiatives were valuable and important in enhancing the quality of education in Fiji. For us, the highlight was seeing some of the students explain to the school leaders what they were doing on the computers and with the robots and how it connected with their schoolwork. In fact, the students' demonstration of how the robots could be programmed to navigate through the Fiji Islands on a makeshift map intrigued all the participants. Two of the teachers, Adam Taylor and Ashneel Singh, did a great job in explaining more about how the technologies could be integrated into their classroom activities. It was very evident that collectively we had made very good progress in a relatively short time. The teachers and students had certainly come a long way!

6 Lesson Learnt – Together We Can Make a Difference

As our time on the ground drew to a close, it became increasingly evident that we all can make a difference in the world by sharing our knowledge and time. This knowledge sharing is not just confined to the field of education. No matter what our knowledge base, we all have ideas and strategies that we can share. Knowledge sharing is not a one-way street either. In the process of sharing our knowledge we also grow because we are presented with a golden opportunity to learn something new and at the same time unlearn and relearn what we thought we knew. This learning is underpinned by experience, which has been identified as a critical element in the learning process by seminal thinkers such as John Dewey, Kurt Lewin, Jean Piaget and David Kolb in the fields of Education and Psychology.

Our time at Naidovi enabled us to understand institutional and societal issues and how it played out in such contexts to a much deeper level (Barbules & Berk, 1999). Without this knowledge, concrete actions which underpin Critical Pedagogy cannot materialise meaningfully. For example, until I went to Naidovi Primary, my knowledge of how foreign aid worked on the ground was minimal. As a citizen of a donor country, we often assume that the financial assistance that is provided to recipient countries actually makes a difference on the ground. There are no doubts that many foreign-aid projects have delivered some very good outcomes. However, in the case of the Fiji Education Sector Program (FESP) which was funded by AusAID, I could not see any significant impact in terms of the quality of education at this school. One of the core objectives of this $28 million project was to enhance the quality of education in disadvantaged schools like Naidovi Primary. In this regard, my observations were consistent with some of the findings of the panel who reviewed this project (Pennington et al., 2010). As an educator and a taxpayer, I was saddened to see the minimal impact of a project that had the generous support of my fellow Australians. We should be asking donor governments more questions about the impact of our hard-earned dollars when they are spent on foreign aid – but where do we start? Australia gives about 22 cents for every $100 of its income in foreign aid (Oxfam, 2017). This is the lowest in Australia's history of spending on aid. As funds become further depleted, the need for models for projects need to change as well. Instead of just relying on governments to support those that are in need, we all can make a difference – no matter what the context.

The students at Naidovi had the potential to be academically as capable as the students that I have taught in Australia. They also possessed two outstanding qualities that is, at this time, on the slide in Australian schools. Firstly, when compared to my experiences of Australian classrooms, behavioural issues at Naidovi were minimal both in terms of frequency and complexity. An argument made by Australian Senator Simon Birmingham (Former Minister for Education and Training) is worthy of note here. He believed that more funding to schools did not automatically "buy better discipline, engagement or ambition" (Balogh, 2017, para. 11). He was reflecting on the Program for International Student Assessment (PISA) results (Thomson, De Bortoli, & Underwood,

2017), which revealed that Australia had once again rated below the OECD average for classroom discipline (Balogh, 2017). As the minister rightly pointed out, self-discipline is critical to student success in schools. Secondly, it was significant to note that teachers at Naidovi were still highly respected by the students, their parents, and the community. Without doubt this would be commonplace throughout the country. Teachers are held in high esteem. Comparatively, in Australia, many teachers reportedly feel undervalued, unsupported, and unrecognised (OECD, 2014). Put simply, in Australia there are times when we do not appreciate how lucky we are to have access to schools with good facilities and qualified teachers. In my mind I have no doubt that the prevailing belief amongst many in Fiji mirrors that of my ancestors – that good education is a passport to a better life. This manifests in students' behaviour and the respect for teachers.

The setting up of a functioning library was a giant leap for the school. Every school needs to have a library. There is a lot of truth in American poet Maya Angelou's profound words that "Any book that helps a child to form a habit of reading, to make reading one of his deep and continuing needs, is good for him [or her]". There is no doubt that the entry point for a child's success in education is largely dependent on his or her ability to read. In a study conducted in a Fijian school, Kumar (2017) concluded that students liked reading storybooks together with other print and digital texts that included newspapers, online books, and religious materials. There was evidence of a correlation between reading story books for pleasure and academic achievement in English exams. This also flowed onto their Language and Literacy Assessment (LANA) results. The objectives of this assessment are similar to literacy and numeracy assessment that is conducted in other countries, such as NAPLAN in Australia. Schools are expected to use the results of these tests for diagnostic purposes. For students to succeed in this assessment, they need to read and comprehend the assessment items. In some instances, they need knowledge and understanding which goes beyond the assessment item. Here again, the value of an effective library cannot be overemphasised. It is one of the few places where students can have access to reading materials.

We had seeded some ideas at Naidovi. Figure 3.4 highlights some of our key activities together with the deliverables. But the real question is, will our ideas be sustained and grow over time? It was evident that teachers needed to be supported, both in terms of their professional learning and access to quality resources. Some of the teachers confided in me and said that there were times when there was no chalk for them to write with on the blackboards. They had some major challenges, but they always seemed to present themselves with a positive attitude. Some of these teachers were also living below the poverty

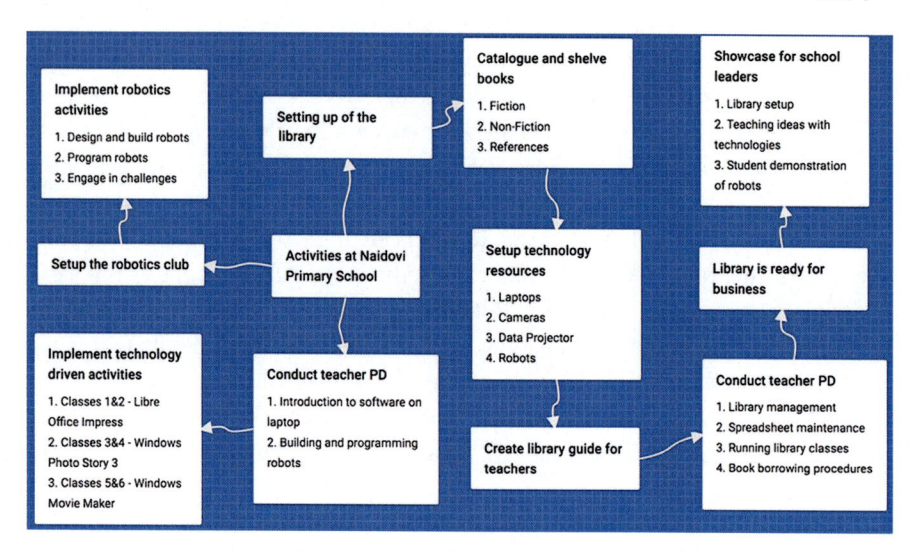

FIGURE 3.4   Key activities undertaken at Naidovi Primary School

line. Thus, purchasing their own computers and other teaching resources was beyond their reach.

As leaders of this initiative we recognised that the professional learning of the teachers had to be continued. One of the most feasible options would be through emails and Skype. From what we had seen and heard from education officers, head teachers, principals, and teachers, the need for teachers' professional development was evident. There seems to be a general view amongst decision makers that all teachers need is access to technology. Once they have this access, the teachers will know how to seamlessly integrate it into their classrooms. This is far from the truth. In some countries, like the US, 97% of K-12 teachers have access to computers on a daily basis in their classrooms (Delgado, Wardlow, McKnight, & O'Malley, 2015). In addition, 93% of these computers have access to the Internet. These findings suggest that developed countries have made significant progress in overcoming the software and hardware barrier, previously the biggest hurdles to technology integration in schools (Hew & Brush, 2007). However, Delgado et al. (2015) also pointed out that despite this significant shift, the actual use of technology from kindergarten through to secondary school classrooms has remained low. It is only through professional learning opportunities of the kind that we created at Naidovi that books, laptops, and robotic kits can be used to their full potential in classrooms. Such initiatives can also justify the efforts of the many donors – not just those who donate resources to schools in Fiji.

There is also a need to develop a culture of self-reliance. Whilst it is good to donate resources to set schools up, it is also important that they do not become over-reliant on the donor. The critical question is, what happens when these resources reach their use-by date. How will they be replaced? Relying too much on donations can create uncertainty and disruptions to school work. Teachers and students both need access to quality resources, but as we found at Naidovi, there were some children who were coming to school with no lunch. When parents are in dire financial situations and living in poverty, how will they find money to support their children at school? At the time of my visit, permanent job opportunities were very few because the once thriving sugarcane farms in the village were slowly dying. A lot of the farming land in the area was once leased by the Indians from the Fijian landowners. As the leases ran out, this land was reverting back to the Fijian landowners. Consequently, many Indian tenants were unemployed with no fixed home address. Other than a small number of openings in the hospitality industry, there are no other significant work opportunities. Social support mechanisms that we have in countries like Australia do not exist and many who remained in the area were struggling. For generations, whenever land has reverted back to the Fijian owners, production levels have not been sustained because of various reasons. On top of this, sugarcane used to be transported by rail from these farms to the sugar mills some 60 km away. Five-star hotels built more recently on the coast have taken over some of the areas that the railway lines were built on. Transport of cane on trucks to the mills is not a particularly profitable option. The slow decay of the sugar industry has impacted not only on families but also other organisations that relied on it. Apart from a few jobs in the hospitality industry, there were no other significant employment opportunities. I spoke to a local I've known since he was a little boy. He used to work for Fiji Sugar Corporation maintaining the railway lines. As an unemployed father of four children, he said fishing every now and then was the only way he could make ends meet for his family.

A possible way to make such initiatives sustainable is by imposing a small resources levy on students each year. For a school of 400 students, a $10 a year levy can generate $12,000 (6,000 USD approx.) over three years. Such a policy can generate sufficient funds for schools to renew their resources periodically. While financial hardship in this community is a given, the locals probably also need to be reminded about the financial contributions that the founders made to build the school, some of who contributed a year's wage to get the school off the ground. I have never heard such conversation in the community. Perhaps, a reflection on the past can be a motivator for the community's reengagement in their schools.

Our three weeks at Naidovi was one of the most rewarding professional and personal learning experiences for Ramila and I. We learnt so much about the context and the issues that the school was facing through our lived experiences. Some of our new knowledge could easily be extrapolated to schools in similar settings in developing countries. For example, we saw both – a digital and a print divide that was hampering the delivery of quality learning experiences. We had taken a baby step towards addressing the bigger challenge of how such issues can be tackled in countries like Fiji. Nonetheless, there were some very positive outcomes and this demonstrated that we had made a difference on the ground. There was clear evidence that there were teachers who want to teach and students who want to learn. For these teachers and students, such a project is most definitely worth doing! As Margaret Mead said, "Never doubt that a small group of thoughtful, committed citizens can change the world; indeed, it's the only thing that ever has". Quietly, and in our own ways, we wanted to be a part of this group!

CHAPTER 4

The Birth of the SEE Project

> Education is the most powerful weapon which you can use to change the
> world.
>
> NELSON MANDELA

The video accompanying this chapter is freely available online
at https://doi.org/10.6084/m9.figshare.10305116

Our visit to Naidovi Primary School in 2011 was an eye-opener. We live on the
same planet, in the same hemisphere, yet I could see evidence of a huge gap in
the quality of education that existed between schools in Fiji and in Australia.
One significant contributor to this difference is the funding model for education in the two countries. In Fiji, the community is expected to make a significant contribution towards the education of their children. On the other hand,
in Australia, the Federal and the State and Territory Governments are major
contributors towards the funding of schools. For example, in 2013, the governments collectively spent an average of $13,298 per student who were enrolled
in Australian government and non-government schools (ACARA, 2016). Education can indeed be a very powerful weapon to change the world. However,
my experiences of working in my former primary school in Fiji demonstrated
to me that many students still lacked reasonable opportunities to acquire this
weapon, largely due to a lack of financial and human resources. These observations and experiences once again pushed me into a state of *critical consciousness* where I was motivated to affect change through actions (Freire, 2000).
The question that kept echoing in my mind was, "Now that you have seen the
situation, with your knowledge, what can you do about it to bring a change that
will create opportunities not only at Naidovi but other schools as well?" This

chapter focusses on the setting up of the Share Engage Educate (SEE) Project. Our visit to Naidovi Primary School in 2011 was the catalyst for this initiative.

1   Needs of Schools

When we migrated in 1986, computers were beginning to be introduced into Australian schools. Parents were starting to buy computers for their children on the understanding that it was going to help them in their education. In addition, libraries were well set up in many schools and they played a significant role within the Australian education system. Many schools had teacher librarians. When we compare this scenario with Fijian classrooms, it is plausible to suggest that the schools in Fiji were at least two or three decades behind in terms of resourcing. The lack of resources in schools has also been acknowledged in studies conducted locally (e.g., Lingam & Lingam, 2013) which impacts on the teaching and learning that occurs in the classrooms. Teachers also have minimal opportunities to participate in professional development activities. From my observations, the lack of resources and the quality of teaching and learning in Fiji was unlikely to change in the foreseeable future. This issue of the huge gaps in the quality of education is not unique to Fiji – it is rife throughout the developing world (e.g., AusAID, 2012). These gaps impact on teacher and teaching quality, curriculum design, and the school environment. All these factors are strong determinants of the quality of teaching and learning that occurs in classrooms (Hattie, 2008).

The children at Naidovi and surrounding schools needed two key resources. First, they needed to have access to high quality library books. As noted previously, this is essential because reading is foundational. Unless they develop an interest and fluency in reading, their chances of success in life and education are significantly diminished. It is a no-brainer that they need to be literate, particularly in the English language. Digital literacy is also becoming essential for all citizens of the world. Without this knowledge, chances are that some citizens will be unable to take full advantage of the opportunities that technologies continue to present. Apart from adding value in classrooms, carefully crafted activities that integrate digital technologies can also develop the 4 C's – collaboration, communication, critical and creative thinking skills that are considered as essential for the 21st century (Kivunja, 2015). In countries like Fiji, where poverty levels are high, parents cannot afford these technologies. Consequently, schools are the only places where students can be educated about new technologies.

Anecdotal evidence demonstrates that computers donated to schools in developing countries are not always used effectively for teaching and learning purposes. Despite all the effort that is rendered towards this initiative by the donors for a perceived good cause, the donations are not used, and as a consequence the exercise becomes futile. This has also been reported in the literature. For example, Hayasaka (2005) pointed out that "computers donated in the name of charity rarely fulfil their philanthropic purpose" (para. 4). If they not used effectively, then they can cause social and environmental problems such as waste disposal. They also occupy space which can be used for other purposes in schools. However, "carefully monitored, well-planned programs" do accomplish their goals (Hayasaka, 2005, para. 11). A similar scenario applies to the donation of books. Traditional methods of book donation in developing countries are "largely useless and harmful" (Hite, 2006, p. 41) if they do not take into consideration the "voices of the users" (p. 42). As Hite noted, books have also been donated with little consideration for the needs of the users. Hite presented some examples of her experiences in sub-Saharan African countries to support her claims. For example, in one of the donations from overseas, she noted that there were multiple copies of the biography of a TV game hostess "whose claim to fame is that she turns letters around on a board" (p. 5) in a game show which had no relevance to the local population. Of concern was also the age of some of the books because some were well past their copyright dates. There were others that were in poor condition with missing pages and some that were riddled with mould and mildew. Hite also highlighted evidence of "an old set of encyclopaedias" (p. 5) where every book was of the same volume. Our experiences at Naidovi and in surrounding schools in Fiji was very similar. In a primary school library, we saw some chemistry textbooks that would have suited students in a first or second year university degree program. The prevailing mentality that was evident amongst some donors was that "we can donate anything" because it is going to a developing country. Little time was devoted to sorting and quality control of the donated items. Zell and Thierry (2015) concurred with these issues by pointing out that while book donation programs start with good intentions, sometimes they miss the mark due to the donors having not taken into consideration practical realities on the ground because of a lack of consideration for cultural and infrastructure implications. As such, it is evident that both book and computer donations in developing countries are faced by similar issues. Of significance, little research has also been undertaken to ascertain the impact of donation programs on local populations (Zell & Thierry, 2015). In our work at Naidovi, we ensured that the resources we identified and shipped were of a high quality and suitable for this school.

2   The SEE Project

Against this backdrop, we founded the Share Engage Educate (SEE) Project. It emerged from what we had learnt at Naidovi and supports the education agenda in developing countries. The underlying philosophy of SEE is to engage with key stakeholders and, in the process, share our knowledge on quality education practices and how they can be implemented in rural and remote schools in developing countries. To transform this philosophy to reality, the provision of print and digital resources together with strategies that had the potential for enhancing the quality of teaching and learning became the lead objectives. There were three key strategies on which we focussed upon to deliver these outcomes in schools. Our first focus was to make resources available. For this to materialise, we expanded our work at Naidovi Primary School and set up a program to donate high quality second-hand digital technologies and library books. Our target was schools in developing countries that were in rural and remote areas. Our second focus was to support teachers through professional development activities so that the donated resources were used effectively. There is no doubt that for any transformation to occur in classrooms, the role of teachers is pivotal (Hattie, 2008; Hollows, 2010). In addition to our individual efforts, I decided to explore opportunities to support the quality of education in developing countries through outreach projects. The idea was to involve university students who would showcase their knowledge of teaching, particularly with digital technologies, in schools where we had developed some connections. Our fourth focus was open-ended and targeted to finding other ways of supporting the education agenda in developing countries. Little did we know that in eight years this unfunded initiative would impact on 15 to 20,000 students, in nearly 60 schools, and in eight developing countries – Fiji, Papua New Guinea, Solomon Islands, Malaysia, Bhutan, South Sudan, Vietnam, and Kenya. This initiative also paved the way for five university outreach projects in Fiji and Malaysia. On a voluntary basis, I also headed a project at UNESCO to develop and implement a program to train master-trainers for the computer studies course in Zambian secondary schools.

The SEE Project donations were not made willy-nilly to schools. We prioritised by encouraging schools to formally write to us with details of their needs, explaining how they intended to use the resources in their classrooms and how they would be managed. The latter mandated some explanations about the physical environment such as the availability of rooms, suitable furniture, and access to a reliable power supply. Schools were also expected to provide updates of how the resources were used. This feedback became a prerequisite for further support. The rationale here follows from a point raised by Damisa Moyo, author of the book *Dead Aid*. Moyo (2009) emphasised that aid efforts sometimes did not lead to productive outcomes if they were given without any expectations. We needed to make our expectations clear and we stipulated that schools had to meet the cost of freight. This was important because sometimes when resources are just given, they are not appreciated. They are undervalued which can lead to an entitlement mentality (Albrechtsen, 2013). By paying for freight, the schools become partners and no longer merely passive recipients. In the case of Fiji for example, freight contributions amounted to about 10% of the value of the donated resources. Most of the digital resources were donated by my university. We bought books and also received donations from family, friends, schools, and the university library. The project website reported on the progress of the work (theseeproject.org).

Graeme Baguley, Director of Queensland University Technology(QUT) International Student Services also teamed with us on the SEE Project. His beliefs and his proactive engagement made a huge difference to the project. He had been working for a couple years with the QUT Alumni in Fiji and the late Geoff Portmann at QUT's Creative Industries. They were sending desktop computers to primary schools identified by the Alumni members. He was concerned about the sustainability of their project in that teachers had no training in the use of ICT as a teaching tool. Hence, many of these computers sat idle and, if anything went wrong, they were not repaired and more likely cast aside. The SEE Project offered an extension on their work where there was a commitment by schools, not only in enduring a place for ICT in the curriculum but also in the maintenance of the equipment.

After returning from Fiji in 2011, one of our first initiatives was to send another 400 books to Naidovi Primary School, so by the beginning of the school year in 2012, the school library had 800 books. This meant that all students were able to borrow at least one book on a weekly basis. As the year started, the feedback from Naidovi was very positive. I interviewed a class 3 teacher at the school (Ram – pseudonym). He believed that, like him, other teachers were buoyed by the opportunities that the new resources were creating. Ram pointed out that a library book borrowing system was in place and all classes were timetabled for one lesson a week in the library. Dorthi Reddy, one of the class 6 teachers showed us the library records for her class (Figure 4.1). She was recording all the details in an exercise book under the following headings – date taken, title, spine label, accession number, and date returned. As anticipated, the students were reading one book every week. The head teacher also monitored teachers' use of the library. It was immensely satisfying when some of the students read to us when we visited their classrooms a few months later.

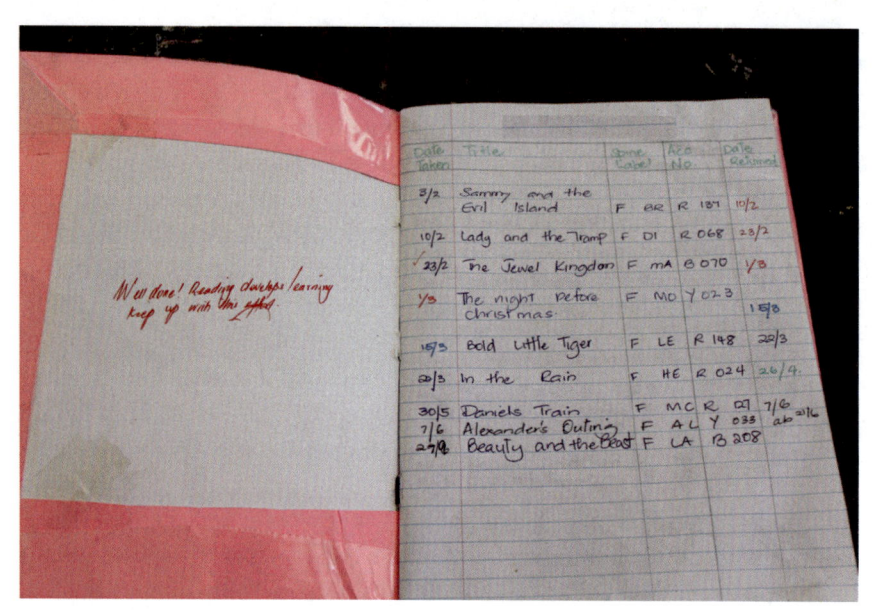

FIGURE 4.1   Dorthi Reddy's library record

When we were at Naidovi, we worked with Ram's class who created a digital story of the local Indian and Fijian communities using *Windows Photo Story 3*. The following year Ram was assigned a new class 3 and he repeated the activity. He started by introducing his students to the basics of the keyboard including terminologies such as mouse, cursor, and touchpad. Hygiene issues such as the need for clean hands before using computers were also explained. According to Ram, while the more able students were able to immerse in the task with ease, there were some others were not only having issues with writing, but they were also struggling with the keyboard. This challenge was understandable given that most students (about 85%) in Ram's class were using a laptop for the first time. Nevertheless, it did not take long before students were able to build their confidence. Ram told me that developing some typing skills was also an important prerequisite. Once students demonstrated their levels of competency in typing, Ram introduced them to *Photo Story*. He adopted a step-by-step approach spread over a few lessons. Eventually all students were able to create their digital stories with photos, text, and sound.

The robotics club which we had set up was also working well. According to Ram, who was one of the teachers in charge of this club, there was a continuous interest amongst the students for building and programming the robots. On the downside, some of the laptops failed, and one was used by the school typist for administration work. Subsequently, there were eight laptops available for classroom use. This meant that there were between four to five students per laptop. Groups of this size can be counterproductive because it reduces the opportunities for active participation. Dorthi reflected that it was always pleasing to the eyes when she saw "students would wait to go to the library for the computer programming lessons with robots". We were glad that the teachers picked up from where we left off, and the wheels of change were slowly rotating.

3 An Unanticipated Start to the SEE Project

There was strong interest from the Ministry of Education in Fiji in the innovative work we had started at Naidovi. At the end of March, about six months after our work onsite, a former Minister for Education, the late Mr Filipe Bole, was going to visit the school. He was interested to see the work we had done with laptops, robots, and library books. School staff and students were eagerly waiting to showcase some of their work – especially with robots. But in the early hours of the morning on the day of the minister's visit, there was a flash flood. The school and surrounding areas were flooded. In some classrooms, the flood waters caused considerable damage, including the library where all the donated resources were stored.

Before this, there had never been a flood either at or in the immediate vicinity of the school. When I was growing up in *Cuvu* (the village) people often talked about the 'big illness' or the 'big cyclone' but there had never been a conversation about the 'big flood'. To my knowledge, there had been no significant changes that could be attributed to local activities (e.g. no major buildings, or roads, or changes in farming practices, or new industries) that could rationalise this unseen and unexpected event. If one looks at the geography of the area (I am no expert in this) it is hard to explain how something like this could occur, all of a sudden. Was this an outcome of climate change? I was unable to find clear explanations about what caused this flooding. Unlike Australia, where questions are asked about why and how a flood occurred after such episodes, in Fiji the focus was primarily on recovery. The weather bureau indicated that there was "violent" rainfall (50mm/hr) for about two hours prior to the flooding (Sharma, 2017). While it was disappointing to hear that a significant portion of the resources that we had donated went under water, hearing the accounts of what some of the others went through in the village made this loss almost insignificant. If you live in an area which has never flooded, how do you prepare for such an event? As the flood waters rose, many seemed to have just escaped with only the clothes on their backs. For the first time, I was able to appreciate the value of social media during a natural disaster. In Australia, the

Pacific Islands hardly feature in mainstream news. Similarly, Australia is hardly featured on the mainstream news in Europe or the United States. However, the members of the school community who had mobile phones were uploading images and videos of the flood in real time on Facebook and YouTube. On this occasion, social media was miles ahead in reporting this event.

Soon after hearing about the flood, I phoned the head teacher of Naidovi Primary. He pointed out that the situation at the school and surrounding areas was quite grave and challenging. His description of the flood and how it had impacted on the residents was almost like a scene from a movie: "In the early hours of Friday morning, people were running towards the school with flood waters almost following them. They ran to the high school because this was the only place in the area with buildings that had a second floor. For some, the clothes on their backs were the only possessions left". For nearly everyone in the village, there is no such thing as house and contents insurance that many of us have in the West. Homes in Fiji are either uninsurable or the insurance premiums are so exorbitant that it is unaffordable. The head teacher went on to say that people in the village had been supporting each other with food, clothes, and shelter. But they were now reaching a desperate situation and needed help from outside. There was no water supply or electricity. It was still raining and, as a consequence, they could not rely on the wood burning open stoves for cooking. I asked the head teacher if he needed any assistance. His response was, "it would be nice if we could provide the students with at least one meal a day because there are many families who have lost everything". He elaborated that, with this provision, parents would have one less worry about caring for their family. For the SEE Project, this was a unique challenge – it was beyond our core business of supporting schools with resources and teacher professional development. On the other hand, it was difficult to shy away from the school community in their hour of need. The head teacher's plea was doable. Our plan was to fund this initiative through the supply of groceries. The head teacher, his staff, and the local community would take charge of the cooking. For this plan to materialise, we had to raise some money. I called a few of my family and friends for donations. We also set a page on Facebook and highlighted the plight of the people as a consequence of the flooding situation in Fiji. As money rolled in, we linked up with one of the food supermarkets in Sigatoka town and instructed the shop owner to supply groceries to the head teacher. We set a tab for grocery purchases.

When the students returned, school staff identified 180 children who needed help as a result of the floods. Cooking for these children got underway. The cost to feed all these children on a daily basis was about 200 FJD (about 100 USD). According to the head teacher, many students came to school "without their school uniforms or bags as they have been washed away". Consequently, we also decided to support the children with their basic school materials like stationeries and class texts. The head teacher estimated that it would cost about 9 FJD per child (about 4.50 USD) to provide these resources. As word got around about the one meal a day program at school, the attendance improved. Adam Taylor, a teacher at the school, reflected on this experience in a Facebook Post as follows:

> The daily distribution of hot meals to the students continue because of the kind gesture by Dr Chandra and friends ... seeing the smile on their [students] faces while serving the hot meals makes me feel how fortunate we are to have people like you who have gone out of your way to donate and help these children. I know the children look forward to their lunch each day and I am sure the teachers look forward to serving them as well. Attendance is improving which is a good sign and classes continue as normal. All care and safety measures are taken to see that the children are free of any likely sickness especially after the flood. There has been a suspected outbreak of leptospirosis and we only hope and pray that none of the students are infected. Our holidays have been shortened by a week as a result of the recent flood so that we can catch up with the teaching hours we have lost and with two more weeks remaining this term, we hope all the children will attend school to catch up with lessons. I am positive things will normalise soon and all it takes is time!! We need to be patient and pray that things will work out for the best!

It was astonishing what we were able to achieve through the collective efforts of our family and friends. More importantly by working with the head teacher, we were able to prioritise how the students could be assisted from the money that we raised. The one-meal-a-day program ran for 18 days and more than 5,500 hot meals were served over this time. Cooking was done on the school grounds. This initiative also generated community spirit. Some people in the village provided their support in whatever way they could. Small donations in cash and kind were made directly to the school. In-kind support included firewood and supply of clean water. Cooking was accomplished by using firewood as there was no access to gas or electric stoves. The school did not have tap water for more than a month after the flood. For the school kindergarten, which lost most of its teaching resources, we shipped 52 sets of brand new toys and games, 15 board books and five picture books. A toy catalogue was created on PowerPoint to assist the teachers to manage their collection. In addition, we shipped 400 second-hand books to re-stock the library. We received many hand-written letters of appreciation from the parents and students. Some of the younger children expressed their thoughts through drawings. Many of the

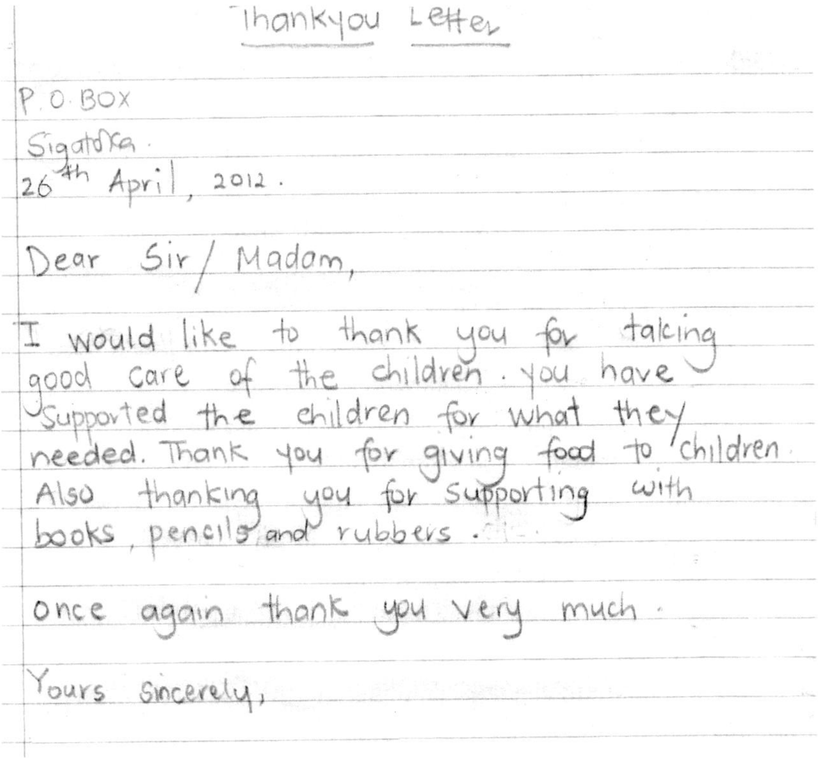

Thankyou Letter

P. O. BOX
Sigatoka.
26th April, 2012.

Dear Sir / Madam,

I would like to thank you for taking good care of the children. You have supported the children for what they needed. Thank you for giving food to children. Also thanking you for supporting with books, pencils and rubbers.

Once again thank you very much.

Yours Sincerely,

FIGURE 4.2   Letter of appreciation from a parent

parents expressed their gratitude for supporting their children in their time of need (Figure 4.2).

This unanticipated participation in a disaster-relief effort was a blessing in disguise because it relayed some powerful messages about communities in developing countries and more importantly about how they respond to first-time adverse weather events. In a Tweet in 2015, former US President Barrack Obama wrote, "Climate change is no longer some far-off problem; it is happening here, it is happening now" (The White House, 2015). I am no climatologist but the violent weather conditions in this instance could have been the result of climate change. In many other parts of the country, the floods of March 2012 were considered to be one of the worst for decades (McNamara, 2013). The areas surrounding the school flooded for the first time. If such adverse weather conditions are one of the products of climate change, then how do the world's poor deal with it, especially when it occurs for the first time? According to most of the local business owners who participated in McNamara's (2013) investigation, the "government failed to provide any warning" (p. 98). This was contrary to the fact that warnings were broadcasted predominantly on radio. The respondents in McNamara's study were from the nearby town of Nadi that is prone to flooding. But no matter how effective the warnings – how does one predict that heavy rain will cause flooding in an area that has never flooded? The role that social media can play in such situations was also noteworthy. Without Facebook and YouTube, it would have been difficult to fathom the gravity of the situation. The mainstream media had limited coverage at the local level. Through social media, we were able to garner support from friends and family. The school community needed our support. Yet again it demonstrated the role that mobile technologies play in the 21st century. According to the head teacher, we were able to provide assistance on the ground long before some of the established organisations stepped in. In terms of aid projects, ours was a "David" in comparison to a "Goliath" of global Non-Government Organisations (NGO's). The SEE Project was light on its feet in responding to need in real time and not held by the bureaucracy that is common in larger organisations. We were able to provide lunch for 18 days, stationery packs, library books, toys, and games for a few thousand dollars. Most importantly all the money was strategically targeted. It went to the school to support them with what they identified as their need. I was amazed to see how far our little contribution had stretched and the real difference it made to the community.

This experience taught us a lot about the context. It gave us a true insight into the challenges and struggles of the school and the community it served. The pivotal role that a head teacher plays in the community as a leader in alleviating pain and suffering following a natural disaster was evident. For the head teacher to succeed in this role, he must be trusted and also have the ability to communicate the key messages with the school community and most importantly with the teachers. It also demonstrated the challenges communities face when there is little or no disaster-relief support mechanisms in place. For example, in Australia every state has a State Emergency Service (SES) which is a not-for-profit organisation that is supported with equipment by the governments. It has thousands of unpaid members from diverse backgrounds who are called upon for action during state and national disasters and emergencies. These volunteers always do an incredible job by working collaboratively with government and non-government agencies. This model of collaboration during emergencies may be worth emulating in developing countries.

4   Understanding More about the Context through Teacher Professional Development

After the floods and nearly twelve months after our initial visit, we went back to Fiji to deliver professional development workshops to primary school teachers in two centres. We funded our trip and delivered the workshops at no cost.

Dr David Nutchey, one of my colleagues from QUT, joined us to present at the second workshop. The main objective was to further develop our understanding of the context. We worked with the Ministry of Education who approved the release of one or two teachers from 20 schools that they had identified. On this trip, we took twenty second-hand laptops – 10 for each workshop that were later donated to the schools. Access to laptops facilitated hands-on-participation of the teachers. We were once again very grateful to the Faculty of Science and Engineering at my university for this donation.

We delivered our first workshop in the town of Sigatoka which is about 12 kilometres from Naidovi Primary School. There was strong evidence that people in this part of the country were still in recovery mode following the devastating floods that went through the area six months earlier. For example, the district education office was significantly damaged. As a consequence, staff were working from a building that was once a staff quarter. I could see their challenges – it was not easy to deliver services – but the team were working well under the circumstances. We delivered the workshop from the Sigatoka District School which was located on the outskirts of the township. This school had recently remodelled a classroom as a computer lab. The attendance was very good – teachers from all of the invited schools joined us. A short survey administered to the participating teachers at this centre revealed they all had either a certificate or a diploma in teaching. All schools had computers. However, the computer to student ratio ranged from 1:7 to 1:170. Two teachers claimed that their school computers were connected to the Internet. Most of the teachers knew of the Microsoft Office Word and Windows Explorer. Some of the teachers were using computers for teaching purposes which entailed activities such as research, creation of PowerPoint presentations, and preparation of exam papers using Word. The majority of the teachers had not participated in any professional development activities associated with digital technologies before. Most of the teachers also pointed out that none of the students in their classes had computers at home. All teachers stated that their schools had libraries but that none of them had a book management system in place.

Our second professional activity was held for the teachers in the Nadi and Lautoka schools. The workshops were delivered at the Ministry of Education's meeting room in the city of Lautoka. A survey was also administered to the participating teachers in this group. Apart from certificates and diploma qualifications, two teachers had bachelor's degrees in Education. The survey showed that the teachers were teaching at either a rural or urban school. All schools had computers, however the computer to student ratio ranged from 1:20 to 1:312. Interestingly in two cases, there was only one computer in the whole school. Most of the teachers knew that their school computers had the Microsoft Office suite together with the Internet Explorer browser installed on them. Five of the schools had Internet connections. Some of the teachers were using them in their teaching for activities such as research, downloading teaching resources, typing drills, and preparation of exam papers. The majority of the teachers had not participated in any professional development activities associated with information and communication technology (ICT). There was evidence of three categories of responses to the item on the percentage of students who had computers at home. One teacher stated that none of the students had this technology to three teachers on the other side of the spectrum who indicated that between 75–90% had access to a computer. All others indicated that a small percentage had this access. Both of these were urban schools. The majority of the teachers had their own computers which they also used for school work. All teachers stated that their schools had libraries. While 40% of the teachers indicated that a cataloguing system was used in their libraries, they were unfamiliar with how it was to be implemented.

The two areas where we conducted the workshops were different largely in terms of the socioeconomic status of the people. There were pockets in the Lautoka/Nadi area where the parents were either more educated with good employment or were business owners. Both these economic indicators delivered good income on a regular basis. In these families, there were more opportunities to support children in their academic pursuits. This explains why more than 75% of the children in three urban schools (30%) had their own computers. None of the teachers in the Sigatoka area reported such high levels of computer access in homes.

On the basis of the data, it was evident that most schools did not have sufficient numbers of computers to give their students reasonable access for classroom use. For nearly all schools, access to data projectors either did not exist or was not used widely for supporting classroom activities. Professional development activities about how to use technology did not occur and were not necessary because teachers did not have access to digital devices in their schools. Nearly 75% of all teachers owned a computer and they were using them for teaching purposes. All teachers expressed an interest in learning more about educational software and how they could be used in classrooms. There was also an interest in knowing more about applications that could be used to design websites. While teachers were enthusiastic, the use and the integration of digital technologies in primary schools was not a priority in the school curriculum. However, plans were afoot to pilot the One Laptop Per Child (OLPC) project in three schools the following year by the Ministry of Education (Ministry of Education, National Heritage, Culture and Arts, 2012).

The feedback from the teacher surveys suggested that most teachers had some knowledge of computers. A significant proportion of teachers also owned laptops which they tinkered with and used for school work. In both of the workshops, through introductory conversations with the teachers, we established that there was little understanding of the achievement indicators in the new outcomes-based curriculum. Their knowledge demonstrated little evidence of how activities and classroom-based assessments (CBA) could be designed to enable students to demonstrate the learning outcomes. Teachers had little knowledge of how digital technologies could be used to design appropriate classroom activities. However, there was a desire to learn more about technology. Thus, our focus was primarily on demonstrating how simple applications that were available at no cost could be integrated into the curriculum. We were mindful of the case study findings of Hollows (2010) in Malawi and Ethiopia who reported that all "too often it is the technology that becomes the focus of attention" (p. 380) and its educational value takes a back seat. This was also evident with this group of teachers in Fiji. However, this is also the case elsewhere and even in developed countries. While many teachers felt that they could deal with content and pedagogical related matters, addressing technology integration issues was far more challenging (Underwood & Dillon, 2011). Teachers lose sight of the fact that technology is only a tool. Teacher conversations and their thinking should start with the content. Mishra and Koehler (2006) developed the Technological, Pedagogical and Content Knowledge (TPACK) framework. I use this framework to teach pre-service teachers in my university courses about how to integrate technologies in their teaching. In my view, it is a common-sense framework and from a teacher's perspective it is underpinned by three key questions: What do I have to teach? [Content], What technologies can I use? [Technology], and How do I teach? [Pedagogy]. There is no-one-size-fits-all. As Mishra and Koehler acknowledged: every situation is unique, and no one single combination of content, technology, and pedagogy will be applicable to all contexts (Koehler, 2012). The context, including access to technology, school culture and support of the school administration, plays a critical role in content, pedagogy, and technology coming together.

Our introductory presentation in the workshops was focussed on the TPACK framework where we highlighted the significance of the three questions that needed to be addressed when teaching with technology. The presentation was supported with examples and how the framework plays out in different contexts. The sessions we presented included creating a digital story with *Photo Story 3*, editing a video clip with *Windows Moviemaker*, creating a game with *Scratch*, developing spreadsheets for libraries using *LibreOffice Calc*, creating 2D and 3D shapes with *Google SketchUp*, and graphing with *GeoGebra*. These were some of the applications that I was also using in the training of pre-service teachers in Australia. There was a presentation on creating websites as teacher feedback forms had expressed an interest in knowing more about how websites could be built for their schools. Apparently, many schools were keen to set up their websites, but they had no knowledge of how it could be done. The cost of getting one done commercially was prohibitive. Dynamic school websites can be an effective way to market the school, upload community announcements, and highlight student achievements. In the context of Fiji, a large percentage of young people leave rural and remote areas and head to cities and even migrate overseas. A school website can encourage the alumni to reconnect and support the schools – both in cash and in kind.

Despite the short duration of the workshops, we were able to cover a reasonable amount of what we had intended. Whilst the workshop sessions were a taster, it was evident that we were also able to seed some ideas that were applicable to the local context. For example, in the culminating activity, teachers worked in teams to propose ideas on how digital technologies could be integrated into their classrooms. The feedback from the teachers was very good. Another meaningful outcome of this initiative was that the teachers agreed to meet regularly under the chairmanship of the education officers from the Sigatoka and Nadi/Lautoka offices. We were convinced that the technology agenda could move forward with this training. However, as we worked with the teachers, the financial challenges faced by schools was evident. A head teacher who was recently appointed to a rural school said that when she started, there were "three pieces of chalk and less than $20 (about 10 USD) in the school bank account". Without the availability of technologies, this agenda was probably going nowhere. Reflecting back on my early experiences as a teacher in Australia I was then confronted with this issue each time I participated in such workshops. It was hard to believe that even in Australia we were challenged by the lack of technologies. We would receive training on some software but when we got to school there were no computers that we could use to put our new knowledge into practice. Even today we hear about similar challenges from teachers – though billions of dollars have been invested in the acquisition of educational technologies.

5 Feedback from Schools

Six of the twenty teachers who attended our workshops convinced their head teachers to email us and make a request for assistance with resources. I had anticipated a higher response rate, but this was a good start, and the response was understandable. Like many schools around the world, school principals and head teachers are the gatekeepers and drivers of change. Fiji is no different. The schools also have a top-down structure where the ideas of classroom teachers are often unheard. If a head teacher or principal lacks the knowledge and does not understand the value of technology in education, then any initiative with focus is pushed aside. Without any doubts many school leaders are also technologically illiterate. As the word got around about the SEE Project, we received another seven requests from other primary and high schools, totalling thirteen altogether in the first twelve months after the project had been set up.

We requested feedback from schools which gave an indication of how the computers were used. Most of the respondents indicated that they were using computers at least once a week with their students. They were also asked to identify the top three activities that their students had completed with computers during the year. The depth and the breadth of the tasks indicated a shift from traditional practices. For example, the teachers were using the computers in activities which enabled their students to create quizzes, self-develop grammar skills, and undertake online research. Their responses suggested that computers were being used effectively and they were highly buoyed by the quality of the intended learning outcomes in their technology-driven classroom activities. It was encouraging to see that the computers were not an add-on. The teachers had a clear rationale for using a certain technology to address the proposed content.

Ram who we started working with at Naidovi Primary School, had come a long way. In one of the activities, students in his class had to identify the different organs in the human circulatory system. Ram created a multimedia presentation with images and videos that were projected onto a screen to show students how the heart worked. According to Ram, in the past "students were only told about the different organs" and a lot was left to their imagination. In many instances students would either copy the notes from the blackboard or complete task sheets in locally produced workbooks. In many cases the quality of illustrations in these publications presented barriers to learning. Ram felt that with the aid of a data projector and resources from the Internet, "students were able to get the idea fast and most of them were able to understand well". Ram was able to show his students in colour the animated parts of the circulatory system. He had another interesting activity where students were given a topic and asked to write a short paragraph using *LibreOffice Writer*. Ram opted for this approach because he felt that "children would learn typing skills" and at the same time with the help of spelling and grammar checking, they would develop their language skills and understand the use of correct grammar. He made a very important point that such an approach would make them realise when they had typed something incorrectly. Instead of being told what to do upfront, on many occasions the students did the corrections themselves, thus developing skills of critical thinking and self-reflection.

We supported a Class 2 teacher's school with ten laptops and a data projector. Mary (pseudonym) shared her experiences of using *LibreOffice Calc* with her students, which enabled them to present data showing water usage for various purposes in a day. She opted to take this approach because it gave the students "a chance to practise typing and formatting skills" and also express data in "tables and as graphs". Mary also believed that *LibreOffice Calc* was effective because of its accuracy and presentation qualities. She noted that the "children were motivated to complete their tasks" and "allowing the use of computers was an incentive for them". Similarly, we supported Latchmi (pseudonym), a class 3 teacher, and her school with the same set of resources. In one of her classroom activities, she focussed on the importance of inter-island ships as a mode of transport between the islands in Fiji. She opted for *Photo Story 3* because it helped "children to better understand about inter-island boats through actual pictures" – especially if they had "not been on inter-island boats". She noted that the activity not only promoted engagement but also facilitated discussion: "While doing the activity, children got to actually talk about the photos and discuss amongst themselves". In addition, the task "actually helps children" to develop digital technology skills such as editing by using "functions like dragging, cropping, and so on".

Villiame's (pseudonym) school was supported with 10 laptops. In Class 8, Villiame got his students to use *Libre Impress* to create a quiz on *Navala* village. They used these quizzes to test their peers' knowledge. This Fijian village is historically significant because it is considered to be the last authentic traditional village that is still standing. The idea was to firstly familiarise the students with some of the features of the software and then develop skills like hyperlinking. According to Villiame, such an approach enabled the students to learn "many facts about *Navala* village" in an environment that excited and motivated them. For their quizzes to work, they had to not only write the questions but also the answers. They also needed to know the content in order to do well in the quizzes that their peers had created. Thus, learning occurred through two pathways. Villiame noted that the lesson was very efficient because students were on task and "no time was wasted". The heightened levels of motivation also ensured that "good behaviour" prevailed throughout the activity. He stated that in the past, lessons on *Navala* village were no more than "a write up only" with students spending their time copying off the board.

The quality of the activities in the high school were equally innovative and impressive. None of the teachers in this group participated in the workshop that we conducted because our focus was on primary schools. The teachers in this group were immersed in workshop activities that were conducted by their principal, Segran Pillay who had an excellent knowledge of how technology could be blended into classrooms to optimise learning outcomes. We supported Segran's school initially with ten laptops. Some of the activities undertaken by his teachers, following the workshops conducted by Segran, were notable. For example, one of the teachers, Shatru (pseudonym) developed an activity where his students in Form 3 researched on the topic of "momentum" on the Internet. Using this knowledge, they had to calculate the momentum of an object before and after a collision. According to Shatru, researching on the Internet enabled his science students to develop an understanding of the concept through different perspectives. As a consequence, the "concept was easily understood by the students" and "most students had good responses to questions" that they were given. I remember learning this concept in school. Apart from memorising the formula (momentum = mass X velocity) that I copied off the board, my conceptual understanding of what it really meant was non-existent. Shatru believed that technologies made the "learning easier and faster". Similarly, Saraswati (pseudonym), a Form 5 teacher, used YouTube videos to enhance her students' knowledge of transformations in mathematics. She opted for this approach because the videos "showed the types of transformations explicitly and students watched the videos a number of times". The convenience of watching the videos multiple times helped the students develop conceptual understandings at their own pace. Like Shatru, she also believed that "computers made learning much faster and efficient". These accounts from the teachers strongly suggested that technologies were facilitating changes to the core business of teaching and learning in their classrooms.

6 Lesson Learnt – Teachers Need to Be Empowered

Working with the Fijian teachers taught us some very valuable lessons. The challenges and issues faced by the teachers at Naidovi were similar to those of their contemporaries elsewhere in the country. Like Naidovi, it was evident that many teachers had the capability to integrate technologies in classrooms. However, some ideas needed to be seeded before they could initiate them. As demonstrated in this instance, short and clearly targeted workshops can be an effective strategy. But there is no point in conducting workshops if teachers do not have the technologies to use when they go back to their classrooms. This is true of training in all fields. Those who are being trained need to have the tools to apply their knowledge in the field. This is the basis for making the initiatives not only worthwhile but also sustainable. In this regard, school principals and head teachers need to have a clear understanding of the big picture. With this vision, they can convince the school management committees of the value of technology to enhance student learning.

Rogers (2003) proposed the diffusion of innovations theory. It is highly relevant to understanding the adoption of technology by teachers in schools. One of the cornerstones of his theory is the 'innovation-decision process'. He defined it as "an information-seeking and information-processing activity, where an individual is motivated to reduce uncertainty about the advantages and disadvantages of an innovation" (p. 172). It is underpinned by five steps: knowledge, persuasion, decision, implementation, and confirmation. In the knowledge step, teachers become aware of an innovation. In this instance, the workshops were one of the strategies to demonstrate how digital technologies can be used in their local contexts. The persuasion step which follows considers the value of using digital technologies in classrooms by taking into consideration factors like the relative advantage to learning, compatibility with the local curriculum, and complexity of making it happen in their contexts. The value of embracing such an innovation at a professional level would also be a consideration. After all, why embrace an innovation if it is not considered important at the school or Ministry of Education level? Once the teachers have weighed the options, the decision step follows. This is a critical stage as teachers decide whether they would adopt or reject the idea of using digital technologies in their classrooms. The role and support of the school principal or head teacher is critical at this juncture. Access to digital technologies is also an essential prerequisite to this decision making. The implementation phase follows if the teachers decide to adopt the idea. Here they think through the ideas, make connections with the curriculum, identify learning outcomes, and then design and implement activities. In the confirmation stage, the teachers evaluate the results of their implementation. If the results are making a difference in terms of teachers' teaching and students' learning, then the use of digital technology continues. In the responses that we received from the teachers, there was strong evidence that all the teachers would continue using digital technologies because they could see that it was adding value to their classrooms.

Rogers (2003) also believed that there are categories within the human population that describe how individuals embrace innovations. He used a normal distribution curve to suggest that within the general population there were five main groups of individuals – innovators (2.5%), early adopters (13.5%), early majority (34%), late majority (34%), and laggards (16%). Thus, Rodgers' categories suggest that not everyone in the general population embraces an innovation at first sight. The widespread adoption of an innovation takes time. Sometimes an innovation is never embraced. For example, Automatic Teller Machines (ATMs) were introduced more than 50 years ago in Australia. However, there are bank customers who still opt to use passbooks and line up in banks to do their banking transactions. Likewise, not all teachers will embrace technology as soon as they are given the opportunity. Workshops, and even access to technologies, do not act as a light switch. After all, if they have been teaching in a certain way for years, no change can be expected to happen overnight. Sometimes a change may never occur because teachers have applied certain teaching strategies that have always worked for them (e.g. teaching addition of fractions in a certain way). As a consequence, a change in technique was not warranted. What is important though, is that technologies should be given to teachers who want to use them in their classrooms. These teachers can be the digital technology champions because they are the innovators and the early adopters. They become a positive influence on other teachers once they start using the technologies. Consequently, these teachers can catalyse a change in their contemporaries. Lev Vygotsky (1978) proposed the idea of a "zone of proximal development" where less able learners work cooperatively with more able peers to achieve a certain outcome. In the context of the adoption of technologies in schools, the digital technology champions can assume the role of more able peers and support other teachers to embrace the innovation agenda. There was strong evidence that some of the teachers that we worked with, and received feedback from, were either innovators or early adopters. These are the teachers that schools in Fiji and elsewhere should focus on to get the digital technologies agenda moving. They need to be empowered!

CHAPTER 5

Student Outreach Projects in Fiji

> No one is born fully-formed: it is through self-experience in the world
> that we become what we are.
>
> PAULO FREIRE

 The video accompanying this chapter is freely available online
at https://doi.org/10.6084/m9.figshare.10305269

In Australia, we take schools with amenities such as ergonomic furniture, taps with clean running water, working flush toilets with toilet paper, and multiple working electric lights in classrooms for granted. Despite these privileges, I feel that in some instances we have gone backwards in terms of student behaviour, respect for teachers, and the value that is placed on education as a whole. After having been involved with education in Australia on the coalface for many years, I wonder if some students realise how lucky they are to be in such well-equipped schools with trained teachers. This attitude is not strictly confined to education but across other areas as well. We take too much for granted. We fail to realise how the majority of the world's population lives because we do not have opportunities to immerse ourselves in such environments. Consequently, it is hard to fathom how three billion people in the world live on less than $2.50 a day (Global Issues, 2013). In addition, the majority of the world's population – about 80% – live on less than $10 a day. As a society, we need to experience and understand this 'another world'. I believe that it is through such experiences we get a chance to value and appreciate what we have and as a result become a better society. This chapter unpacks the impact of service-learning outreach projects that were undertaken in rural and remote Fijian schools by Australian university students.

© KONINKLIJKE BRILL NV, LEIDEN, 2020 | DOI:10.1163/9789004406872_005

1   The Importance of International Engagement

There were many compelling reasons for undertaking the outreach projects in Fiji. Given the connected nature of our world, universities in particular have a responsibility to provide opportunities for their students to develop an international-mindedness that challenges preconceived ideas about who they are as global citizens (Hill, 2012). Through such opportunities, students can become multi-literate and also develop a deep understanding of global dependencies (Giroux, 2011). According to the literature, a critical strategy for students to develop international-mindedness is to engage in some form of outbound mobility volunteering and service-learning outreach programs which incorporate a focus on critical, reflective thinking and civic responsibility that is mutually beneficial to both parties (Baker-Boosamra, 2006; King, 2004). Through such experiences, students can also develop new knowledge about the beliefs and values of different cultures and the worlds where they exist. Service-learning provides experiential learning that encourages students to regularly negotiate and make sense of multiple meanings and values in new environments, which challenges them to think other than what they have come to understand as the norm in their world. Trilokekar and Kukar (2011) described such encounters as "disorienting" experiences that create "disequilibrium" where one must discard old ideas and habits to adapt to new ways of thinking and behaving. Working through such a disorienting process encourages students to become competent communicators who have developed the skills and attitudes necessary to break down cultural barriers (Eisenchlas & Trevaskes, 2007) and establish international-mindedness (Hill, 2012). There is substantial research evidence to suggest that well-structured international service-learning and volunteering projects can deliver highly desirable benefits to students (Birdwell, 2011; Lough, 2009).

Applying critical pedagogies with the intention of creating a socially just and equitable society is a cornerstone of effective volunteering and service-learning programs. Immersing Australian university students in Fijian schools was an ideal way to increase such awareness. For such an approach to materialise, teaching and learning activities need to focus on "developing students' intellectual and moral attributes" (McLean, 2006, p. 128) so that they gain an opportunity to think more deeply about societal problems. However, for students to develop these attributes, they have to step outside the walls of university classrooms. By doing so, they momentarily step outside their dominant culture and are able to see their surroundings from a different vantage point. Immersion in real-world contexts also gives the students the opportunity to think critically and creatively and at the same time be challenged to "act responsibly with others to ameliorate the problems" (McLean, 2006, p. 128) on the ground. Drawing upon the theories of Freire, Lough (2009) highlighted that such programs encourage participants to take on meaningful roles, reflect on their experiences, and act accordingly. University students have the intellectual capacity to engage in this way and make a difference. What they need are meaningful real-world opportunities which create a win-win situation for the students and the society they are immersed in. Consistent with the theoretical perspectives of critical pedagogy, the students need opportunities to go beyond observing and understanding a context to actually doing something on the ground to make a change. On paper, the rationale for the international engagement of university students sounds convincing. But how this can be achieved in reality is another matter.

2 The Overarching Ambitions of the Outreach Projects in Fiji

I believed that students from our university had the capacity to be challenged to work through some of the problems and complexities that confronted schools in rural and remote parts of the country. Over two years of leading the SEE Project, I had developed sufficient understanding of the school system and I was convinced about the real-world learning and knowledge sharing opportunities that outreach projects would present to our students. After all, I had started taking some proactive steps as a critical educator and in my view outreach projects presented unique opportunities to "raise ambitions, desires, and real hope" of our students who wished to tackle "the issue of educational struggle and social justice" through concrete actions (Giroux, 1988, p. 177). There is no doubt that "the look, sound, feel, and even smell of another country cannot be completely felt by description or grasped by study" (Wessel, 2007, p. 74) undertaken on a university campus. Giving some of our students a chance to experience a developing country first-hand could go a long way to shaping who they may become in the future. I was also convinced that such an experience would also align with QUT's distinctive identity as "a university for the real world". I thought one of the ways to give our students *in situ* experiences was by offering them an opportunity to travel with me to Fiji to learn first-hand how they could be of service to the community. In return the community would also get a chance to serve them in their learning. The aforementioned evidence in the literature also convinced me that there was real value in running outreach projects for our university students.

One of the units that I taught focussed on technology education. This unit was a neat fit to the outreach project because it prepared pre-service teachers to teach children from kindergarten (three years old) to year 10 (fifteen years old) on using technologies to learn. This unit had a two-pronged focus. It taught students how to integrate digital technologies across all the subjects in the Australian Curriculum by selecting appropriate pedagogies. The pre-service teachers also developed specific knowledge about how to teach the two subjects (Digital and Design Technologies) from the Technologies Curriculum. For one of the assessments, students had to demonstrate their knowledge and understanding of how technology driven activities could be designed for Australian classrooms using the Technological Pedagogical Content Knowledge (TPACK) framework (Mishra & Koehler, 2006).

I felt that I could tweak the focus of the assessment from the Australian to the Fijian curriculum for those students who wanted to participate in outreach projects. After all, university education should enable students to apply their knowledge internationally. Thus, the challenge for the students would be to design and implement classroom activities based on the Fijian curriculum. One of the main constraints was to propose technologies that were affordable and teaching strategies applicable to the local context. This task also positioned the students to connect their ideas to a range of social and contextual issues (Giroux, 2011). I also wanted my students to work in transdisciplinary teams because a real-world challenge needs to be viewed and tackled from multiple perspectives. Giroux (1992, 2001) argued that disciplines generally operate in a silo mentality. Knowledge is closely guarded and not shared between disciplines. As a consequence of this mentality, real opportunities for working in collaborative learning spaces that lead to productive outcomes for the students are lost (Giroux & Giroux, 2004). Such an attitude has been prevalent throughout my life as a student, a teacher and a university lecturer. To overcome this challenge, Giroux (1992) proposed that universities should do away with the discipline model and embrace either an interdisciplinary or a transdisciplinary approach that paves the way for the creation of new knowledge. However, implementing such a strategy is not easy. The model that I decided on was for students to work in transdisciplinary teams of three to four that included students from other faculties at QUT. The disciplines included Science, Information Technology (IT), Engineering, and Creative Industries. While the participating pre-service teachers from my unit would lead the teaching teams, students from other faculties would provide complementary support such as expert knowledge on how some of the technologies could be used. Thus, the challenge for each team would be to design and teach an activity (usually over a week) that was aligned with the Fijian curriculum and showcase the use of digital technologies. The activity would be delivered in a rural or remote school with a caveat that the head teacher or principal would be a stakeholder in the identification and design of the activities.

With these ambitions in mind, Graeme Baguley and I started applying for grants that would enable our students to participate in outreach projects in Fiji. Our model of engagement was well received because we were successful with our applications on three occasions over three years. These grants enabled three groups of students to engage in service-learning projects in three rural and one remote island school in Fiji between 2013 and 2015. All these schools were like Naidovi, built by the local communities, with many of the founders possibly illiterate like my ancestors. Grants from our university and the Australian Government's New Colombo Plan covered most of the students' travel and accommodation costs. Each school was either a rural or remote primary or high school. The following sections describe our initiatives and subsequent experiences at each school.

3   2013 – Sabeto Central and Sabeto District Schools

On June 26, I flew out to Fiji with staff and students from our university. For me, this flight was a history-making event – it was going to be the first time that I would have the opportunity to lead an outreach project at the Sabeto Central and Sabeto District Schools. On this occasion, our students would engage in teams and deliver digital technologies-based classroom activities. They would also participate in community activities at the Sabeto Village. Both of these were rural schools in the Sabeto Valley which is approximately a 15-minute drive from the Nadi International Airport. Most of the children who attend these schools were from low socioeconomic backgrounds. A lot was going through my mind. The experiences and the outcomes of this project could either make or break our initiatives of enhancing the quality of education in developing countries. I am sure that the students shared similar views – for many it was their first trip overseas. One of the students reflected on her initial thoughts as follows, "I knew how important it was to challenge yourself and do something different ... step out of your comfort zone". Therefore, apart from the challenge of teaching and interacting with the members of a community that was very different to theirs, they also had to adapt to an unseen and unfamiliar classroom environment. They were going to engage with adults and children from a very different culture to theirs. But all of us were pumped, excited, motivated, and looking forward to what was to unfold.

This project was made possible through our university's Engagement Innovation Grant. The late Geoff Portman and Professor Martin Betts were joint applicants with Graeme and me for this grant. Full-time students from the Faculties of Education, Science and Engineering, and Creative Industries who were enrolled in the selected unit were invited to participate. From the expressions of interest that were submitted, thirteen students were selected. This project had two parts. I led the first part where the students delivered classroom activities using technologies at the two schools. The Sabeto Village was the focus of the second part of our engagement. Geoff, who had prior connections with this village community, led this part of the project with his wife Annette. In the village, students with disciplinary backgrounds in fashion led teams to teach the local women dressmaking skills. The students who were enrolled in the Film and TV course led teams that produced a documentary of the village and captured audio recordings of the local choir group. One of the students, Ratu Epeneri Korovakaturaga, had a dual role. He was a Fijian student on an AusAID scholarship studying architecture. Aside from being a participant, he also played the part of a cultural ambassador. In this capacity, he became the go-to person on matters relating to the local context and especially Fijian customs. Dr Carly Lassig was also a part of our team and worked with the students to deliver the activities at Sabeto. She has a strong background in inclusive education and her rationale for participating in the project was as follows:

> I was most drawn to the Sabeto project in Fiji because it provided an opportunity to engage in work that could make a real difference to schools, students and families in a developing country. I find it particularly rewarding when I can be involved in work like this that has a tangible impact. As an academic working in inclusive education, I was also particularly drawn to the social justice component of the project. In the school, which was my main focus, I strongly supported the goals of not just providing resources (although the school certainly appreciated the technology that was donated), but also teaching staff and students so that they could continue to develop their own ICT knowledge and skills.

Zarina Shahban from the university's international student services helped in the classroom by teaming up with local students in activities and also liaised the out of school activities. While the teaching staff had part of their trips covered through the grant, Zarina met all the costs herself. We were very grateful for her commitment and support in this regard. Zarina had a strong belief in supporting disadvantaged communities. As a former resident of Fiji, she was well versed on some of the difficulties that schools faced in delivering quality education, particularly in rural and remote areas.

Our approach to outreach was unique and there were no similar projects that we could emulate – we were the trailblazers, and everything was done from scratch. A lot of preparatory work had to be done before departure. We developed the classroom activities in collaboration with the head teachers. This collaboration started months before our trip. At my own expense, nearly a year before the project got underway on the ground, I met both head teachers and the school management committees in Fiji. Geoff also made a trip about three months before the students arrived to ensure that the schools and the village community in Fiji were ready for the students. It also gave him an opportunity to address some of the concerns of the partners. Through ongoing consultations with our Fijian counterparts, we agreed to work for a week and run two full-day programs at each school. On the first day, our teams would work with classes 1, 3, 5, and 7. On the second day, the teams work with classes 2, 4, 6, and 8. On the last day, students from both schools would showcase what they had learnt and how technology had been used in their learning. At each school, we would also donate and setup a computer lab with 10 second-hand desktops. These would be shipped from Australia to Fiji in preparation for our arrival with the university students. Neither school had any useable computers, so we also made arrangements to borrow some iPads and cameras from the university so that we had technology resources for all classes.

I was very grateful to the staff in Graeme's office who assisted with some of the travel issues. Our project coincided with the university's June/July winter semester break. Incidentally, these dates also overlapped with the Australian school holidays which meant that many people were travelling to Fiji for their island experience. This meant that the airfares were not only exorbitantly high, but we also had to ensure that we got the flights that we wanted. Some of the staff had different arrival and departure dates, and this added another layer of complexity. We also had to locate and book affordable accommodation that was within proximity to the schools with rooms that could be shared between students. Given the size of our group, finding suitable ground transport (like a minibus) was not easy. Imported products that catered for students with dietary requirements were hard to find because there was no demand for this from the locals. The awareness and knowledge about dietary conditions did not seem to exist amongst many on the ground. Luckily, we had some advisory support on logistical issues from QUT's Alumni in Fiji. We also had to ensure that all students were well versed about the local context and particularly Fijian and Indian customs. Before departure, all students participated in an induction workshop which dealt with these aspects. We were fortunate to have the support of the South-East Queensland Fiji Students Association. They alerted the students to some local customs and traditions that they were likely to encounter, and which required sensitivity and tact. Our student cultural ambassador Epeneri was also the president of this association, which made things a lot easier. *Kava* was one of the discussion topics. The root of this plant is highly significant to the indigenous people in the South Pacific Islands. When the plant matures, its roots are sun-dried and pounded into a powder. When the powder is mixed with cold water and passed through a muslin cloth, the mixture that passes through is also called *kava*. This drink, also known as *yaqona*, is traditionally drunk in *bilos* (dried coconut shells) during ceremonies and on social occasions. There are specific protocols that need to be followed when serving and drinking *kava*. The drink produces numbing and sedative effects. For social occasions, it is sometimes drunk as a substitute to alcohol. But unlike alcohol where ethanol makes people drunk, with *kava*, the sensations are due to a group of compounds called kavalactones. Given that our students were going to participate in Fijian ceremonies, this background knowledge was necessary because kava drinking is an integral part of the proceedings.

3.1   *Getting Started at the Sabeto Schools*

When we arrived in Sabeto, we were very warmly welcomed by the village and school communities. Leading up to our activities in the schools, we were invited to participate in some traditional festivities at a neighbouring Fijian village. Cultural activities like traditional dances that were on show was an eye-opener for many of us (Figure 5.1). It helped our group develop contextual understandings about the schools and the communities they were serving.

FIGURE 5.1   A Fijian cultural dance performed at a neighbouring village

Both schools were close to each other and had a good working relationship. Sabeto Central mostly had Indian students with a small percentage of indigenous Fijian students. Prior to its name change in 2011, it was Sabeto Indian School. Like all other 'district schools' in the country, Sabeto District was located adjacent to the local village (Sabeto Village). The majority of the students at the district school were indigenous Fijians. Like the Central School, prior to the name change, it was known as the Sabeto Fijian School.

Our university group was divided into four mixed teams. The integration of the technologies was closely aligned with the expectations of the achievement indicators in the local curriculum in each year level. Here too, we found that teachers had minimal understanding of how this new curriculum could be implemented in their classrooms. The first team taught in Classes 1 and 2. Class 1 students presented a cultural dance which enabled them to demonstrate a series of movements associated with a song. Students in Class 7 videoed their performance. Class 2 students had to act and role-play in front of an audience. This activity enabled them to develop and demonstrate their dialogue, costume, and character skills. Students in class 8 videoed their performance. The second team taught Classes 7 and 8 and their main objective was to develop video camera filming and editing skills, which they used to capture and present the dance performances of the children in the lower grades. Through this video, the Sabeto students were expected to explain how their culture had changed over the years. This activity targeted the achievement indicators in Social Science. Class 8 students worked in a similar way. The videos were edited using a software called *Openshot* and then uploaded to the desktops. In Class 8, students were working towards achievement indicators in English.

The third team taught in Classes 4 and 5. In Class 4, the team worked towards developing their students' knowledge of food and water contamination in Health Science. The students then participated in an experiment where water was purified through reverse osmosis using materials such as plastic bottles, activated charcoal, sand, gravel, and cotton wool. The team leaders adopted this idea from similar projects that were done by Engineers Without Borders (2011) in countries like India. Students used their knowledge about water quality to explain what they had done in a video using *iMovie* on iPads. In Class 5, students conducted experiments on series and parallel circuits. They used their knowledge to explain how these worked by creating digital animations with the *myCreate* app on iPads, addressing achievement indicators in the Fijian Science curriculum. The fourth team targeted students in Classes 3 and 6. In Class 3, the students were asked to write a story about their school. This activity involved the arrangement of digital images (taken with an iPad) with text. In Class 6, students also created a digital storybook. However, they were immersed in a process that engaged learners in the critical aspects of story writing, including developing a storyboard. From this foundation, the students sketched the pages of their story. Digital images of these pages were captured using the iPad for their creative outputs. This activity focussed on the English curriculum.

This first outreach project was a truly satisfying experience. It was apparent that it had made a difference to everyone who was involved. The feedback from our university staff and students was exceedingly positive.

> My experience with the Sabeto project was extremely rewarding and memorable. I thoroughly enjoyed the work that we did in the schools and seeing the difference that the project made to the community. Equally memorable was the relationships I created with other QUT staff, QUT students from various Faculties, and the teachers, students, and families in Sabeto. It was rewarding to collaborate with QUT students in multidisciplinary teams and see them thrive in such a new and challenging environment. Getting to know the children and families in the villages is something that will stay with me forever. Their positivity and approach to life was inspiring for all of us, particularly in reflecting on our own privilege and how we take our lives for granted. On a personal note, as my first trip to Fiji, it was wonderful to see the real Fiji and be immersed in the culture and how Fijian people live. (Dr Carly Lassig)

> We are leading different lives and growing up differently but universally we are all connected because ... we are all humans ... I was surprised at how strong that connection was and how much we shared. (Film & TV student)

> I did not realise how easy we got it here [in Australia] with the amount of resources and the amount of help. (Education Student)

For the teachers and their students in both the Sabeto schools, the classroom interactions, with a predominantly white group of teachers from overseas, was a once in a lifetime opportunity. The revitalised classrooms were a breath of fresh air with a real change from their chalk-and-talk lessons. The quality of the work produced by the children was, on the whole, very good. The parents were also able to see evidence at the open day. Like Naidovi, this experience once again reaffirmed my belief that no matter where the children are, they will engage as long as the classroom activities are of a high quality and also relevant to the local context.

Like the teachers we had met at Naidovi, we found that there was little knowledge about designing classroom activities for the listed achievement indicators in their new curriculum in the Sabeto schools. Hence, here too, the teachers needed new ideas. But for their ideas to manifest into reality there was a need for more than just technology resources. For example, in the digital stories activity, the students sketched drawings for each of the pages in their stories. In one of the schools, there were no coloured pencils for students to use. We had one set of pencils as a backup that students shared to complete their activities. The lack of basic resources was more evident in one school than the other. How can children succeed if they do not even have the basic necessities for their education?

My experiences at Sabeto demonstrated that well-thought-out university outreach projects that are designed and developed collaboratively with local communities can deliver productive outcomes for both parties. Unlike some other outreach projects, our services rendered to the schools were both inno-vative and responsive to their needs. We also donated computers and other resources so that the students' learning could continue for some time. At a per-sonal level, I was thrilled because the teacher-student relationship had been redefined. I was teaching and at the same time learning with my students. In some respects, I was working towards a model of pedagogical practices where we had collectively become "agents of change" by "actively questioning and negotiating the relationships between theory and practice, critical analysis and common sense, and learning and social change" (Giroux, 2011, p. 172). Such experiences are rare in university classrooms.

One good thing can lead to another and I was thrilled when our student cultural ambassador Epeneri approached me and said, "It would be terrific if we could take a QUT group to Somosomo District School on the island of Taveuni". This school was adjacent to Epeneri's ancestral village. He went on to add that, "From what I have seen here at Sabeto, such an experience would benefit the Somosomo students immensely. It will be a real shift in how the teaching occurs in their classrooms". I was quite pleased to hear that Epeneri saw the value of the work we were doing. His interest motivated both Graeme and me, and we decided to target Somosomo District School as our next outreach project.

4   2014 – Somosomo District School

The journey to Somosomo District School on the island of Taveuni began almost nine months before the actual trip. An application for the Australian

Government's Short-Term Mobility Program Grant was successful, which set the wheels in motion. Taveuni is a remote island to the north-east of the country and is also known as the 'Garden Island of Fiji'. It boasts some of the idyllic gifts of nature such as crystal-clear ocean waters, a scenic coastlines, clean air, and breathtaking waterfalls. The friendliness of the locals adds another dimension to this island. It is quite fitting to say that it is an island where humans and nature have co-existed for ages. Nestled on the western coast is the chiefly village of Somosomo and the district school. Many prominent Fijian leaders lived here at one time or another and attended this school. Perhaps the most notable was the late Ratu Sir Penaia Ganilau. He was a former Governor General, deputy Prime Minister and also the country's first president. He was also Epeneri's grandfather.

Prior to the trip, direct communication with the head teacher was not possible because she did not have access to either a phone or a computer with Internet connectivity. We communicated verbally with the school though Epeneri and his uncle, the late Ratu Jone Ganilau who lived in the village. Nearly six months prior to the trip, when Epeneri was on holidays in Fiji, he had travelled to the island at his own expense to meet the head teacher, the school management team, and other members of the school community to explain the details of the project and the anticipated outcomes. In keeping with the local protocols, Epeneri also had to seek permissions from the chiefs to bring the project to Somosomo because it was their school. On this occasion, I had to apply for temporary teacher registration for all the team members with the Teacher Registration Authority in Fiji. This was new development and on the part of the Ministry of Education. It was a step in the right direction as it gave some certainty to ensure that volunteers, especially from overseas, were vetted before they entered schools as 'teachers'.

Our first outreach project to Sabeto was highly successful, but it also taught some useful lessons. In keeping with the tenets of action research (Chandra, Chandra, & Nutchey, 2014), we reflected on our experiences regarding those aspects that worked and those that needed further refinement. Some of our strategies were very effective, and we repeated them for this trip. For example, student induction occurred prior to the trip in much the same way as the trip to Sabeto with the support of the South-East Fiji Students Association. The timing of the project was almost the same and it overlapped with our students' winter semester break. The transdisciplinary team approach was very productive. However, engaging students with multiple disciplinary backgrounds in meaningful classroom activities was challenging because it was difficult to find a common thread between students' disciplinary experiences. Thus, for the trip to Somosomo, we focussed on students from only Education and Information Technology (IT) faculties. We also felt that engaging with two schools within our timeframe diluted the effectiveness of our work. For this reason, we opted to focus on one school. Regarding teaching, our approach was similar to what we did at Sabeto, however there were assessment tasks for all the participating students. For the pre-service teachers, the task entailed teaming up in groups of two or three to design classroom activities that they would implement in two classes. In each activity, the ultimate objective was to enable the students at Somosomo to create a digital product using the technologies. Each education team also collaborated with an IT student who provided technology expertise. The pre-service teachers also had to create a website using *WordPress* and upload their planned activities. The rationale here was to facilitate the sharing of their teaching ideas with their contemporaries on the World Wide Web. Some websites are still active with many visits from users throughout the world (e.g. Fishing for knowledge, https://kggroup422014.wordpress.com/). Before departure, like the rest of their peers in the cohort, the groups had to deliver a part of their proposed activity in a micro-teaching session. The teams also had to create a sample of the product that they expected their students to produce. Upon their return from Fiji, the pre-service teachers reflected upon his or her experiences using Edward De Bono's Six Hats (De Bono, 1991). The IT students also had real-world-focussed projects in their unit. They had to document and reflect on their experiences from an IT-in-society perspective.

Prior to departure we established that Somosomo District School had two campuses. Classes 1 and 2 were on the lower campus which was right next to the sea. The rest of the school was up on a hill. It took about fifteen minutes to walk from one campus to the other. For logistical reasons, we decided to deliver the teaching activities to students from Classes 3 to 8 at the campus up the hill. Like Sabeto, teaching would occur from Monday to Thursday culminating in an open day on Friday for the parents and the community. The school also did not have a library, so we decided to set up a learning centre with laptops and books – much like we did at Naidovi Primary on our first visit. The Short-Term Mobility funding for the trip covered most of the costs for travel and accommodation for ten students. The grant also included a portion of my expenses. Likewise, the university subsidised part of Epeneri's expenses. Two other students with backgrounds in engineering and nursing joined us at their own expense. I was grateful that Zarina and Ramila were able to team up with us. They gave up their holidays and travelled at their own expense to assist in the setting up of the library at the school. In total, we had a team of 16 staff and students who spent a week at the school. We were fortunate to get administration support from my school at the university for travel arrangements. For the project to materialise as planned, we took 14 second-hand laptops which were donated to the school. The participating students were very familiar with the struggles experienced in Fijian schools regarding resourcing. At her initiative, Christa Miyoni, one of the students on this trip, set up a crowdfunding webpage, which raised about a thousand Australian dollars (about 750 USD). Another student, Lauren Edmondson managed to get support from one of local Rotary clubs, which enabled us to purchase classroom resources such as stationery and kits for science experiments. A Brisbane Catholic primary school, together with our friends and relatives, supported us with library books. We ended up taking 500 books with us. Like Naidovi, a spreadsheet was created to assist the school in keeping track of the books. The school had converted a classroom into a library and built shelves for books, but they did not have any funding to buy tables. As a team, we chipped in, raised some money and donated a few tables.

The school did not have access to electricity which presented a challenge to our students. How could they run the laptops without electricity? As the IT students in our group were tinkering with the problem and brainstorming feasible ideas, a miracle happened. The South Korean Government donated a diesel generator to the school a few months before our team arrived. Our students were then confronted by another problem. How can we provide online resources to the students on the laptops without the Internet? The IT students came up with the idea of building a device that would enable the students at Somosomo to access useful resources on their laptops. They drew inspiration from the RACHEL PI Project (2014). The objective of the RACHEL PI Project is to enable users in developing countries access to a range of online resources without the need for connecting to the internet. It uses low-cost hardware such as the Raspberry Pi technology and an SD card to make the device affordable. The Raspberry Pi is a palm sized low cost computer that can be programmed and be used as an integral part of hardware in range of digital technology projects. In this instance, the technological device that was developed was called the *SEE Box*. It enabled multiple users to access online resources such as Khan Academy videos, the Wikipedia Encyclopaedia, and eBooks from Project Gutenberg without the need for an Internet connection. World Possible makes these resources available to users under a Creative Commons License (RACHEL PI, 2014). The *SEE Box* was a great idea because it had the potential to create new opportunities for teaching and learning. The offline Wikipedia resource would enable students to undertake research activities. Similarly, the Khan Academy videos could be helpful for self-paced learning for both teachers and students to develop and enrich their conceptual understandings.

When compared to Sabeto, this trip was logistically far more complicated. Managing the resources that we took with us added another layer of complexity.

We had to fly into Nadi, then travel on a bus for five hours to the country's capital Suva. We were so fortunate that Epeneri's mum and the members of his family hosted our team for lunch at their own expense. For our university students, the delightful food, lovely music, and the friendliness of Epeneri's family was a unique and unforgettable introduction to the Fijian culture and their hospitality. We spent a night in Suva and then boarded a ferry that took 18 hours to get us to Taveuni (the return trip was more straightforward because we flew directly from Taveuni to Nadi and then boarded a connecting flight back to Brisbane). Four modes of transport later, we finally arrived on the island. On the Sunday of the school week, we were warmly welcomed with traditional ceremonies by the community in the village church. We quickly learnt that nearly all 300 children who attended this school were from low socioeconomic backgrounds. Evidence of poverty in the community was high, driven by a lack of any significant economic activities on the island. The only notable activity was the construction of the island's new hydroelectricity plant which was a Chinese Government aid project. However, the workers on this project were predominantly Chinese nationals who were presumably in the country on work visas. Most of the residents were subsistence farmers. They grew vegetables, kava and other root crops such as dalo (taro) and cassava. Sometimes they sold their surplus crops either locally or to the middlemen who would ship them across to the mainland. Dalo and cassava are important staple foods for the islander communities, and there is an export market for kava and other crops overseas. Middlemen buy fresh dalo on the island for about 0.50 USD. By the time it gets onto the supermarket shelves here in Australia, the price increases more than tenfold.

There were three student teams on this trip. Like Naidovi and Sabeto schools, nearly all students at Somosomo were going to use laptops for the first time. Team 1 worked with students in Classes 3 and 8. They started their Class 3's with the basics of the keyboard. In the second part, with the assistance of the classroom teacher, their students performed a traditional Fijian dance (*meke*). Filming occurred as the students translated the meaning of the dance in the Fijian and English language. In Class 8, this team taught their students to create short digital stories that were inspired by Fijian myths. They used *LibreOffice Impress* to create their e-books, which, when completed, were to be shared with students in Class 3. Team 2 delivered Science lessons to students in Classes 5 and 6. The lessons focussed on electricity and the activities targeted two concepts – conductors and insulators; and series and parallel circuits. The idea was to get the students to a create multimedia presentation using *LibreOffice Impress* where they explained what they had learnt using the software *RecordMyDesktop*. Andrew Iddles, one of the group members, recalled his experience: "Most of our students had never used a computer before". This presented an unforeseen challenge. However, there was flexibility in planning which "allowed more time for creating the presentations with *LibreOffice Impress*". Andrew also noted that while the group had to forgo their plans to record the presentations using *RecordMyDesktop*, they had "great success with our session teaching basic computer skills". He also added:

> One of my most memorable moments teaching these skills was when groups of five students happily shared one computer, and cooperatively played games and as a consequence developed their typing skills. This was a sight that I have never seen in Australia.

Team 3 focussed on sustainable fishing practices in Classes 4 and 7. This theme was chosen because it was highly relevant to the students' lives – both in the short and long term. Given the proximity of the school community to the ocean, understanding the impact of environmental and economic factors on the marine environment is an essential priority in this part of the world. In terms of the Fijian Curriculum, the activities targeted achievement indicators in Science and English. Students researched and created e-books with messages of sustainable fishing practices using *Libre Impress*. To develop their storyboards, they brainstormed ideas to understand the status quo and issues associated with fishing in the local context. They created mind maps using software called *Freemind*. To assist the students with the basics of the keyboard, the team members helped them one-on-one. However, they noted that once a Somosomo student picked up an idea, they were also very quick to share their newly acquired skills with their peers. Eventually, the students were able to create some very interesting e-books which amazed their parents and the members of the community when they showcased them at the end of the week.

Apart from students' lack of familiarity with technology, all teams also noted literacy as another barrier that impeded students' full participation in classroom activities. There were reasonable numbers of students in each class who struggled with reading, writing, and speaking in English. This deficiency also impacted on their abilities to listen and decode the English text which was spoken by the 'teachers' in a foreign accent. On the basis of these observations, the setting up of the school's library was a step in the right direction. Hooking children into reading is one of the strategies that can develop their English language skills. The setting up of the library was a challenge in itself. When we arrived at the school, the shelves were still being built. While there was nothing too flash about the design of the shelves, it was nonetheless pleasing to see that the school had taken proactive steps to convert one of the classrooms into a library. However, the rate at which the work was progressing was an issue. To speed up the process, Ramila and Zarina helped the carpenter with some of the painting. By Thursday of the week, the library was ready for the staff and students. Ramila talked about the importance of reading and the care of books to the students. She explained the procedures for borrowing books and suggested ideas for library activities to the teachers. Seeing the children with a book in their hands was an emotional moment. I have never seen children so happy to flick through pages of a book. As soon as they grabbed a book from the shelves, they found a small place on the bare concrete floor and in small groups started looking through it. They began to interpret some of the images in their mother tongue. It was apparent that some of the students were familiar with the Disney characters from the videos that they had seen on DVD (Figure 5.2). To me personally, the opening of the library at Somosomo shed new light on what books mean to the underprivileged. What we take for granted in the developed world was a piece of treasure here.

FIGURE 5.2   Children seated on bare concrete floor to read the new library books

Our engagement at Somosomo District School once again reaffirmed my belief that no matter where children are, they will engage in learning as long as the activities hook their interest and curiosity. There were so many instances at Somosomo that validate this view. This episode is worth sharing. I was standing outside the Class 5 room when the students were learning about static electricity using balloons. This was a special moment for them. It was a real shift from chalk-and-talk lessons. What was even more exciting for the students was that if the balloon was rubbed on their hair, it picked little pieces of paper from the floor. There was excitement across the classroom as they made this observation. I threw in a question to add more fuel to this excitement – "Why does the balloon pick the paper?" and I added – "I will give a prize to whoever can answer this question correctly". And then I walked away. As soon as the school bell rang at the end of the day, the majority of the students from this class came running to me. I was working in the library at that time, and they lined up to answer the question. I was amazed – I had never seen this level of interest in an Australian school, even though I had posed similar questions to my students. They kept guessing and finally they asked for a clue. I said "somewhere in the answer, there is a word that starts with 'C'". The next morning, I was perplexed. They were waiting for me to arrive so that they could answer the question. To my amazement, one student had found an old dictionary in the village, and he was trying his luck with all words that began with C. Through perseverance one of the students worked out "charge" as the answer. She was thrilled with the pens, pencils and rubber that I gave her as a prize. For this student, these were much-needed resources for her schoolwork. She told me that she wanted to be a soldier and would happily be my bodyguard when I visited Fiji in my old age! I left Somosomo feeling very proud of our team. I was convinced that we had made a difference to the children at this school. Who knows what these new opportunities may bring them in the future?

5   2015 – Balata High School

In Fiji, children attend primary schools from Class 1 to either Class 6 or Class 8. The high school enrols students either from Form 1 to Form 7, or Forms 3 to 7. We started working with Balata High School in 2014, through the SEE Project. This rural school is 5 km from Tavua town on the main island of Viti Levu. At the time, the school had about 250 students on its roll in Forms 3 to 7. It also had a vocational centre for boys. Much of the credit for our connection with Balata goes to the school principal, Segran Pillay. In response to his request in 2014, we donated 10 laptops, a data projector and a digital video camera to the school. Six months after receiving the donations, Segran emailed me a detailed report. Despite limited resources, I was truly amazed by what he had been able to achieve by working collaboratively with his staff, especially considering that his school had been seriously ravaged by a cyclone only a few months earlier that year. The innovations we instigated at his school included the setting up of a computer lab that was accessed by every class once a week for research activities and online quizzes that included external exam papers with examiners' reports. A lecture theatre and media room was also setup for presentations. Students also had the option of borrowing laptops so that they could work on their projects. One of the laptops was also used for entering school data into the Ministry's database. Segran's resourcefulness was evident in how he set up the digital resources. For safety, he decided to put burglar-proof grills in the room that had the laptops. He collaborated with the vocational education teacher and arranged for his students to work on a project to build the grills onsite. Instead of buying a screen for the data projector, he improvised and bought white canvas fabric locally which was much cheaper than the commercially available option. The technologies were also facilitating self-paced learning especially for remedial classes conducted after school and, yes, on Saturdays and in the evenings too. External exams are part and parcel of the lives of high school students and their teachers in Fiji, so many schools offer after-school classes to assist their students. Segran was working towards a school policy that would mandate all teachers to save lesson plans, notes, and other necessary content as soft copies for viewing on a school server. These changes showed Segran's commitment and that of his staff towards technology integration. Most of the outcomes were the result of Segran's innovative capabilities. He led by example and seeded new technology ideas in his teachers. In my mind, principals like Segran fall in the category of innovators and early adopters (Rogers, 2003) and they can truly change the landscape of schools almost anywhere in the world. The evidence he produced showed what was possible in schools and what outcomes good leadership can generate (Chandra, 2016). For Segran,

> The Integration of ICT at Balata High School in partnership with the SEE Project brought about a new dimension to teaching in a school that enrolled students predominantly from the farming background. The journey that began in 2013 with an initial donation of 10 laptops and a projector led to revolutionary attainments for students and the community.

Given the connections we had developed with the school, there was mutual interest in running an outreach project. It would be different to the first two projects because our university students would be working in a high school for the first time. According to Segran:

The outreach project provided us with many opportunities to achieve our vision. Secondly, the school already had a connection with Dr Chandra, QUT, and SEE Project. We were very grateful for the thousands of dollars of equipment that had been donated to our school. This outreach project was going to open up new pathways, ideas and assist our students and teachers in grasping new methodologies. This was Balata's opportunity to showcase projects and student achievements to the community, the Education Ministry in Fiji and the others with a vested interest in educational technology.

When compared to our trip to Somosomo, ground transfers were more straightforward because all we needed was transport from the airport to our accommodation near the school. For most of the students, this trip was made possible by the Australian Government's New Colombo Plan. In addition, the university financially supported two Deans Scholars from the Faculty of Science and Engineering who joined our group. As per previous trips, Ramila and Zarina volunteered their time and funded their trip. Dr Richard Medland from the Chancellery and the Learning and Teaching Unit also joined us and self-financed his expenses. He was a real bonus to our team because of his strong background in Science, Technology, and Mathematics. His rapport with his students was admirable. According to Richard:

> The intent of the SEE project fulsomely aligned with my own values while achieving professional milestones. The design and development of the *SEE Box* also married up a challenging international immersion experience and real-world research project for students I supervised and mentored as part of STIMulate. The collaborative in-situ teaching and training with peers and local teachers and students I would argue also changed lives for the better. The *SEE Box* and work by our team exposed rural/remote schools and communities with minimal ICT infrastructure and experience to the power and accessibility of cheap, low-power, embed computing.

I had started the discussion with Segran and the teachers almost eight months before we arrived at the school. Our model of engagement was similar to previous years. In total, we had 12 students who were enrolled in courses at QUT that would lead to degrees in Education, IT, and Engineering. Segran was very proactive in identifying the teachers that our students were going to partner with for their teaching activities. Thus communication via email started between some of these teachers, and our team, a few weeks before we arrived. This helped some of the teams refine their ideas. Like our other trips we donated laptops, robotic kits, and cameras.

As in previous years, all students who put their hands up for the project wanted to make a difference by sharing their knowledge and at the same time learn more about other cultures. And for most of them, it was their first overseas travel. One of the pre-service teachers with a migrant background articulated her reasons as follows:

> I have always been interested in going on volunteer projects overseas. One of my goals in life is to travel and teach anywhere and everywhere. I can't wait to participate in this project because I believe that it will provide me with the opportunity to help and make a difference in the lives of the students. My parents come from a migrant background where it wasn't easy to get a good education, and they taught me to really value it. I believe that a good education can really change somebody's life and being part of a project like this one can provide students with this opportunity to learn and develop skills that are very important in today's day and age. I really want to inspire the students to be interested in learning and their education. I intend to do this by having a positive and encouraging attitude.

Without a doubt, some of the planned activities would have been a first for Fiji. Even by Australian standards, all activities were very innovative and of a very high standard. The size of our group enabled us to deliver activities in five different classes. In a Form 5 class (16–17 years old), we presented an activity which had a Science, Technology, Engineering, and Mathematics (STEM) focus. There has been a lot of talk about STEM and for some, particularly in political circles, it means no more than enticing more students to study these subjects in schools. In countries like Australia, current employment trends suggest that 75% of the fastest-growing occupations in the country require employees to have STEM knowledge and skills (Australian Government, 2014). However, the uptake of these subjects in Australian schools and universities has been on the decline for a few decades (Marginson, Tytler, Freeman, & Roberts, 2013). Student interest in pursuing careers in STEM has fallen or stagnated. This decline is strongly associated with the recycling of more of the same teaching and learning ideas where STEM education is driven by a silo-based approach that fails to enthuse and excite our students (Bybee, 2010; Hogan & Down, 2015). Research strongly suggests that a transdisciplinary approach to teaching STEM can have a positive impact on learning outcomes (Hattie, 2008; Marginson et al., 2013). Thus, when I design STEM activities, I purposely situate the learning tasks in real-world contexts that facilitate hands-on engagement and at the same time enable students to explore conceptual connections across these disciplines.

At Balata, our approach to STEM was simple. We organised the students in Form 5 to design, build, and program robots so that they travelled in a straight line (Engineering and Technology). The students gathered data on the motion of the robots (Science) to draw graphs (Mathematics). We used these graphs to consolidate their understanding of how these lines connected with equations explaining the meanings of terminologies such as *intercept* and *gradient*. They also used graphs to identify the point where one robot would pass another and in the process got to view simultaneous equations from a different perspective. They extended this knowledge to kinematics by looking at specific types of graphs (distance/displacement-time, speed/velocity-time, acceleration-time etc.). These activities laid the foundations for more challenging contextualised problems, such as this one that was posed: "The distance between the towns of Tavua and Rakiraki is 30 km. A car leaves Rakiraki and travels at an average speed of 60 km/h. Another car leaves Tavua and travels at an average speed of 75 km/h. Draw graphs to determine where the cars will pass each other". The problem can be extended to incorporate the point where the paths of the two cars will cross using Google Maps. Graphs can foreground students' understanding of solving equations algebraically. We took this activity further and used the video game *Angry Birds* and software *GeoGebra* to teach students about parabolic graphs. Our approach allowed students to have a play first. We then taught them to take a screen capture. This was embedded on a *GeoGebra* page and from here the students determined the equation of the graph that aligned with the path followed by the birds. Only four students in this class had access to computers at home! For all students, building and programming robots and the software *GeoGebra* was a new experience. Surprisingly no one at Balata had played *Angry Birds* before even though the game was relatively well known to the younger generation in Australia.

I remember doing these types of problems in Physics and Mathematics when I was in school. There was no imagination or effort on the part of my teachers to find interactive strategies to enable us to develop a more meaningful understanding of the tasks at hand. We developed and implemented this task with a high level of success because the Mathematics and Physics teacher at Balata was very motivated about using technologies in his classroom. He reflected on his experiences by pointing out that his students had enjoyed all the lessons. Personally, he viewed the lessons as professional development as he had learnt a lot about teaching and learning by participating in our classes. He noted that thoughtful use of technologies makes teaching and learning more productive and increases the effectiveness of the process. He believed that *GeoGebra* is an important tool for teaching Mathematics because it created interactive opportunities to learn concepts in geometry, algebra, and calculus in an environment that was very user-friendly. He was also confident that *Angry Birds* could be used to teach concepts such as quadratic graphs (as was done in classes) and projectile motion in Physics and pointed out that his students learnt most of the concepts that were taught using robots. He was grateful to the robotics kits and the laptops that we donated to the school specifically for Mathematics and Science students.

For a Computer Studies class in Form 5, Richard and the IT students designed and implemented an activity that explored the use of Pizazz robots for teaching two programming languages – *Python* and *Scratch*GPIO. These robots use the Raspberry Pi technology and are programmed using sensors. Like the STEM activity, this was a wholly new experience for the students at Balata. The activities designed by the team went beyond what is stipulated in the Year 11 Computer Studies syllabus in Fiji. One of the QUT students from the IT Faculty reflected on his experience by pointing out that teaching was not something that he had ever considered, but from this opportunity, he had realised that he genuinely enjoyed it and his only regret was that he only got to teach for four days. He was buoyed by the enthusiasm of the students when they finally got the robots moving despite all the network complications. Another IT student expressed his thoughts as follows:

> ... the highlight of the trip for me was the incredible enthusiasm that the [Balata] students brought into the classroom. There was never a moment when I felt that they had lost interest, and on several occasions, they even volunteered to stay back over lunch to keep working on the problems that we had set. Further, the students surpassed our (ever higher) expectations at each stage and as a result we were able to progress beyond our initial planned activities and cover almost a third of a semester worth of university-level content in only four days.

Another group focussed on the environment in their activity. I feel quite passionate about this topic. Each time I visit places like Fiji and see breathtaking sceneries, I begin to wonder about the future of the planet. One of the questions I ask myself is, "Will my grandchildren, and future generations, see this same view from where I am standing?". Most times the answer is in the negative. One of the ways to tackle this challenge is by educating the younger generation about nurturing our planet. Within the Form 4 (fourteen- to fifteen-year-olds) Science curriculum in Fiji, there is an environment-centred unit.

One of our teams focussed on this topic which led to the production of a short documentary where the Balata students developed storyboards, scripts, and ultimately performed and recorded their stories. This activity took a step in the right direction. If students throughout the world become more conscious of their environment, then their actions can pave the way to a healthier planet. The Science teacher working with this group expressed her thoughts by pointing out that the outreach project was "very beneficial to my students and me". She learnt a lot as to "how ICT can be used in the Science classes. The step-by-step details of how to go about engaging students to make a video on a particular concept has been a beneficial form of professional development". She also learnt that making a video was more than just grabbing the camera and taking the shots. She learned that the creative process involves "camera angles, camera functions, planning by completing the story board ... taking shots ... consideration of background noise and ... using *Openshot* video editor software". She strongly believed that her students were actively involved in the activities, which made all the difference in their understanding of the concept. One of the pre-service teacher's was amazed by the pace at which the students had engaged and learnt to use the technologies that were entirely new to them. For this student:

> ... the best part of the whole teaching experience was seeing the Balata students' faces light up as they watched their final products on the projector ... just seeing them smile uncontrollably when they saw all their hard work and effort on screen meant the world to me, it showed that we had taught these students a new skill that they were proud of.

Another pre-service teacher noted that the experience had taught her a lot about the "teaching profession and also myself" because she was able "to gain valuable insight on the different ways knowledge can be constructed through the use ICT inside the classroom. After this trip, I feel very confident about my teaching abilities".

The Form 4 English curriculum includes a unit that covers *girmit* and the Indian indenture system (See chapter 2). I was so glad that this was now a part of the curriculum. Back in my time, we had no such opportunities. One of the teams developed a classroom activity that explored *girmit* through role play and drama. This topic was also used as a focus to teach English through the structure of narrative and develop skills such as reading, writing, spelling, and comprehension (Figure 5.3). Students at Balata developed story-boards, scripts, and ultimately performed and recorded their role-plays. Ramila, Zarina, and I participated in role play and acted as *girmiteers* to give students a perspective of the country's past. An unplanned and highly significant outcome was a very popular Hindi song – *chal akelaa chal akelaa, chal akelaa, teraa melaa peechhe chhootaa raahi chal akelaa chal akelaa*. The late Mukesh sang this song for a Bollywood movie released in 1968. The words directly translates to 'move alone, move alone, move alone, your people have been left behind, keep moving alone'. This song was inspired by Ramila and Zarina to intertwine the musical talents of the Balata students with the theme of the activity on *gir-mit*. The lyrics of the song also summed up the journeys that were undertaken by the *girmiteers* ... they left their comfort zones and kept walking alone into the unknown. Perhaps the song also relates to the journeys undertaken by many migrants today. Personally, the singing of this song was quite significant because all students, irrespective of their ethnicities, joined in to sing. One of the Education students recollected the moments that she would treasure for-ever from the week at Balata High School. She was very moved by one of her students who gave a touching speech about what she and her classmates had learnt during the week and finished up by thanking the teaching team mem-bers. "Hearing a student so appreciative of what you tried to do for them, and seeing that the time and effort you put into a unit or a lesson had paid off, was an incredibly special and proud moment".

FIGURE 5.3   Class discussing the issue of *girmit*

In the Form 4 Social Science syllabus, a historical unit of work covers the period from "Early Settlers and the Society of the Early Fijians" through to "Offer of Cessation", which is an important era in Fiji's history. Such a unit enables meaningful conversation not only for assessment purposes but also about the history of the country. I like this quote from the award-winning novelist Pearl S. Buck – "If you want to understand today, you have to search yesterday". One of the teams delivered a classroom activity that explored some of the historical players and facts from the 1800's that eventually led to the cessation of Fiji to Great Britain (See chapter 2). The culminating activity was the production of a current affairs type video clip that highlighted the events from that era. The outcomes both for the teaching team members and for the students were outstanding. One of the Education students expressed her thoughts about the unique learning opportunities at Balata, as follows:

> Working with my fellow QUT students and overcoming technology and lesson challenges within the week built our teamwork skills immensely. Teaching the students was just so much fun. I do not have words to describe how much fun I had and how many skills I developed. I feel like the students taught me just as much as I taught them, and I will never be more grateful to have experienced something like this.

Apart from teaching activities, a number of excursions and visits to local communities and schools further enriched our university students' knowledge and understanding of the context. They visited a primary school and a Fijian village that was located in the interior. They also spent some time at the Ra Special School where we donated some laptops. This visit gave them an insight into inclusive education and how it was delivered in the country. Our students thoroughly enjoyed and appreciated the activities that were presented by children at this school.

According to the Principal, Segran Pillay, he received very encouraging feedback from the teachers and the school community about the outreach project. The teachers were very happy because "it was an eye-opener and a refresher passé for them as they gathered some unique teaching ideas on how to teach the curriculum using technology". For example, the Science teacher shared with other colleagues how documentaries were made by different groups on recycling. She mentioned how startled she was to see her students adding subtitles, titles, background music, and editing the videos to get them "ready in less than 2 days". This was the first time such an activity had been undertaken in her classroom. Upon reflection the history "students opened up" and pointed out that their "boring lessons suddenly came alive" with the use of technology. The Mathematics and Physics teacher "was amazed to see the involvement of the low achieving students as they built the NXT LEGO robots". He was astonished to see the students program the robots "to demonstrate their understanding of some of the more challenging concepts in his subjects". The principal was also amazed by his seven-year son's curiosity about LEGO and *Angry Birds*. "But, I believe most children of today are attracted to technology and games which can be used in a very positive way to engage students in a classroom". He added that the showcase which was staged on the last day of our project at Balata was "a very rare event in Fiji". It demonstrated the highlights of our engagement including student achievements and it "opened many eyes". All participants including leaders from other schools and the Senior Education Officer commented positively on the project and its achievements.

Upon reflection, I was thoroughly impressed by the breadth and depth of the content that was covered, how it was delivered and the technologies that were used. Some of the content was also unknown to our students, for instance *girmit*, and Fijian History. Like previous trips, the teams did an excellent job, delivering and sharing their knowledge fittingly in an unfamiliar context. Our university prides itself as being the "university for the real world" and I could see the evidence here. The students had the capacity to not only apply their knowledge in unseen contexts but also deliver outcomes that had the potential to seed new ideas. Every university student should have such an experience! Richard reflected on "his fond memories of Fiji and team" and he felt that "the overall experience was marvellously fun and I learned a great deal through my exposure and immersion".

6   Lesson Learnt – A Win-Win Situation

My observations, conversations, and interactions with all key participants (university students and staff, head teachers, principals, teachers, students, parents, and community members) resoundingly pointed to one conclusion. They were all winners who were touched by the experiences in special ways. Teaching in such contexts enables both the teachers and their students to develop new knowledge. Paulo Freire (2001) aptly stated this duality as: "whoever teaches learns in the act of teaching, and whoever learns teaches in the act of learning" (p. 31). The success of these projects was largely due to the fact that we understood the context very clearly. We built strong bridges with the partners before engaging in outreach projects. Our engagement was also meaningful on the ground. It was well thought out, and the context was integral in the planning of the activities. According to Segran:

> Programs of this nature benefits all stakeholders. I am glad that QUT students and lecturers also gathered much from their experiences in Fiji.

Apart from classroom experiences, the visit to a local farm, a long dusty bus ride to a Fijian village in the interior, local food dishes, and our lifestyle of Western Fiji would be remembered for some time. I am glad that Fiji was chosen as a destination for this outreach. I am sure the program did not happen by chance. It must have taken months of planning and preparation.

There was strong evidence that teaching in Fijian classrooms taught our university students new lessons about themselves, their disciplinary knowledge, other cultures, and this part of the world. I felt that the project ticked many boxes meaningfully regarding the aspirations that the university had for its students and their learning experiences (QUT, 2017). The classroom environments were foreign and challenging. Some of the students were not even training to be teachers. However, they persisted and delivered the intended outcomes with pride and gusto. By doing so, they demonstrated their ability and resilience by employing different ways of thinking (QUT, 2017). All the teams worked highly efficiently – this showed the students' abilities to be "effective collaborators and communicators" in both "disciplinary and interdisciplinary contexts" (QUT, 2017, para. 5). The outreach projects also created a unique opportunity for the students to demonstrate their abilities to apply digital literacies and use technology to deliver highly engaging classroom activities (QUT, 2017). They were able to adapt in a unique global context by adopting the accepted protocols of the local culture together with the guidelines set by the schools and the Education Ministry in Fiji (QUT, 2017). In doing so, the university students made a positive contribution that had a real impact on the students and teachers in the respective schools (QUT, 2017). The students were able to demonstrate these attributes because the outreach project provided authentic learning experiences and the transdisciplinary makeup of the teams exposed the students to each other's disciplines and their ways of thinking (QUT, 2017). They also got a chance to engage with learners with diverse cultural perspectives and in the process, utilise and apply a range of learning technologies and tools (QUT, 2017). Collectively these are some of the qualities of international-mindedness that all university students should be able to demonstrate in the 21st century (Chandra & Tangen, 2018; Hill, 2012).

The reflections and the feedback from the university students spoke volumes. All students who provided feedback after the trip rated their overall experience with scores of nine or ten out of ten. Students supported their reasoning for their scores with comments such as, "This trip was probably the most amazing experience of my life (9.8/10)" and included sentiments such as considering the outreach project as "a dream come true, cultural trips ... were eye-opening, I learnt a lot about my teaching profession and also about myself". The reflection of one of our Engineering students who led the water purification activity in the Sabeto schools highlights the significance of well-thought-out classroom activities to the local communities. The student recalled that word had got around the school about this miraculous activity that delivered clean water. A student from another class became very interested and wanted to build one at home.

> I was pretty excited when the student approached me ... and ... said ... I want to build my own water filter for home and I said have you got a problem with your water? He said, "yeah it usually comes out dirty like when we turn the tap on". I asked him, are you drinking this water anyway, he said yes, we drink it every day, and ... sometimes it does make us sick and I think it is from the water ... and so I said right ... I will get some stuff and show you how to build it ... so I got a piece of paper because I already had the experiment drawn up on the blackboard for the open day ... so I showed him how to build it [water filter] and he was really motivated and he was writing down the things really quickly and asking me all the questions ... then I got him a sample of everything so he could go home and build his own water filter and that was really awesome ... I was really moved by that ... I got him all the gear and ... he said thanks and ran off.

Here was an example of real-world impact, showing what university students can do through outreach to ameliorate local problems. While I have done similar experiments in Australian classrooms where we made muddy water in science lessons and passed them through a filter paper to remove the sediments, in developing countries like Fiji water quality is a real issue. Many are powerless, with no choice but to live with whatever they can get from taps (if they are lucky), wells, ponds, and rivers. The QUT students were "proud" and at the same time believed that their activities "had an impact on the students and their learning". A pre-service teacher's reflections on her experiences probably also sum up the views of many who participated in the outreach projects:

> This trip to Fiji has been without a doubt the greatest experience I have ever encountered in my life. Words cannot express how invaluable an experience this trip has been in regard to not only developing my teacher identity I guess you could call it, but also developing an admiration for the Fijian culture and developing lifelong friendships with those that we went on the trip with. One thing I loved about this trip was that we as

students were really able to be immersed into the cultural side of Fiji as opposed to the tourist side which I believe majority of people who travel to Fiji tend to do. I really have a newfound respect and admiration for the Fijian culture and it has really opened my eyes to their welcoming nature. It was just amazing to recognise that those who live with so little were the happiest and kindest people I have ever met.

The teaching aspect of this trip was absolutely amazing, and it has made me really want to travel back to Fiji and teach in different schools. The staff and the students at Balata High were so kind and so welcoming and the students who we had the opportunity to teach were all amazing in their own ways. Although this teaching experience was all about us as teachers teaching the students, I really believe that I learnt more from them. I could go on writing for hours but overall this has been an amazing experience, I have loved every second of it and would like to thank you Vinesh for giving me this invaluable opportunity that I will never forget and am so grateful to have experienced.

For me, this was also one of highlights of my teaching career. For once, I thought I really made a difference to my students. I taught, and I learned, but most importantly, I could actually observe what my students were able to do in the real world. This is one opportunity that many university lecturers never get. Their positive comments about their experiences spoke volumes. It also added a new dimension to their university education. They all learnt something new about themselves and their future professions. It was a win-win situation for everyone!

Student Outreach Projects in Malaysia

> The goal of education is not to increase the amount of knowledge but to create the possibilities for a child to invent and discover, to create men who are capable of doing new things.
>
> JEAN PIAGET

The video accompanying this chapter is freely available online at https://doi.org/10.6084/m9.figshare.10305281

Our success in Fiji gave us confidence and we were convinced that these outreach projects were having a positive impact on both the university students and the school communities. Leading and running such projects is hard work. Nonetheless, they are worth doing as they deliver a range of benefits and outcomes that cannot be achieved in conventional classrooms. Graeme Baguley had strong connections with Malaysia. He had previously worked as an Australian Volunteer Abroad and also as a member of the Australia diplomatic corps in Malaysia for about five years. He also had a strong circle of friends in Malaysia from his university days, but more recently he had developed significant partnerships with the QUT Alumni in Malaysia. According to Graeme:

> As much as I have personal connections and a love for Fiji, I have a strong affinity with the people of Malaysia developed through the time I have worked there and through the many close friends living there. Extending the SEE Project to Malaysia gave me the opportunity to introduce the rich and wonderful cultures of Malaysia to our Australian students and to invite the Malaysian students to meet and work with some great Aussie kids. Besides the positive impact on the Orang Asli children in the

schools, deep intercultural learning for all involved was the underlying objective of my involvement in the project.

One of our graduates, Dr Siti Suriawati Isa at the Universiti Putra Malaysia, expressed an interest in outreach projects that would mutually benefit students at the two universities and the communities they served. Graeme and I started to explore grant opportunities to take a group of QUT students to deliver outreach projects in Malaysia.

Like Fiji, Malaysia too was once a British Colony and it gained its independence in 1957. It has a much larger population (more than 30 million) but is multi-ethnic in composition (Samuel, Tee, & Symaco, 2017). Every country has its unique set of attributes. The Human Development Index (HDI) that was created by the United Nations Development Program provides an opportunity to assess development in 188 countries and territories around the world (UNDP, 2016). It was "created to emphasise that people and their capabilities should be the ultimate criteria for assessing the development of a country, not economic growth alone" (UNDP, 2016, para. 1). The HDI is an aggregation of three different indices – life expectancy, education and gross national income (GNI). Using this index, the United Nations Development Program generates a rank order of countries. On the basis of this index, Australia is ranked at 2 (HDI = 0.939), Malaysia at 59 (HDI = 0.789), and Fiji 91 (HDI = 0.736). Thus, these indices provide a relative measure of human development in the three countries.

Malaysia, like Australia, has come a long way in advancing the education levels of its citizens. At the time of the country's independence in 1957, only 6% of school age children had completed secondary education (Samuel et al., 2017). About 50 years later, it rose to 82%. There are five distinct levels of education (pre-primary, primary, lower secondary, upper secondary, and post-secondary) that come under the control of the Ministry of Education (Samuel et al., 2017). The ministry takes charge of managing the school system, developing policies, and overseeing the curriculum and assessment. The education system is highly centralised. While progress has been made with improvements in overall access to education, the Ministry of Education "acknowledges that serious problems remain with the quality of education in a period of rapid expansion of educational opportunity" (p. 10). A World Bank report also noted that the quality of education could not be blamed on the lack of financial resources (Samuel et al., 2017). It is noteworthy that while hundreds of millions of dollars had been spent on the acquisition of technologies for schools, there was "little impact on transforming teaching and learning practices" (Tee & Samuel, 2017, p. 97). According to the Ministry of Education (2013, as cited in Tee & Samuel, 2017), "teachers were not adequately prepared to integrate technology effectively into teaching and learning" (p. 97). As we know, in schools, technologies on their own do not make a difference, teachers do.

Malaysia has also faced challenges over the position and the relevance of English as a medium of instruction (Nor, Leong, & Salleh, 2017). More recently, Malaysian students' poor performances in international testing (e.g. PISA – mathematics, science, and reading) has served as a driver for changes in the curriculum (Hwa, 2011). The Standard Curriculum for Primary Schools (KSSR) that was introduced in 2010 incorporates the teaching of the core basic modules (literacy, numeracy, and spiritual development) through subjects such as English. 'Basic ICT' is also one of the skills that students are expected to develop. On the basis of some of this research, it was evident that more could be done in terms of teaching with technologies and conducting classroom activities in English. This background research combined with Graeme's prior knowledge, experiences, and connections inspired us to undertake outreach projects in Malaysia.

There were some significant differences between Fiji and Malaysia. In both countries, the integration of digital technologies in education presented a challenge. Mastery of the English language was a more significant issue in Malaysia than in Fiji. I believed that the model that we had developed for our outreach project in Fiji could be extended and adapted to Malaysia as well. The focus would primarily be on delivering classroom activities that showcased the integration of digital technologies and at the same time develop students' knowledge of English. The mix of our teams would be transdisciplinary, although this time also transnational, with Dr Siti Isa's students as part of our teams. The prospect of working alongside a colleague and her students from Malaysia was exciting. Our grant applications for Malaysia were successful on two occasions. The first grant was from QUT in 2015 while the second was from the Australian Government in 2016. This enabled us to run two outreach projects in two schools in the State of Pahang. The two participating primary schools were *Sekolah Kebangsaan* (SK) Temai and *Sekolah Kebangsaan* (SK) Sungai Mas in the State of Pahang. As with the projects in Fiji, prior to our departure we ran induction workshops to familiarise the team members with the proposed classroom activities, Malaysian school system and culture, and the Universiti Putra Malaysia (UPM) team. We were supported by some locals in Brisbane who were either former Malaysian nationals or had working knowledge of the context.

1   2015 – SK Temai

This outreach project to SK Temai Primary was funded by QUT's Short Term Outward Mobility Program. It was run on a shoestring budget because the grant only partially covered the costs of the students travel and accom-modation. There was no funding for staff. Despite these constraints, 10 students with disciplinary backgrounds in Education (4), IT (3), Health (1), Film and TV (1), and Business (1) joined us on the trip and also met some of their expenses. Another student with a background in Design joined the group, funding all her expenses. Four staff members – Graeme Baguley, Dr Richard Medland, Ms Jocelyn Tan (International Student Office) and I funded the trip ourselves.

Much of the credit for the project coordination on the ground goes to Siti. She was able to muster support from her university, the Office of the Chief Minister of Pahang State, Pahang Tourism, and the QUT Alumni which collectively lowered the financial burden of the project team members. To give a real taste of the local culture, Siti was also able to put together an overnight home-stay for the team with parents and other families who lived near the school. As Siti recalled, coming up with an effective program on a tight budget was not easy (The SEE Project, 2015, para. 6):

> A significant hurdle was that the budget for the project was limited. I had to come up with feasible options to ensure that everything was doa-ble at a minimal cost. I was glad that my faculty and the university were very supportive and provided financial assistance to cover some of the expenses. A few weeks before the QUT participants arrived, I managed to secure two dinners for all participants that were sponsored by the Office of the Chief Minister of Pahang, YAB – Dato' Sri DiRaja Hj Andan Yaakob and the Chairman of Tourism and Culture Pahang – YB., Dato' Sri Hj. Mohd. Sharkar Hj. Shamsudin, the local representative of Bebar in the Pekan parliament – YB. Mohammad Fakhruddin Mohd. Ariff helped identify between 10–15 families from the local community to be our 'foster parents' for one night. Everything was planned and we looked good for our QUT guests who were to arrive on the second day of Eidul Adha celebration when most of the Malaysians would be on leave.

Siti also organised the school and our channel for communication with the school. SK Temai is a primary school in Pahang, Malaysia. This school had 160 students and 40% were of Orang Asli background. The Orang Asli are the indigenous people of Malaysia. Siti reflected on her initial thoughts and experiences as follows (The SEE Project, 2015, paras. 4 & 5):

> Finding a school with high Orang Asli enrolment was personally satisfy-ing. The Orang Asli community around the school comes from the Jakun

tribe who live at Kampung Permatang Siput, located approximately 15 km from the school. The Jakun tribe are considered to be the most advanced in the Malaysian peninsular. While they maintain their traditional culture and lifestyle in many ways, they have also been very progressive. This is also reflected in the students at the school. Over the past 20 years, the school has maintained an excellent record of graduates of Orang Asli background. I firmly believe that the Orang Asli children, particularly at SK Temai, have the potential to succeed if they get the right exposure and opportunity. With the mix of university students from Australia and Malaysia – this project had the potential to present some good role models to the children at SK Temai.

My strong connections with a few people enabled me to choose the right primary school for the project. While gaining approval from the school at Sekolah Kebangsaan Temai, Pekan, Pahang was easy, I also had to get approval from other parties since all schools in Malaysia are under the jurisdiction of the Malaysian Ministry of Education. I also decided to include the State Government of Pahang in this project since this would be the first time QUT staff and students were coming to their state. I wanted the QUT participants to experience the Malaysian culture and also have the opportunity to visit some interesting tourist attractions. I also wanted these tourism destinations to be different from what Australia offers. Though the arrangements and planning took a lot of my energy and time, I enjoyed doing it because deep down inside I felt that this project would benefit many people and would also provide me with a great experience ... Community development work has always been very close to my heart. This was probably another reason I was excited about this project.

By working collaboratively with Siti, we were able to develop a program that would enable all the participants to share disciplinary and cultural knowledge with each other. The timing of the visit was crucial. The only time that the trip was doable for the QUT students and staff was during the week-long mid-semester break at the end of September. This time also coincided with *Eid al-Adha* which is an important festival in the Muslim calendar. However, our Malaysian counterparts were very accommodating.

1.1   *Going to Sekolah Kebangsaan Temai*

Our trip began from the Brisbane International Airport on September 25. The first leg of the flight was from Brisbane to Singapore. When we landed, the airport was blanketed in haze and visibility was poor. According to newspaper reports, the haze was the result of bushfires in Indonesia that were lit by irresponsible palm oil, paper and pulp merchants who were clearing land to further advance their business ventures. In short, this was an act of environmental terrorism. At this time of the year, fires are lit in parts of Indonesia with little thought about the consequences for the flora and fauna (including people). According to the Guardian Newspaper, "tens of thousands of people in Indonesia and Malaysia" had to seek "medical treatment for respiratory problems. The annual burning is decades old, and Indonesia has faced mounting pressure to end the practice. Scientists say the pollution could surpass 1997 levels when the haze created an environmental disaster that cost an estimated US$9 billion in damage" (Holmes, 2015, paras 5 & 6). This haze played havoc on our week-long trip. It also gave all of us an unexpected insight into the vandalism that is inflicted on our environment through such actions.

After a five-hour stopover in Singapore, we landed at the Kuala Lumpur International Airport. Dr Siti and about a dozen of her very enthusiastic students greeted us at the Kuala Lumpur Airport. It was the first time I had experienced a welcome of this sort. Some were holding up a banner to welcome us as we emerged from passing through customs and immigration. This gesture on the part of Siti and her students was very touching and what made it even more meaningful was that this was about 11pm on a Friday night that also coincided with a significant festival in the Islamic calendar. How many Australian university students would show this level of commitment? In my mind, this warm welcome was an indicator of the partnership that we were going to develop with Dr Siti and her students.

We spent our first two nights at the Sultan Idris Shah Forestry Education Centre in Selangor which is also one of the campuses of the Universiti Putra Malaysia. This centre has a unique history. Through the efforts and the foresightedness of Sultan Idris Shah, it was set up in 1996 after the Selangor State Government gave the university a 99-year lease to manage and conduct educational activities that would foster forestry development. The forest had since become home to hundreds of plants and animals – some of which have been on the endangered list for some time. We toured this very well-managed facility with Siti. Following this expedition, our students teamed up with their Malaysian university counterparts to go through the activities that they had developed for the SK Temai Primary School. The Malaysian student group was comparatively large. A number of ice-breaker activities followed which provided opportunities for the students to socialise and get to know each other.

After two days at the Forestry Centre, we packed up, boarded a Universiti Putra coach, and headed to our destination. Our visit to the Kuala Gandah Elephant Sanctuary along the way was a great experience. It showed the country's efforts toward wildlife preservation. After nearly seven hours of travel, we arrived at the Pahang campus of Universiti Malaysia. We spent the next four nights in shared student accommodation. It was the most affordable accommodation within proximity of the SK Temai Primary School. Throughout the campus there were signs about dengue fever with advice on how students could protect themselves from mosquitoes.

Our proposed teaching activities were to start with classroom observations on Monday (28 September). As I woke up in the morning, the first thing I did was to look outside the window in my room. The haze looked a bit thicker than on previous days. During breakfast, Siti advised us that due to the haze all schools were closed for the day because pollution levels were higher than the recommended levels in many parts of the country. For the first time in my life, I was experiencing school closures due to pollution levels. It was a sign of what the world could become because of the greed of a handful of people. While the cancellation of the school day was a downer, we still went to the school because it was a normal school day for the teachers. Upon our arrival we were greeted by the head teacher and his staff. Two of his staff members gave us an overview of the school. These presentations were very informative and gave us a good idea of how we could proceed with the classroom activities. We also explained our purpose and our intentions.

We had four teams, and each focussed on a theme: Culture and History (Class 3), Environment (Class 4), Deforestation (Class 5), and Alternative Energy (Class 6).

From Tuesday through to Thursday the classroom activities flowed well. While students from QUT were leading the activities, the students from UPM also played a crucial role in the classroom. They acted as a bridge between QUT students and the students at SK Temai. This bridge was critical because of language barriers. As described earlier, literacy in the English language was an issue for most staff and students. This is common in other countries as well where the spoken language is different. In such instances, a mediator can play an important role – one who understands both languages. Thus, the partnership and presence of UPM students made a significant difference. This was aptly explained by a QUT student as follows:

> The combination of UPM and QUT students worked well, giving us the ability to explain our lesson preparation and receive feedback based upon local knowledge and incorporate ideas and games from UPM students into the classroom. In the classroom, some of the children found speaking in English very daunting which challenged us to think about other ways of interacting, however the UPM students were fantastic at encouraging the children to speak and this gave them the confidence to have a go!

> I think I can say from all of us at QUT that the UPM students made it lot easier and played a big role for us regarding our engagement with the kids. There were times when we struggled with communication, but having the UPM students by our side, meant that they were able to clarify things for the children.

We were quite fortunate that two primary school teachers, Syarifah Nazurah and Nurhezrin Anuar, spent their week with us at SK Temai. Both had attained their degree qualifications in Education from QUT a few years earlier. They drove from Kuala Lumpur to join us. This was truly appreciated, and their presence made a significant difference to our work. Their input and advice were invaluable because they had a good understanding of education in the two countries.

By the end of the week, all the teams worked well and attained the desirable learning outcomes as planned. The head teacher and teachers were very supportive throughout and they did everything that was possible to ensure that our teams adapted to their classroom activities with ease. These tasks were context-based and very similar to what other teams had achieved in Fijian schools. For example, in Class 3, the students created stop-motion videos using the software *OpenShot*. For this activity they incorporated a story that was in English and replaced the characters with Australian animals. The task set for their students was to create a similar story that also used masks in their role play. One of the team members who was a former Malaysian national was buoyed by her experience, pointing out that she was amazed at "how quickly they learned to navigate and use the laptop to create their digital story ... even though some of them had never used a laptop before". Her team had to regroup and find additional activities because the students were very good, and they covered most of what they had planned in the first few days. However, she found that the language barrier was an issue. "Being able to converse in Bahasa Malaysia, I found myself speaking mostly in Malay to the Year 3 students as they had trouble understanding me in English. Some of the students were too shy to respond in English even though they may have understood some of the questions that were being asked".

In Class 5, the students created video clips, with deforestation as the theme. One of the UPM students noted that she had a lot of fun assisting her Australian counterparts and at the same time enjoyed helping the students in class to draw their story book illustrations. Her group created a story entitled "Homeless Orang Utan". They read their stories aloud in order to record their voices and also made puppets using to illustrate their stories (Figure 6.1). While she was not training to be a teacher, the experience taught her a lot about working with children under time constraints. Overall, she appreciated the teamwork and was very pleased that the students at SK Temai understood what we tried to deliver to them. The English proficiency of some of the students was impressive as evidenced through their abilities to read and understand the language. At times she had felt challenged, especially when some of "the computers froze and the groups had to reboot and redo the video". This took time. The task also became harder because some of the students knew nothing about computers, however they persevered and "having a student in our teaching team who was so good with computers made a difference". The students in her group took interest and helped each other to complete the video clip. Another UPM student in this group was a Korean national. He remarked that the "teaching at SK Temai went on smoothly". However, he was very apprehensive at the start and some of these questions crossed his mind many times – "Can I teach them? How do I communicate with them? I also do not know English well, can I help my friends?" He felt that the students at SK Temai were very kind and honest. There were "no behaviour problems – so we could teach them easily". By the end of the week, the students made some *excellent* videos and he felt that they had achieved a lot and he was proud of his students and his group. One of the most memorable moments for a team member from QUT was "when we got the children to read to us. I was amazed at how well the kids can read". He concluded that there was no doubt that he had worked with intelligent kids who were eager to learn – all they needed were opportunities.

FIGURE 6.1   Students with their masks for the stop motion activity

In Year 6, students got to experience new technologies as they explored the theme of alternative energy. They had hands-on experiences with a technology called *Little Bits* and they also learnt how to create games using *Scratch*. SK Temai students were deeply immersed in the activities and they really wanted to optimise their learning opportunities. For one of the students from QUT, his favourite moment on the trip, was when the students in his class "did not want to go to lunch but would rather stay and keep working on their projects". Another student made similar observations, pointing out that "the skills and capabilities of the Year six students were far better than we had anticipated, with the students picking up concepts much quicker than we had planned". This presented a challenge because they had to come up with increasingly more demanding tasks that had not been previously prepared. But for one QUT student, "the absolute highlight ... was seeing the Year six girls grow in confidence over the course of the week". This student, who had a strong background in IT, noticed that on the first day, the "female students were very hesitant to ask questions or engage with the hands-on activities, outside of what they had been instructed to do", whereas by the end of the week, "they were laughing and asking questions, and playing with the *Little Bits* in a much more confident and creative way".

Like our projects in Fiji, there was a parent/community showcase where some student groups from SK Temai talked about their outputs that were created using digital technologies. Standing on a stage, with their laptops connected to a data projector, they explained their experiences with a very high level of confidence. This was a satisfying moment and I was convinced that we had seeded some changes at this school. There were some very good vibes throughout the week. In every classroom, there was strong evidence of the teaching teams engagement with their students in a range of rich tasks. Most times, the students were actively engaged, obviously interested and enjoying what they were doing. While the incorporation of digital technologies into the activities presented a moderate level of challenge, it was a change from the daily classroom routines. We had some feedback sessions during the week. The feedback from the teams was positive. Our experiences in classrooms at SK Temai mirrored what I have seen elsewhere. When classroom activities are interesting, enjoyable, challenging, well-scaffolded, and connected to the student's real world, learning happens, irrespective of where the children are. While the school had a relatively modern computer lab, we also donated a class set of second-hand laptops. They had received more than 40 brand new laptops from the government about six months prior to our visit, but they were still sitting in their boxes. As pointed out in the literature (e.g. Tee & Samuel, 2017), the teachers may not have had the knowledge of how to set up and use the computers in their classes. This probably explained why the boxes were not opened.

The people that our team members engaged with were overwhelmingly welcoming. They gave special insights into their Muslim culture beyond what can be achieved without person-to-person engagement. It has become quite trendy these days to paint people with a common ethnic or religious background with the same brush. This is not the way the real world works, and generalising can be harmful to people who are wrongly portrayed. One of our QUT students, a former Malaysian national, reflected on his pre-trip experience:

> I have to say I had mixed emotions about the trip. I was anxious, and a bit apprehensive, but, for the most part, I was excited. I was looking forward to returning to my home country for the delicious food, and I couldn't wait for the new experiences and challenges that were to come. Malaysia has a population of about 30 million. Islam is the religion followed by more than 60% of the population. My religion too is Islam. What would my colleagues think of my country? More recently some in the media, for example, have not portrayed Islam for what it stands for. Mercy, compassion, and beauty are some of the words that can be used to describe my religion. Regrettably, it is sometimes interpreted as a religion that is intolerant, backward, alien and so on. What exactly is Islam? That in itself is a whole other topic that requires much scrutiny and time, but it was not why we were on this trip. It's such a big part of the experience, and, therefore, I felt it needed to be addressed. One of the greatest things about our project was the cross-cultural experience.

Overwhelmingly, students' reflections of their cultural experiences demonstrated their new knowledge about Malaysia and its people. Being in a country where Islam is one of the main religions was never an issue. Quite simply, religion did not dictate how the country was run. There were some very deep reflections such as "Walking into this program I had little expectations ... Malaysia invaded my being, dug a hole and found a special place to exist". Cultural excursions such as the overnight stay with a local family presented new insights about the everyday people. For a QUT student:

> The homestay was the highlight of my experience. At one point I remember sitting at the dinner table surrounded by piles of dishes of amazing food ... it was the first time I felt like I really experienced the culture of a foreign country.

The hospitality of the Chief Minister of the State and Pahang Tourism also added new dimensions to students' cultural experiences. I was quite moved by the actions of Dato' Ahmad Farid Abdul Jalal, Director of the Pahang State Museum Authority. After one of the dinners, Dato' Farid's special invitation enabled us to visit the Masjid Sultan Abdullah Pekan Museum. He arranged his staff to open the museum for our team (yes – the museum was re-opened especially for us at 10pm). What we saw was breathtaking. Ingenious design skills and innovation appeared to have been creatively melded in this newly renovated heritage-listed building. This mosque was built in 1929. As the population grew, a larger mosque was built later on in Pekan. For the past two years, work had been carried out to convert this building to a mosque museum. Dato' Farid showed us around and highlighted some of the main features of the building. The displays and the architecture were remarkable. Strategically positioned lights heightened the workmanship of this great building. As pointed out by Dato' Farid, the museum is a place to visit for people of all races and religions. It is the first time I saw and visited a mosque museum, and it was a privilege. What a great idea and a way forward for world peace? But more importantly this kind gesture gave us all another unique insight into the Malaysian culture and Islam that we not have had otherwise. It was a leap forward in terms of our intercultural understanding.

The interactions between university students from two different countries with diverse populations created new opportunities to meet and work with new people, build new friendships and gain new experiences. For one Malaysian university student, "I will have long-lasting memories of the experiences that I had with my mates from QUT and UPM". An Australian university student mirrored these thoughts pointing out that the UPM students, "with their warm generosity, and hospitality, were some of the friendliest, most down to earth, and most genuine people I have met in a long time". Richard Medland, one of our very hard working colleagues reflected on his Malaysian experiences as follows:

> Malaysia was a trying time with a severe pollution emergency impeding our efforts, the immersion was quite fascinating regardless. The SEE *Box* had been revised and further developed for our visit and the local orders of the technology for independent use after our visit are heartening.

Likewise, the overall impact of the project on the students was very positive and this was evident in their comments. According to a QUT student:

> The ten days spent in Malaysia as a part of this project have been one of the highlights of my degree. The trip provided me with a real experience of culture that would be difficult to obtain on a holiday or a quick visit. I have gained insights and experiences that will stay with me for the rest of my life ... The QUT students and staff are some of the coolest, most

down to earth, intelligent, and a dedicated bunch I've met. I found it a bit intimidating at first (because I'm the total opposite). But these qualities of our team members motivated me to work hard.

2   2016 – SK Sungai Mas

After the success of our outreach project in 2015 in Malaysia, we lodged another application. The Australian Government's New Colombo Plan Grant was successful and each student was awarded $3,000 towards travel and accommodation. It also provided a small allowance to cover some of the costs for staff travel and accommodation. In comparison to 2015, we could afford a few luxuries such as accommodation in a budget hotel. We teamed up with Siti who was once again supported by her university. We were also very grateful that one of her colleagues, Dr Evelyn Lim Ai Lin was able to join us on the trip. Siti was once again instrumental in getting the support of Dato' Sri Haji. Mohd Sharkar Shahbudin (Chairman of Pahang State Tourism) and Dato' Ahmad Farid Abdul Jalal, (Director, Pahang State Museum Authority). Siti identified SK Sungai Mas as the primary school for our project. This is a small school near Kuantan, the state capital of Pahang and it caters for children from the local Orang Asli Village. Ten undergraduate students, ranging in disciplines from Education to IT to Science, and two staff members from our university participated in this project. The project was managed by Graeme. I was responsible for leading the students and their activities in the classrooms. As in previous years, the challenge for my students was to design and implement a unit of work that showcased the use of digital technologies. They also had to align the unit as closely as they could with the local curriculum. For the QUT students on this trip to Malaysia, I upped the ante. Their unit of work had to focus on coding and computational thinking. Coding and programming go hand-in-hand. Back in my time, various codes constituted a computer program. Now a single code on its own can be a program. There are various interpretations of computational thinking. The Australian Curriculum and Reporting Authority (ACARA, 2017), describes it as "a problem-solving method that is applied to create solutions that can be implemented using digital technologies. It involves integrating strategies, such as organising data logically, breaking down problems into parts, interpreting patterns and models and designing and implementing algorithms" (para. 7). This is a generalised explanation which has more scope in schools, but for the Malaysian context, we wanted the students at SK Sungai Mas to solve problems through coding. In addition to developing knowledge and skills in this concept, the classroom activities also had to be structured in a way that created opportunities for the children to develop their English language skills. Given the size of the Sk Sungai Mas school, the students worked in three teams to deliver activities around coding with *Bee-Bot* robots in Years 1 and 2, coding with *Edison* robots in Years 3 and 4, and coding in *Scratch* in Years 5 and 6. We had used *Scratch* in our last engagement, but we had not used the *Bee-Bots* and *Edison* robots previously. The *Bee-Bots* introduce young children (Kindergarten through to Year 2) to the world of problem solving and coding without the need of writing codes. The *Edison* robots are Australian-designed for students from Year 3 onwards. At the introductory level they can be programmed with bar codes. At the more advanced level, they can be programmed with codes using programming languages that can be downloaded from the *Edison* website.

According to the rules of the New Colombo Plan Grant, all students received their grants individually and as a consequence made their own travel arrangements. This caused a few issues with team members arriving in Kuala Lumpur at different times. Siti and her students were very patient – accommodating our team as they arrived. Fortunately, we all arrived in time to commence our coach ride to SK Sungai Mas on the morning of 25 October. Our ten students were joined by 31 undergraduate and postgraduate students from UPM. Most of the faces were familiar from the previous project. These students were enrolled in an undergraduate tourism degree program. Other students were studying for postgraduate qualifications in science. In comparison to the student population at the school, the size of our team was relatively large. The UPM students played such an important role as go-betweens. From my experience in 2015, the proficiency in the English language was low for both teachers and their students. When language becomes a barrier, these UPM students become the conduit to transfer messages from English to Malay and vice versa. Without these students, our project would be either difficult, or almost impossible, to implement. We were looking forward to working with them once again. We arrived at our hotel in the evening after a day of stopping off at tourist attractions. This hotel was going to be our accommodation for the next five nights. I liked this property – it was welcoming, clean, with all the basic amenities including a western toilet. This hotel is in the township of Sungai Lembing. It is also sometimes known as a living museum because the hotel is surrounded by buildings and machinery from the mining era. The area was known for tin mining which was started by the British in 1880's and closed down in 1986 due to poor yields and high production costs.

SK Sungai Mas was about half an hour from our hotel. However, our coach could not get us all to the school. There is a feeder road that connects the school and local community to the main road. While the condition of this road was relatively good, it was only designed for light traffic. It was too narrow for a bus to go through. We could not walk it either because it would have taken us a while to make the journey from the main road. There was a UPM mini bus that transported some of us to the school, while the rest found themselves hiring a local 'ute taxi'. This open-air transporter was an adventure for the students. While it had seats built on the tray, the passengers had to hold on tight – otherwise they would risk being thrown out.

The Orang Asli community that the school serves draws some of its income from their rubber plantation. Sap from the trees is drained into containers which is sold for processing. Rubber production has been an important staple of the Malaysian economy for more than 100 years. In 1988, it was the third-largest producer and the top exporter of this commodity (Hays, 2008). However, in recent times production levels have dropped. Thus, there is a need for the locals to explore new job opportunities outside the community. This is contingent on a good background in literacy and numeracy. The government funds literacy and numeracy classes for some of the adults in the village. These classes are run by the head teacher at Sungai Mas. The participants are paid as long as they attend these classes. Employment prospects within the community, however, remain limited.

The homes in the village adopt a western style construction but are very simple in design. The walls are built from the local *merenti* timber with corrugated roofs. Many families have very basic possessions. Close to houses are water tanks on stands which are connected to taps. This was consistent in many other villages that I have visited in the past. The locals faced challenges as literal as wild elephants that ransacked their gardens and farms at night. Some of the elders guard these areas regularly to keep the elephants away. Despite the problems that the elephants were causing, it was very pleasing to hear that the they were not harmed in any way. In Malaysia, these elephants are trapped and transported to wildlife sanctuaries.

My first impressions of the school were very positive. I found it very clean and tidy and very inviting. It was colourful. Walls throughout the school were peppered with text and images. Most were designed to capture the students' attention momentarily in the hope that it would deliver some positive message that would add value to their learning. The assistant headmaster welcomed us to the school. We were able to communicate in English with the head teacher and some other teachers, which made our work easier. We were shown to our classrooms. Given the small size of each class, combining Years 1 and 2, 3 and 4, 5 and 6 was relatively easy. The three groups were ready to work as planned. Monday was the day for observations. However, as soon as our teams got into the classrooms, they were thrown into the deep end. They had to spring into action and take charge because the teachers handed the class over to them almost straightaway. Language barriers may have prompted the Malaysian teachers to take this step. For our teams, a few variables came into play almost simultaneously. They were not only pushing their boundaries by immersing themselves in an unseen environment, they also had a very unique group of students who they had not worked with previously. Conversing with these students in English with an unfamiliar accent and through interpreters presented another hurdle, not forgetting teaming up with a rather large team of contemporaries from Australia and Malaysia, none of whom had a teaching background, added to the complexity of the context. The local indigenous language presented another layer of difficulty. Even the Malaysian students had difficulties understanding it. Despite all these challenges, the Education students from QUT coped very well. Their leadership skills in this environment were flawless. As per all other outreach projects, here too I felt very proud of what they were able to demonstrate at short notice.

At SK Temai Primary (the last school) they had a modern computer lab plus another 40 brand new laptops that were waiting to be set up. Based on this experience, we were unsure if we really needed to take second-hand laptops with us, but in the end, we decided to take ten as a backup strategy. In addition to these laptops, we also took four *Edison* robots, six *Bee-bots* and a range of other resources which were purchased from the project funds. In total, all this would have been worth about 20,000 *ringgits* (about 5,000 USD). Prior to our trip we were informed that the school had a computer lab. We were quite excited as we took our shoes off (practice in Malaysian schools) and walked into a modern computer room. Our excitement was very short-lived, however, as we were told by the school's computer teacher that none of the computers in the lab were working. This was the first time I had had such an experience. In most computer labs I have been in, there would be at least some computers that would be working if the others had broken down. In this case, the monitors and keyboards were connected to a central server. In such situations, when the server fails, none of the computers worked either. According to one of the teachers, a commercial organisation had set up the computer system in the lab for a cost of about 100,000 *ringgits* (about 25,000 USD). As part of the deal, they also agreed to provide after-sales service. Despite the school's attempts to get the company to rectify the problem at hand, there was no progress. Each time they tried to ring the company, there would be no one to answer their call. The dust that had gathered on the screens and the keyboards was testament to the fact that students had not used these computers in a while – a few months at least. It was very disappointing to see that a lot of money was invested in building and resourcing this room. It was well-designed with adequate space for the students to move around and for teachers to interact with them. There were tiles on the floor and the room was also air conditioned. Many teachers and students around the globe would have envied their contemporaries at SK Sungai Mas for having such a modern computer room.

Research has shown that in many schools, the lack of technical support is a major barrier to technology integration (Hew & Brush, 2007). The situation at SK Sungai Mas was a typical example. The use of computers comes to a halt if there is no technical support to address technical issues. It is similar to car troubles. They cannot be fixed unless a knowledgeable mechanic can address the problem. In a small number of cases, tech-savvy teachers may be able to fix some of the problems on a small scale. But these teachers also have their limitations. When the computers do not work, a chain reaction starts. Teachers get disheartened, so they resort to their traditional practices. For some, technology failure also becomes a good excuse for not using computers even after they are fixed. If they are not used for extended periods, then they end up occupying space which could be better used for other classroom activities. For example, the computer room at Sungai Mas would have been ideal for a range of other activities, especially on hot days.

Luckily, we did bring a class set of ten second-hand laptops, though the failure of technology did have a ripple effect on our teaching plans. Two of the three classes needed computer access for their activities. As a consequence, the laptops had to be shared and parts of the activities were either trimmed or modified. Students' familiarity with the technology was also an issue. It was taking at least "two sessions to cover one concept". As teachers, we need to understand that "each teaching and learning context has its unique dimensions that must be dealt with individually. Our understanding of educational purpose is also shaped by the complexity of these contextual appreciations" (Kincheloe, 2008, p. 32). Thus, for us teachers to survive in classrooms, we have to acknowledge this fact and respond accordingly. The Year 5 and 6 team had planned to use the online version of *Scratch*. They had planned to challenge their students to design a simple game that involved the players interaction with "falling objects on the screen". Their idea was to develop students' knowledge by utilising coding strategies such as sequencing, branching, iteration, and user inputs. They planned to assess their students' coding skills through the flowcharts and the quality of the games that they created. In their original plan, the students were going to work in teams of two because such an approach has been found to be very effective (Werner, Denner, & Campe, 2014). The creation of a game using *Scratch* requires students to have greater access to computers because they have to execute and debug their codes continuously. However, they ended up in teams of five or more which was not the

FIGURE 6.2   A group activity on *Scratch*

ideal scenario and can sometimes be counterproductive (Figure 6.2). Such a
situation minimises active participation of all students in the activities.

This issue was compounded by the *Edison* robots which were also malfunctioning. We had brought these for Year 3 and 4 students. The teaching team had
planned to initially familiarise the students with these robots through simple
activities, then increase the complexity of the task where the students would
be challenged to navigate their robots through a maze. Using this experience,
they wanted their students to create and share e-books that would demonstrate how *Edisons* can be programmed to go through a maze. Such a resource
would also be valuable for students in other grades. The *Edison* robots can be
programmed either using barcodes or codes written and transferred via a computer interface. The robots – surprisingly, the whole set of them – were not
reading the barcodes, and this was a real conundrum. It was a first for me –
the *Edison* robots had always performed well whenever I used them. Somehow the barcodes on the robots were not being read and they were performing
actions that were inconsistent and were contrary to the intended program. If
the robots were programmed to avoid obstacles, they would start to go around
in circles instead. This was disappointing for the university students, especially
when these children were being introduced to the robots for the first time.
After numerous troubleshooting strategies to fix the malfunctioning robots,
it became obvious that the robots were not going to work. While the malfunctioning of the robots was a downer, for one of QUT students repeated troubleshooting "became a lesson in persistence ... which was good too" because
all technologies can present failure and challenges from time to time and it is
important that we do not just give up. As humans, this is the type of attitude

that all of us need. It is a message that I also share with my students in class. We should not be scared of failure because failures lead to reflection and thinking outside the box. It raises questions such as: "Why is something not working? What is causing the problem? How can the problem be fixed?". Through these questions, we develop new knowledge. However, given the time constraints, the team decided to change the activity to a *PowerPoint* presentation where they showed what they had done during the week. This too was a first-time activity. Thus, students had to be first taught how the software worked. There were only ten laptops that were shared between two classes and like the *Scratch* activity, there were between six and seven students per group. This situation was challenging but the students had to make do with what they had.

The language barrier with the students at SK Sungai Mas proved a challenge. The Orang Asli people have their own languages and dialects like all of us. It is different from the Malay language (*Bahasa Melayu*) that many speak in the country. While the students from UPM were fluent in the Malay language, they too had difficulties conversing with the students in this community. The teaching teams came up with their own strategies to break communication barriers. The most common one was play. Reflecting on the strategies, one of the QUT students indicated that play developed a "nice little bond after that first day", which was not only an ice-breaker but also generated an atmosphere of mutual trust between all the parties in her classroom. Games like *Simon Says* were very effective in not only overcoming cultural and communication barriers but also in introducing the concept of sequencing, which is critical in coding and computational thinking. According to a pre-service teacher from QUT, *Simon Says* could be treated as a game which "kind of involved coding". Children were taught terminologies like 'forwards' and 'backwards' so that they could progress with the coding and in the process, they got used to giving and following commands – to and from each other. More importantly, commands were not executed unless 'Simon' said "it". Therefore, in this game, a player responding to "Simon says put your hand up" and "put your hand up" conveys different meanings. Similarly, for codes to be executed, they need to mean something to the computer. Like *Simon Says*, they have to be explicitly coded to make sense. These analogies were making a positive contribution in enabling the children to develop an understanding of the coding syntax.

The students at SK Sungai Mas were placed in composite groups. The teaching teams noticed that the age gap between the students had an influence on how quickly they picked up the concepts. In some of the groups this was an issue because those who could not pick up the concepts became disengaged and as a consequence they could not keep up with the faster students. One of the team members working with students from kindergarten to Year 2 noted that while some of the older students understood the basics of coding the *Bee-Bots*, some of the younger children in the group still felt challenged. The teaching teams felt that more information about the SK Sungai Mas students and their prior knowledge would have helped to facilitate differentiation more effectively so that they could work at a manageable pace. I endeavoured to obtain information about the students we would be working with and their possible capabilities from the school because direct communication with them prior to our visit was not possible. In real-world teaching, while it is ideal to know your students before implementing learning experiences, this is not always the case. Even in Australia, most classroom teachers' get a whole new class of unknowns and have to be ready to work with them on day one; relief teachers walk into the unknown every day; specialist teachers in primary schools teach each class for about thirty minutes a week and never get to know any group like their class teacher does. In some respects, I was pleased that these experiences were giving my students an extreme up-front taste of real-world teaching!

Some of the issues that the teaching teams confronted were not unique to Malaysia. Even in countries like Australia, access to specialist staff who are able to troubleshoot technology problems onsite is an issue. From time to time, teachers also face language barriers with their new students, especially if they are from a background where English is not a first language. In schools where there are multi-age classes, teachers can be challenged on how they deal with children of varying cognitive capabilities. Despite challenges in the Malaysian context, the pre-service teachers were able to deliver a number of the intended outcomes that they had planned. Understanding how they dealt with these issues is critical. For the pre-service teachers, their frames of reference were only what they had seen and experienced in Australian primary schools. One of the pre-service teachers explained that despite the contextual barriers, the content remained the same and they had to find pedagogies with common themes between the students that enabled the building of a "shared experience" that was not dependent on "our cultural backpack" for communicating. Consequently, the pre-service teachers applied a range of pedagogies that promoted the use of visual cues. Kinaesthetic learning strategies that facilitated communication through movement were also effective. An analysis of the feedback from the pre-service teachers suggested that they adopted a five-step process in their teaching to teach coding. It involved introducing ideas through play and games; building conceptual understanding with physical actions and objects; connecting concepts with the software; practicing coding with examples; and creating designed solutions to problems.

On one of the days, we had visits from teachers from local schools who were very keen to see our activities in operation. The feedback from the teachers was very good and they were also excited to explore robotics as classroom activities in their schools.

2.1 Parent Showcase

Consistent with our approach in other projects, on the last day at SK Sungai Mas, there was a parent showcase. The head teacher expressed some doubts about parents' attendance. He was unsure if they would attend or not. The system in Malaysia is different to what we have in our schools in Australia. Usually, for such events letters are sent to parents either in hardcopy or via email. Some schools also publicise such events on their school website. But at this school, it appeared that messages were relayed by word of mouth. I was sure that the teachers would have informed their students about this event. The head teacher also conveyed this message to the village elders. Our plan was to start the parent showcase at 9am. I was quite surprised that they arrived before the scheduled time. At this school, like many schools in Malaysia, there is a guardhouse at the entrance of the school gate. Visitors at the school see the guard before they enter the school. Next to the guardhouse is a small shed with a couple of benches. It is not architecturally designed with flash building materials, it is a basic shelter for the community to drop by when they feel like it or when they are waiting to see a teacher or pick up their children. On the morning of the showcase, the parents, all mothers and grandmothers with only one male relative among the crowd, arrived before time and they were waiting for further instructions. Apparently, this was also part of the group that attended the adult literacy and numeracy classes at Sungai Mas.

Before the parents went into the classrooms to participate with the children in their activities, I had a quick chat with them. One of the students from UPM acted as my interpreter. I told the parents about our outreach program and explained what the children did over the week. I highlighted what I had seen in the classrooms and emphasised that what their children had done was very good and their work was as good as what children in Australia would have done within the timeframe. I felt that this was an important point to raise. Sometimes people living in developing countries have an inferiority complex that is based on a false assumption that they are less smart than those who live in developed countries. I wanted to dispel this cultural myth. I also stressed the importance of parental support towards their children's education. As the teachers told me, the local community believed that their children should not be forced to attend school. This probably explained the number of children on motorbikes who rode past the school throughout the day. I believed that quite a few of them would have been primary school-aged. A parent or community elder would have probably owned the bike and also met the cost of fuel and maintenance. So why would anyone let a child who was underage take charge of a motorbike at any time of the day, let alone school hours? On one occasion, I saw a child who was probably no more than ten years old riding a bike with two other children as passengers and none of them had helmets. The one at the back would have been around five or six years old and the one in the middle appeared to be a lot younger. While the riders demonstrated good control of the bikes, I heard stories from the teachers about motorbike accidents with some resulting in serious injuries and even death of the riders. I also gathered that police road patrols were uncommon in this part of the country. Whilst I did not raise this issue, because it was not my role, I talked about the importance of education in general. I am not sure how well my messages were received but I was truly impressed in the way the parents engaged with their children in the classrooms. The university students likewise noted the level of excitement and enjoyment amongst the parents. They were making a real effort to not only understand what their children were doing but also engaging in their activities hands-on. Like their children, all the parents were confronting educational robots and coding for the first time. As one of the parents pointed out, it was also the first time that they had a chance to participate with their children in their classrooms in this way. Our time at SK Sungai Mas came to an end with a formal ceremony which was attended by the local member of parliament. It was very pleasing to see that the parents stayed on until the formalities were over.

3   An Evening with Her Royal Highness, the Crown Princess of
       Pahang

For all of us, the dinner with Her Royal Highness, The Crown Princess of Pahang, Tunku Hajjah Azizah Aminah Maimunah Iskandariah, was a significant moment. We were given a unique taste of the Malaysian culture with a royal twist. According to Siti, the princess was very passionate and proactive about the education and welfare of the Orang Asli people, which explained her particular interest in our work. The Director of the Pahang State Museum Authority, Dato' Ahmad Farid Abdul Jalal, was also very supportive of our initiatives in the state. To acknowledge the significance of our efforts, the Pahang State Museum Authority hosted the Royal Dinner at the Art Museum. Through the grapevine, I learnt that about 100,000 *ringgits* (about 25,000 USD) was spent on this evening, which was close to the cost of our whole outreach project. We were immensely grateful to Dato' Farid for finding the resources to make this an event of a lifetime for our team, and to Siti, who played a significant part in making all this happen.

For many of us, it was the first time that we got a chance to get close to royalty in Malaysia. But for the locals, it was probably an even bigger moment. The museum was in a colonial building that was originally designed and built by the British in 1910. In the early 2000's, it was transformed into the Pahang Heroes Museum, and more recently it was relaunched as an Art Museum. The inner courtyard of this building was transformed with dinner tables and a makeshift stage to mark this special occasion. Dato' Ahmad Farid and his staff left no stone unturned to ensure that the venue was well and truly fit to host the princess and other invited guests. All the tables were strategically placed. The stage was directly across from the royal table. As expected, the princess sat at the head of the table. The tables, the chairs, and the cutlery were all selected and placed thoughtfully to mark the occasion. A red carpet was laid to welcome the princess. Twenty hours earlier the place looked very different as our team had been invited to participate in the rehearsals. It was a hive of activity. Many hands joined together to transform this venue. Wherever you looked something was going on until the transformation of the venue was complete.

About fifteen minutes before the princess arrived, I was told that I would be sitting at the royal table with the princess and other guests. I felt this to be an honour but was not quite sure about how I was expected to engage with the princess and others at the table. I was also unsure about the table etiquette. I had never had dinner with a princess, before, however, I believe in the saying 'live and learn'. I was on a steep learning curve and I convinced myself to do my best to learn how to dine like royalty. Invited guests arrived and took their seats, and then everyone waited eagerly for the princess's entrance. The Gamelan orchestra played in the background to keep the audience entertained. In a very timely manner, the royal party arrived. The princess graced the red carpet as she entered the museum. The guests rose to welcome her as per the protocols in Malaysia. To greet the princess, guests put their palms together in a prayer pose and raised them to their foreheads. Once the princess was seated, everyone else took their seats.

A puppet show, with quirky characters set the tone for the evening (Batik & Bubbles, 2016). This was a showcase of local talent in puppetry. "The Wayung Kulit (Shadow Puppet) show puppeteers served as the emcee for the evening, giving little quips and anecdotes in between speeches and entertainment" (Batik & Bubbles, 2016, para. 23). This art appeared to have been passed on from one generation to the next and was very clever and creative. The puppeteers sat behind a white screen. Well-placed lights created well-defined shadows of the puppets on this screen. Music was interwoven with dialogue in the local language, and the voices and variations in the tones made it engaging even for those to whom the language was foreign. My name came up in the puppets' conversation a few times. My interpretation was that they were probably talking about the guests and making the conversation interesting and humorous at the same time. Whilst I did not understand what was being said, I was not alone. Batik and Bubbles (2016, para. 23), a local publication, reported that "judging by the uproarious laughter of the other guests, we assumed it must've been pretty funny alas, it all went a bit over our heads as the puppeteers spoke in a thick Kelantanese accent!" I was thoroughly impressed to witness this unique cultural performance.

One of my roles for the evening was to present a speech on behalf of the staff and students from QUT and UPM. It had to be approved by the princess's staff beforehand. I began my speech as follows:

> Her Royal Highness Crown Princess of Pahang, Tunku Hajjah Azizah Aminah Maimunah Iskandariah; Yang Berbahagia Dato' Sri Haji Mohamad Sharkar Shahbudin, Chairman, Pahang State Tourism; Yang Di Hormati Dato' Ahmad Farid Abdul Jalal, Director, Pahang State Museum Authority; Professor Dato Dr Mohamad Shatar, DVC UPM; Professor Dr Mohamad Zakaria, Dean of Faculty of Forestry UPM; Mr Humdan Bin Ahmad, head teacher SK Sungai Mas Kuantan, teachers from Sk Sungai Mas, colleagues and students from QUT and UPM.
>
> Tonight, represents a once-in-a-lifetime opportunity for us all that will remain in our memory forever. Your royal highness, the staff and students of the Universiti Putra Malaysia and Queensland University of Technology would like to express our deepest gratitude and appreciation for your attendance at this magnificent dinner tonight. We are deeply honoured to be in your company. We are also grateful to Dato' Ahmad Farid, Director of the Pahang State Museum Authority, for hosting the dinner and making this evening possible in this modern museum that tells us the story of the significance of this state.
>
> It is always a pleasure visiting your country, Malaysia, and more so your lovely state, Pahang. Teaming up, sharing our knowledge, and learning from our colleagues and students from the Universiti Putra Malaysia and local school communities is a deeply enriching opportunity for us all. On this occasion the staff and students at SK Sungai Mas Kuantan have been truly magnificent. It is indeed very heart-warming to be embraced and welcomed in this way. From our first arrival, we have felt very much at home.

Our engagement in schools has a short but highly successful history. I will share it briefly as it sets the context. About six years ago, I visited my primary school in Fiji. I was quite overwhelmed when I learnt that the school did not have a library. Forty years earlier when I attended this school the scenario was the same. Throughout my childhood I never had a chance to read library books. Looking back on this, this situation was unacceptable and confronting. How could we still have schools in this day and age where students are deprived of learning opportunities?

And I went on for another five minutes. According to the evening's program, the princess was not scheduled to speak. As soon as my speech ended, I joined her at the table and the emcee started to move to the next item, but then she interjected politely and indicated that she wanted to say something. Responding to some of the comments that I had made, she spoke for about fifteen minutes, weaving in some very interesting episodes of her experiences. Her speech echoed her affections towards the Orang Asli people, education, forests, and the environment.

At the dinner table, we talked on a range of different topics. She was interested in the work we were doing in developing countries with libraries and technologies. I was also quite fascinated by her interest in cooking. I learnt that the princess had written a cookbook and she also had her own cooking show. The first publication of the bilingual cookbook was sold out. What was unique and interesting about her cookbook was that she travelled to remote and rural areas to get recipes that families had used for generations. She was looking for recipes that used local ingredients in food preparation. I felt that this was such a significant initiative. Over time, as we get more accustomed to imported ingredients and packaged food items, we tend to forget the local recipes that have stood the test of time. Though this was my first interaction with royalty, I found her royal highness more 'natural' than most people I have met, and she was very down to earth. Her willingness and her desire to make a difference in the lives of the underprivileged was obvious.

After dinner, we joined the princess to view the artefacts that were displayed in this lovely art museum. Whilst this was not particularly large, in its very special way it portrayed and presented some intriguing stories that were historically significant in the state of Pahang. As we toured these rooms, the princess shared her knowledge and her connections with what was on display, and when the tour of the museum rooms ended, the princess had one last duty to perform before she retired for the evening. In front of the stage area, a table was set with a birthday cake for the princess. To me it appeared that it was a surprise addition. Apparently, it was the princess's birthday recently. No matter where you go, no birthday parties are complete without the 'happy birthday' song. The singing started in earnest "Happy birthday to you, happy birthday to you, happy birthday dear ... happy birthday to you". There was confusion in terms of what was to follow after "dear". Did we have to take her name, her title or just call her the princess? After the cake was cut, the guests, and in particular the students, made the most of getting as close to this special guest as possible. She was swamped and treated like a star from Bollywood. As expected, she was not frazzled by the attention that she was getting. She mingled with her admirers and engaged with them in conversation and a little later the princess left, when the evening came to an end. We were very grateful to the princess for her time as well as to Dato' Ahmad Farid and his staff for all the hard work. On my way back to the hotel, I kept wondering, "How many participants in outreach projects get to enjoy a dinner evening with a princess and experience another culture in this way?"

4   Lesson Learnt – "In-situ" Experiences Cannot Be Substituted

The Malaysian outreach project was, despite its challenges, yet another feather in our collective cap on our steady path to improving outcomes in a small way for children in remote locations, demonstrating once again that well designed classroom activities will facilitate learning irrespective of where they are delivered. For many Malaysian children, the week they spent with university students was different to their regular school routine. Apart from learning about coding and developing English language skills, the students also had fun. One aspect that was unique was the level of support and interest that was shown by various stakeholders who have a genuine interest in promoting global education. This collaboration made a huge difference to the project, though of even greater significance was having a partner like Siti on the ground who shared common values about education and social justice. Transnational intercultural outreach projects work best when a genuinely interested local is there to guide the visitors through expected protocols and customs of the host community.

University students' reflections such as these yet again highlight the point that there are some things that cannot be taught within the four walls of a university classroom:

> Before leaving Australia, as a non-Muslim, I was a bit nervous about being in a mostly Muslim country. The reason for this was due to the way practising Muslims often get portrayed in the media. I was expecting to be disliked everywhere I went. This couldn't have been further from the truth.

The Malaysian university students I met over there were kind, funny and lovely people. It didn't take long for me to develop my friendship with them.

I feel very blessed to have had this opportunity. I envisaged that I would learn more than I taught and that was certainly the case. I pride myself in being one to embrace diversity and find the good in most, but this opportunity highlighted to me how I had allowed my viewpoints of the Muslim culture to be socially constructed by the perspectives portrayed in mainstream media. The stereotypical Muslim doesn't exist. What I discovered was the warmest, most caring, engaging, astute and nurturing group of people I have ever met.

The student's reflections here reinforce the importance of *in-situ* experiences. They cannot be substituted. Such experiences give credence to a point made by Giroux (2011) that critical pedagogy should go beyond just enabling students to think critically and act accordingly. Their immersive experiences should give them opportunities to "question deep-seated assumptions and myths ... that structure every aspect of society and to take responsibility for intervening in the world" (p. 172). We need to experience the world first hand and not take what we see or hear from second and third parties as gospel truth. Thus, students need to be immersed in contexts where they get a chance to think critically and draw their own conclusions about the world and its people.

CHAPTER 7

Bonding with a Community in the PNG Highlands

In a gentle way, you can shake the world.
MAHATMA GANDHI

 The video accompanying this chapter is freely available online
at https://doi.org/10.6084/m9.figshare.10305293

We used to store the second-hand computers in a derelict building on our uni-versity campus. The rooms in the building were very dusty, dark, and were fall-ing apart. There was no electricity. Given the state of the building, it had become home to many species from the animal kingdom. Whilst this building had its issues, we learnt to coexist in this environment. We made the most of what we had. And in our line of work we always see the glass as half full. We were cer-tainly very grateful that the university had given us space to store the computers.

Our relationship with Saint Theresia Kuruk Primary School, in Mount Hagen, Papua New Guinea (PNG) began through this building. It started with Paul Ogil. He had previously worked as a security guard at our university. One day when he was on duty, he came to unlock the room so that we could load some of the stored computers for a school in Fiji. As we began our work, Paul became very inquisitive. He wanted to know where the computers were going. We responded to his question and told him more about our project. Almost immediately he said that it would be nice if computers were also donated to his former primary school in Mount Hagen. We were buoyed by the interest and enthusiasm that was shown by Paul. He strongly believed that we all lived in "a global village" but the odds for full participation "were stacked against" the marginalised and the underprivileged, particularly in developing coun-tries. However, he felt that fluency in digital technologies had the potential to "level the playing field" particularly in the jobs market. According to Paul,

© KONINKLIJKE BRILL NV, LEIDEN, 2020 | DOI:10.1163/9789004406872_007

the first-time students found a chance to use technologies in PNG was when they got to university. For the majority of young Papua New Guineans, such an opportunity did not exist because there were no technologies in schools. We agreed, in principle, to support him with the proviso that if he could find a way to transport the computers, we would find computers for him. Little did we know that this meeting with Paul would give the SEE Project a new direction and challenge with no grant money or university students. Like my ancestors who joined hands to build a school, this partnership too would demonstrate how the beliefs and the goodwill of a small group of people could go a long way in supporting remote schools in Papua New Guinea.

We did not see Paul for a few months. He had found new employment at the Brisbane City Council as a bus driver and quit his work at the university. Paul kept working on his dream of getting computers to his school and did a lot of the background work with his people in Mount Hagen. Firstly, he had to convince the school head teacher, Andrew Colin, that computers were an essential tool for learning in this century. As children, both Paul and Andrew were classmates at Saint Theresia Kuruk Primary School. When they were students, the school was different. Their classrooms were bush huts, but the school landscape had changed over time. In recent times, bush huts were replaced by new buildings with a western influence and made of materials such as bricks, mortar, corrugated iron, and timber. Much of the credit for this change goes to Andrew who had played a significant role in working closely with the local community and the government to bring about this transformation. It was evident that Andrew was a visionary in his community and as a consequence, he could see the importance of computers and of giving children access to technology. According to Paul, Andrew's knowledge about digital technologies was minimal and he "sat down with him and outlined the reasons why his students needed to be technologically literate in the digital age". For Andrew, the decision to embrace technologies was a giant leap – both for him and his school. He also trusted Paul and the manner in which a case for technologies was articulated. While Paul had won the head teacher over with his idea, his next big challenge was getting the computers to the school. To get computers across, they had to be shipped from Brisbane to the Port City of Lae in PNG. From here the computers would need to be transported on a long road trip to Mount Hagen. Unlike Fiji, an additional challenge was the cost of custom and excise duties and charges for the importation of these second-hand computers into PNG. In Fiji, imports of second-hand goods by schools for educational purposes are exempt from duties. It was Paul's determination of surging forward that kept alive his dream of relocating the computers to Saint Theresia Kuruk. His good friend Kelly Kerua came to his rescue. Kelly worked for a company that regularly imported machinery into Papua New Guinea from Australia. He agreed to assist with the transportation of the computers from Brisbane to Lae. The transportation also included customs clearance costs. In October 2014, 30 desktop computers made their way to PNG.

1   Getting the Computers to Saint Theresia Kuruk Primary School

Once the computers landed in Lae and cleared customs, Andrew volunteered to pick them up. He drove a twenty-five-seater bus from Mount Hagen to Lae to collect them. Ten teachers from his school volunteered to travel with him to pick up the computers. This trip took him more than eight hours. Like many developing countries, the condition of the roads often challenges drivers. The country roads of PNG are very poorly maintained and littered with potholes. The Papua New Guinean landscape offers another layer of complexity. The country boasts an array of mountains and rivers, and while these features are part of what make the place so scenic and picturesque, the difficult terrain coupled with extreme weather conditions make the building and maintenance of the roads in such environments challenging. The return journey, however, was longer. He factored in the fragile nature of the goods that were on his bus and also ensured that he made the trip when it was daylight. Consequently, he started his journey early in the morning in Lae. The ten teachers who had travelled with Andrew, ensured the safety of the computers. They carried some of the boxes on their laps and kept the others on the seat next to them. This ensured that the boxes were not thrown around on the bus. Nearly 11 hours later, he returned to Mount Hagen with all the computers intact. According to Andrew, he had to "drive slowly and carefully … during the day" to ensure that the computers arrived safely. Andrew recalled the moment he arrived at the school with the computers. "As soon as I turned off from the main road, I put on the lights and the blinkers and I tooted the horn on the bus". It was a moment to cherish in Andrew's life. Many in the village had gathered to welcome the computers. "They were all waiting, they shouted, and they clapped as if they were welcoming a human being". From day one, the community was involved. Andrew had convinced the villagers that the computers were there for the benefit of their children in education. In spite of the bad press about crime in Mount Hagen, it was probably this community ownership that developed a deep relationship with this newly acquired asset. The computers were set up in a classroom with limited security. Louvre blade windows in this classroom had no burglar-proof grills on them, yet they were very safe where they were. The world often sees Papua New Guinea as a place riddled with crime; indeed, according to the Australian Government's (2016) *Smartraveller* website, "Crime rates [in Papua New Guinea] are high, particularly in the

capital Port Moresby, Lae, Mt Hagen, and other parts of the Highland provinces".
It is probably the 'community ownership' factor that ensured that school assets
such as computers are respected and valued, and they do not become targets of
criminal activities. For such a connection to be developed, more head teachers
like Andrew are needed so that the community understands the big picture and
why school assets are to be respected and necessary for school use.

For Andrew, there were other challenges. Firstly, his school did not have
a reliable town power supply. By working with the school community and
through the funds received from the government, Andrew purchased a diesel generator that powered the desktops. Temporarily he set the computers
in the teachers' staffroom. Yet another problem emerged once the computers
arrived at the school. As in previous deployments, we also shipped some USBs
that contained the *Edubuntu* operating system with relevant software for the
classrooms. This strategy had worked very efficiently. Teachers had no problems in setting up the computers by downloading the software from the USBs
we supplied. But for some reason, the USBs just didn't seem to work at Saint
Theresia Kuruk Primary School. Through troubleshooting and by setting up
an identical computer in Brisbane, we realised that the problem was in the
disk boot sequence. The computer was looking for the operating system files
on the hard drive which did not exist. As a consequence, the computer pro-
cessor did not go 'looking' any further. There was a need for some technical
expertise because the users on the ground had to interrogate the Basic Input
Output System (BIOS) setup on each computer to make changes. For someone
who knows computers, changing the boot order can be achieved relatively easily. On the ground at Saint Theresia Kuruk, teachers had limited knowledge
of this process. However, there was one ray of potential sunshine. Luckily,
the head teacher's daughter Anthinda Collin, a university student, had some
basic knowledge of computers, although her ability to troubleshoot computer
systems was very limited, as is the case with many users globally. We know
how to use a computer, but our knowledge of how it works is either minimal
or non-existent. It is like driving cars; most of us know how to drive without
really knowing how the engine and the rest of the components come together
to make the wheels move. I tried to give some instructions over the phone to
Anthinda about accessing the BIOS. The operating system installation process goes step-by-step and usually takes about 10 minutes. For some reason,
the steps in the installation process went haywire. From our point of view, the
files on the USB somehow must have been corrupted. While Anthinda was trying hard to assist, we were not making much headway and calling PNG also
became quite expensive. For these reasons, we abandoned this approach and
began thinking of other possibilities. I suggested to Paul that we post some
new instructions and videos. Paul's response was that the postal service in PNG

is unreliable. The posted item may get lost or arrive at the intended address months later. A few weeks afterward, new hope emerged. The school was able to make contact with a local who had some knowledge about *Edubuntu* operating systems. He worked with some staff members and showed them how the issue could be addressed. One of the teachers who had a background in typing was assigned the task of installing the systems. Eventually, all the computers came alive, and they were ready to roll. Apart from issues with BIOS, this experience also showed that in transit, the USBs need a physical shield to stop the files from being corrupted. Personally, I realised the challenges of communication with technology in developing countries – something that we take for granted. PNG was so near, yet was so far!

Once the software was installed, the school was ready to engage with the new technology. However, for the staff, the next step presented a real conundrum. Their big question was "What to do with the computers?" They wanted me to visit the school and conduct professional development activities. My semester had been busy. I was also very concerned about safety. Papua New Guinea is not a country whose control over crime is highly regarded and reported in the media. Apart from safety concerns, there are also issues about mosquito-borne diseases such as malaria. I have been a blood donor for some years, however the blood bank does not accept the donation of travellers to Papa New Guinea for at least three years. According to the Australian Red Cross, "if you have travelled to Papua New Guinea (PNG) ... there is a risk of relapsing malaria in that country. Even if you return a negative result for malaria antibodies, we will only be able to use the plasma portion of your donation for a period of 3 years on your return from PNG".

Despite these concerns, and after numerous assurances from my friend Paul, I made up my mind to go and visit the teachers at the school. I contacted one of our past students, Matthew Brown, who had previously made the trip with me to Fiji, to see if he was interested in joining me on the trip. After graduation from QUT, Matthew had joined a large banking corporation. As I proposed the idea to Matthew over a cup of coffee, I asked him to closely read some of the information that was available about travel to Papua New Guinea. I wanted him to make his own judgment. I was also quite determined not to rope Matthew in on the trip if he did not feel confident about where he was going. Matthew is an adventurer and wasn't the least bit perturbed by the warnings and the media gossip. Consequently, Paul, Matthew and I agreed on a date, and took time off work to make the trip.

When I told my colleagues and friends that I was travelling to Papua New Guinea, the responses from many of them was similar. "You must be brave" and "Really?" While they all meant well, what they were saying aligned with my initial thoughts of travelling to PNG. The concerns about safety and diseases are real, and they play on the minds of people. We all tend to form opinions about people and places based on what is reported, predominantly through the media. Only a few weeks earlier there had been terrorist attacks in parts of Europe. However, if I was travelling to Paris, I'm sure the response would have been very different. "Wow Paris, have fun!" There are many deep and meaningful views about our perceptions and how they impact on our thinking and actions. Quotes by some famous people eloquently sum up the connections. In the words of Ralph Waldo Emerson, "People only see what they are prepared to see" and the "eye sees only what the mind is prepared to comprehend" (Robertson Davies). Consequently, "no two people see the external world in exactly the same way" (Penelope Fitzgerald). Yet we form opinions based on what we have read or heard and sometimes take the conveyed messages for granted.

2 Our Journey to Support Saint Theresia Kuruk Primary School

As we prepared for the trip we packed some second-hand laptops and other digital technologies to support the teachers. We had three laptops in a small bag, and the rest was going to be in our handheld luggage. To make sure that the laptops arrived in PNG in one piece, we had the small bag securely wrapped in plastic at the airport. However, as we tried to check in the bag with the laptops, we were stopped by the airline's customer service agent. Apparently, the laptops could not be transported as checked luggage. This directive was news to us. A few weeks earlier when I made a trip overseas, the airline staffer who processed the check-in formalities stated that laptops in bags were fine as long as there were no spare lithium batteries. There seems to be a lot of confusion about the transportation of these batteries and the digital devices that rely on them. The risk is that these batteries can catch fire. Decisions seem to vary between airlines, airports and also staff who process check-ins. As a result of this ruling by the staff member on the day at the Brisbane airport we had to leave some laptops behind.

We were booked to fly on Air Niugini from Brisbane to Mount Hagen. It was the first time that I was going to fly with this airline. I must admit that I had some preconceived ideas. I was flying on an airline that was predominantly manned and managed by citizens from a developing country. In my mind, I was convinced that the service and the flight was going to be mediocre. But well and truly I was wrong. I was quite amazed at the efficiency, both regarding the flight and the quality of service. Of all the airlines that I have known in the world, I would rate Air Niugini very highly. After a brief stopover at the

Jacksons International Airport in Port Moresby, we boarded the flight to Mount Hagen. On this sector, I had visualised travelling on a small plane, similar to some of the ones I had flown in Fiji. But here too I was wrong. We flew on a modestly sized Dash 8 aircraft. We arrived in Mount Hagen as scheduled, late in the afternoon. The weather was very good. Kagamuga Airport in Mount Hagen is surrounded by high mountains. On rainy days when these mountains become covered by clouds, flights are often cancelled. Many locals choose to fly domestically because roads do not exist. Even in developed countries building roads through the mountainous terrains is very challenging and expensive.

When we arrived at Mount Hagen, we were greeted at the airport by Andrew, the head teacher at Saint Theresia Kuruk Primary School. We also met Peter Mughkerhegl, one of Paul's friends who is a local businessman. We were going to be accommodated for three days in one of Peter's apartments which he rents out to employees of non-government organisations. As we headed to the car park, the steel grills on Andrew's Land Cruiser caught my eyes. Apart from a small square opening on the driver's side, all the windows were protected by grills. However, not all vehicles were like Andrew's. He explained the reason for protecting the windows in his car. He pointed out that when riots break out, throwable objects such as rocks, metal, and wood pieces become projectiles for the rioters. If a driver was unlucky and had to drive through a riot, the chances were that some of these projectiles could possibly land on vehicles, smash windows, and damage the bodywork. Occupants of the vehicle could also be injured. I was also amazed that there were no cars in the carpark. All I could see were large vehicles, and most of them were four-wheel drives. Later I realised that there were no cars on the roads in Mount Hagen because of the condition of the roads. Despite being covered by bitumen, the main roads were very poorly maintained. Big potholes were common, and some of these were reasonably large. Also, there were a lot of feeder roads which were predominantly unsealed and in need of ongoing repairs. Thus, driving cars on roads in Mount Hagen was a big no-no.

Travelling into a developing country also raises concerns and thoughts about food. By the time we left the airport, it was almost dinnertime. Andrew and Peter drove us to a rather modern local Chinese restaurant. The menu was not much different to the choices that we see in many Chinese restaurants around the world. The food was freshly cooked with local ingredients and quite tasty. This first meal allayed my concerns about food. Peter gave us a tour of the township as he drove us to our accommodation. We were very quickly getting accustomed to the potholes. There were many of these, and drivers were sometimes challenged to navigate through them. Apparently, they had been the cause of many accidents in the past. As drivers navigate to avoid these potholes momentarily, some forget other dangers. If they veer to the other side of the road, collisions with oncoming traffic become a real possibility. I also noticed that many homes were surrounded by high fences with burglar-proof grills on doors and windows. In some places there were lots of people by the roadside, buying or selling local produce, predominantly betel nut. The locals call it *buai*. It is the seed of the fruit of the areca palm. The nut is chewed for a few minutes and then a bean-like green mustard (*daka*) coated with lime powder (*kambang*) is bitten. This mixture sets off a chemical reaction. In addition to the perceived benefits, this reaction makes the teeth and the lips turn red. According to the locals, the nut induces a mild stimulant effect that reduces stress, heightens awareness, and suppresses hunger. Betel nut chewing is also an important cultural practice in some other countries in the Asia-Pacific region.

I learnt from Andrew and Peter that employment opportunities were limited here, similar to the communities that we encountered in other countries. This scenario was similar to many parts of the developing world where unemployment is high. Many people leave villages and head to towns and cities in the hope of work and a better life. However, when these opportunities do not materialise, people resort to other options to make a living. This includes petty crime. The privilege of unemployment benefits that are a part of the welfare system in western countries such as Australia does not exist in PNG. As we drove around the town, I learnt some interesting facts about Mount Hagen. Western civilisation arrived in this part of world only in the 1930's. This was also marked by the introduction of Christianity in the region and today the churches play a significant role in the delivery of education and medical services. In the early days, access to school was limited. According to Paul:

> There was a time when children in his village had to leave home after completing grades 1 and 2. There were no roads, they would walk for miles, and camp overnight in the bushes before reaching another part of the country many hours later. To attend school, they would board with people who they hardly knew for a term or so each time before they returned home during the holidays. Over time things changed, and I did not have to travel like the others because Saint Theresia Kuruk Primary School had opened. However, I had to cross three rivers to get to school. If my clothes got wet, I was in trouble because I only had one pair of uniform.

We arrived at Peter's property early in the evening. It was far enough to be away from the hustle and bustle of the city centre. The accommodation was comfortable and very clean. It was better than some rooms that I have come across in hotels and motels in more affluent parts of the world. Matthew and I stayed here, and Paul opted to stay with his parents and family in the village. While the room was very clean and tidy, my only concern was mosquitoes. I saw a couple of them in my room, and I made sure that they stopped flying – forever. However, my worry was that more would appear through the small cracks and crevices of the building as I slept during the night. It is amazing how the human mind thinks and how the body responds as a consequence from time to time. Like most westerners, I was loaded with high-quality sprays and roll-on insect repellents, and I did use them as best as I could. I also wore appropriate sleepwear that covered my whole body, but I was still apprehensive to a certain degree – what about the parts of the body I might have missed, like the tip of the nose or the forehead? As I lay on my bed, these thoughts disappeared as my body was too tired to think anymore. I had a good sleep and did not hear the noise of any buzzing mosquitoes overnight. There was no electricity, and water supply was also cut off in the early hours of the next morning. However, Peter's property had its own water and power supply, so we had no real issues.

After a quick breakfast at a local hotel, we made tracks to the school. The drive to Saint Theresia Kuruk Primary School took us about 40 minutes. The populated areas quickly thinned out as we drove away from the city. Paul was the driver, and he pointed out places of interest along the way. He showed us some of the places that he was connected with as a child and as an adult when he lived in PNG. I found the Mount Hagen's 'World Trade Centre' quite interesting. This is the place where the locals come to trade. It is very different to many trade centres that we come across in the developed world. There were rain showers earlier, and so the trading was taking place on a ground that was very muddy with pools of water everywhere. People were navigating through parked trucks, four-wheel drives, and minibuses to reach the produce and the animals that were up for sale. The hustle and bustle of this 'centre' was not much different to what one experiences in open air markets in some other parts of the world.

As Paul drove us to the school, he told us more about his village. I was quite startled to hear that the average annual income per household would be about 100 USD. Work opportunities were minimal, and most people were subsistence farmers. They grew crops like tobacco, sugar cane, broccoli, carrot, and cabbage. To generate some income, they would sell some of the extra produce in regions where these crops did not grow well such as in coffee growing areas. Communal support was strong, and everyone chipped in to help because "everybody's' problem was your problem". Most students had the bare minimum in terms of educational needs and according to Paul, "about 1% would wear shoes to school". Most homes did not have access to electricity or town water supply. Television sets were also rare in the village. As we neared the school, our excitement level grew and Matthew and I were really eager to meet the school community.

When I met the head teacher the previous day, I told him that I would like to start working with the teachers as soon as I arrived at the school. In this way, we would get a chance to work solidly over two days. He indicated that the staff, students and the local community had put together some performances to share their culture and customs with us. He said that this would probably take 30 minutes. I agreed. Our day at the school was scheduled to begin at 9:30am. As we drove towards the school on a bumpy feeder road, we went past many people. They were all walking towards the school and some were barefoot. As we approached the school, the first thing that I noticed was that the playground was packed with people of all ages from the local community. There was a hive of activity, and the locals were dressed in many colourful costumes to welcome us. It was a very touching and humbling moment in my life. I nearly cried. What was going through my mind at the time just cannot be described. I could not believe that so many people had put in so much effort to welcome us. It was a Friday, and it was also a public holiday. The commitment and interest of the people was unbelievable.

As I stepped out of the four-wheel drive, the head teacher and some members of the school community greeted us. We were then led to the presentations that were stationed strategically throughout the playground. In the words of Andrew, the community wanted to welcome us and also say thank you for the computers. The first in the chain of activities was a dance item. It was almost like a guard of honour for us with the participants covered in traditional body paints and costumes dancing on either side. As we continued our walk, we went past more groups that were performing dances that reflected the tribal origins of the participants. Some of the groups were chanting in English and also in their local language, "thank you for the computers", while some of the other performances focussed on their lifestyles. One group demonstrated how customary musical instruments were made and played using local materials. We were also shown how fires were lit without matches when the community went out into the bush. One of the groups showed their interpretations of how their ancestors were forced to carry large logs for the European settlers when they first arrived in the region. For the locals, sweet potatoes are a very important ingredient in their diet. The students, under the watchful eyes of the community elders, showed us how they cooked the yams and potatoes. Three strategies were shown – cooking on hot coals, cooking inside bamboo stems, and cooking in underground ovens. We got a chance to taste the students work. The freshness and the cooking method made the sweet potato very tasty.

In another part of the playground, children were showing us how funeral rites and protocols are observed in their community. Here again, my words do not do enough justice to portray what the children were demonstrating. These children were probably 11 or 12 years old, but the manner in which they demonstrated the mourning and other rituals performed individually and in groups revealed how death played out in their real worlds. In another part of the ceremony, the children showed how members of other tribes are welcomed as they join in the grieving process and offer their condolences and respect to the deceased. There was another group that performed cultural dances that are entwined with death in their customs. Traditionally these dancers are believed to drive away the evil spirits. While each performance showcased the richness of this culture and how effectively it seemed to have passed on from one generation to the next, the portrayal of how funeral rites are observed in this tribe was thought-provoking. One of the questions that went through my mind at the time and even now is how many children of the same age in the developed world would be able to demonstrate the protocols and procedures that are observed in their cultures when someone passes on?

The amount of time, effort and energy that had gone into these presentations was almost mind-blowing. The manner in which the acts were performed was flawless. There was no budget, no fancy marquees erected or steering committees to stage the event. People seem to have engaged out of the goodwill of their hearts and the traditions of welcoming visitors that have been passed on over many generations. They just wanted to be there. The commitment of the whole community to participate in the way they did on a public holiday was heart-warming. I was amazed to see the elderly and the parents who had joined in with the staff and students – not just as spectators but as actual performers. I wonder how many other schools and communities worldwide would welcome donors in this way. Some people had just turned up to shake our hands. It was a truly overwhelming experience!

There were some speeches to mark the occasion. The members of the community sat in the playground on this hot sunny day without any shelter, chairs, sunscreens, or hats to listen to the speeches. The speakers included a member of the community, a senior student, a teacher, Paul, and me. All the local speakers reinforced the importance of embracing this new technology for the education of their children. They all expressed their gratitude for the donation of computers and alluded to the new possibilities that these technologies will present to the teachers and their students. They acknowledged that much of this was the result of one of their own villagers, Paul Ogil, who was seen as a 'bridge builder'. A community leader also emphasised that much of the AusAID that came to the country never reached the disadvantaged in rural and remote areas. Thus, there was optimism about the opportunities that the new bond between the school community and the SEE Project would create. I was humbled by the appreciation that this community had shown towards this technology. One of the senior teachers, Mrs Andakis, remarked that while they were very appreciative of what they had been given, they had nothing to offer in return. What the community probably did not realise was that through their cultural performances, they gave me an insight into their lives that could not be obtained through other avenues – no matter how hard I tried. It showed the richness of their culture and their many talents. While I might have been technologically knowledgeable, I learned so much about this community just by witnessing what was on show. Without knowing, they had given me so much. The end of the speeches did not stop the performances. It was a day of celebration and these kept going until later in the day. For me, what I had witnessed on the school playground was an unforgettable moment – it is one that I will never forget.

We had experienced a great start to the day. Once the speeches were over Matthew and I joined the teachers and headed towards their staffroom. This room had become the home for the computers. I was quite impressed as I walked into the room. The computers were thoughtfully set up. They were all covered by pieces of cloth just to prevent dust from settling on them. Luckily, we had taken a data projector with us. Without this technology, it would have been difficult to engage effectively with the 25 teachers. Another huge bonus was that all the teachers could speak English. I asked them, "You have had these computers in your school for more than six months. What have you done with them so far?" The response from almost all the teachers was the same. "We used the computers once. We turned it on and turned it off". The unanimous response from the teachers was that they did not want to do anymore because they feared that they might break something. Thirty years ago, I felt the same when I first dabbled with personal computers. I was also very fearful and did not want to "break anything". In those days computers were less stable and more prone to freezing which led to the loss of unsaved work.

We did not know the background of the teachers. We also did not know how the computers were set up and used. One of the teachers had typing skills. As a consequence, she was given the responsibility of setting up the computers. In some parts of the world, computers are still viewed as an upgraded typewriter because they have a keyboard. The underlying belief is that if one can type, they should be able to operate a computer. Our initial chat with the teachers set the scene on where the professional learning should start. Most teachers had little experience with computers. While two or three had computers at home, their machines had the Windows operating system installed on them. The computers at the school were operating on the *Edubuntu* system. While it was user-friendly, it was still different, and all the teachers needed to develop an understanding of how the icons and the preloaded software worked. So, our first task was to focus on login steps and the desktop. Using the search icon, we got the teachers to locate *Tux Paint, Tux Math* and *Tux Typing*. These applications are very intuitive, and first-time users get the hang of them very quickly. Most importantly they all have an educational value. As an initial activity, we had the teachers play with these applications. Within a very short time, they knew what they had to do.

We then showed them how to access programs such as *Libre Open Office* which had worked very well in other countries. Our main focus here was on word processing. We got them to write a paragraph about their school. One hour later, many were still struggling with the task. Getting used to the keyboard is a daunting task, and we were not expecting any miracles. Our motivation was to develop the teachers' awareness of the program and how it could be accessed. With this knowledge, the teachers had the potential to develop their capabilities over time. Matthew had built the next model of the *SEE Box*. Like the previous versions, it had all the resources that included the full version of *Wikipedia, Khan Academy* videos, and a variety of digital texts and library books. The teachers were thoroughly impressed when we projected the Mount Hagen page from Wikipedia on the screen. It was the first time many saw this page. We then showed the State of Origin page – this was well and truly exciting for them. The State of Origin is a National Rugby League (NRL) competition that is played between teams from States of Queensland (Maroons) and New South Wales (Blues) in Australia. Apparently, in PNG this competition is very closely followed with strong supporters for each side. It is taken so seriously that there have been reports of "physical aggression" and "tribal combativeness" between the supporters that has led to "horrifying consequences" including death (Matthey, 2015). There have also been calls to ban live broadcast of these games in PNG. On this occasion there were no uproars or squabbles even though everyone was a supporter of one of the teams. I was pleased there were more supporters of Maroons than Blues! We then focussed on the research possibilities that Wikipedia offered. I divided the teachers into class groups and challenged them to think about how this resource could be used to facilitate research in their classroom activities. After brainstorming and discussion it was pleasing to see that they all came up with a range of ideas that could be integrated in their classroom activities.

We changed gears and our next step was to delve into *Scratch*. We had used this in Malaysia. This is a free programming language that was developed by the Massachusetts Institute of Technology. It is a very powerful program that enables users young and old to create interactive stories, games, and animations. The rationale here was that if the teachers picked up the basics and shared it with their students, then a new wave of activities that promoted problem-solving together with critical and creative thinking could start in the classrooms. To get the teachers onside, we started off by going through the *Scratch* interface and some of the relevant terminologies. The interface is divided into sections, each with its specific purpose. There is a stage where the actors known as sprites do the 'acting', which is based on how they are programmed or coded. The coding occurs in another section of the screen by using coloured program blocks. A significant advantage of *Scratch* is that it gives users instant feedback. The default sprite on the screen is a cat. I started off by getting the teachers to start coding the cat by using the 'move 10 steps' block. This is probably the way many start their journey with *Scratch*. When this block is dragged into the scripting area and clicked, the cat moves ten steps. The teachers were able to do this without much hassle. It was an instant success. However, 10 steps in *Scratch* is different to ten steps as we know. There is no movement of legs as such – the whole-body glides '10 steps'. While this may sound confusing, it is very easily understood. Most got the hang of what this meant and had their "cats" not only moving but also performing other actions on the screen. Despite struggles with the keyboard, the addition of other blocks with a "meow" sound or drum beats was also done quite easily. *Scratch* has many built-in tutorials which are very useful in helping users understand how the program works. For the teachers at Saint Theresia Kuruk, I had them go through the 'getting started with *Scratch*' tutorial which comes packaged with the software. I have used this tutorial with my students whenever I have introduced this application in my classes. While the program has many capabilities, this tutorial gives an overview of what can be achieved through this program. By bringing this tutorial to the attention of the teachers, I was also increasing their awareness of what was available with this software that could be used to enhance their knowledge and understanding of how the program worked. For teachers in this part of the world, these offline tutorials were vital because they did not have any other options for learning. Teachers in Australia would be able to access a range of resources to enhance their understanding of the software and how it was used in classrooms. They could access the Internet, view YouTube videos, borrow library books, connect with online forums and so on to develop the knowledge and understanding. For these teachers no such options were available. The on-board help that comes with *Scratch* can make a huge difference.

However, for tutorials to make a difference, a paradigm shift needs to occur. For many teachers who are very used to being told what to do, a shift needs to be made to prioritise and value self-paced learning which can only occur through self-motivation and determination. All this does take time.

Once the teachers got the hang of how the program worked, I presented them with some simple challenges. The Irish Software Research Centre has produced a series of lessons in *Scratch* for use in classrooms. The layout of these lessons is worthwhile because they start off by building students' skills in coding and culminate in activities where they are presented with challenges. Each lesson also shows how it connects with concepts in other subject areas. For the teachers at Saint Theresia Kuruk, we photocopied the first five lessons before we left. We quickly realised that while our idea was good in principle, the black-and-white printing was a hindrance. *Scratch* programming blocks are colour coded. The dark blue blocks, for example, are for coding the motion of the sprite, the purple blocks add sound and so on. If we had printed these tutorials in colour, the teachers would have been able to follow the steps with greater ease because they were using *Scratch* for the first time. We did not have access to a colour printer on the site or anywhere else, so we could not print coloured worksheets. In the developed world we take access to such hardware for granted. Our next best strategy in this context was to load the files in the SEE *Box*. Teachers were able to access the lessons, though this was not the ideal solution because they had to switch between screens to view the lesson, then switch to the *Scratch* screen and vice versa. Given that the teachers were very new to the keyboard, performing this switching execution was not easy. Some tended to forget the keys to switch between screens. I understood the challenges that they were facing in this regard. I tend to have similar issues myself. Nevertheless, the teachers that we were working with were quite determined. By the end of the session, most had completed the first lesson.

My strategy with these teachers was to seed some ideas and give them time to have a play until we met next time. If they could view the on-board lessons on *Scratch* and explore the software on their own, then this would be a positive change. I was not expecting any significant changes concerning the development of innovative activities for their classrooms using *Scratch*. If teachers could consolidate their understanding of what they had learnt, then this would be a step in the right direction. Rome was not built in a day and on the same vein, I was not hoping to move any mountains on this trip either. These activities were a taster, and my experiences as a classroom teacher and researcher show that one-off professional development does not work. Learning how to use new technologies takes time and fortunately I was able to work with these 25 teachers over the two days. Based on my previous observations such an initiative can impact on teachers in three ways. First there will be a group that will emerge as digital champions and lead the change at the school. According to the diffusion and innovations theory, this group be the identified as the innovators and early adopters (Rogers, 2003). The second group will watch for signs that the waters are safe before they embrace digital technology as a teaching tool. They fall in Rogers early to late majority adopters' category. There will be a third group that may run so far away from technology that they may never want to get anywhere near it again. They would be the laggards (Rogers, 2003). But we will wait and see.

The feedback from all 25 teachers was very positive and encouraging (Figure 7.1). Many pointed out that they had no prior knowledge of using computers. They also did not have any opportunities for participating in technology-focussed professional learning activities. But the two days had given them lots of ideas and they were confident that they would be able to transform this new knowledge into meaningful classroom activities for their students. One of the teachers remarked that she was learning so much that she did not want to go home. "The presentation was powerful, and I loved it". Another pointed out that it was a real transformation in their journeys from "stone age to computer age" and the "memories of your presentation will remain". In any new context, designing and delivering professional learning activities is a challenge. This is largely due to the lack of knowledge about the teachers' prior experiences, interests, strengths and weaknesses. Thus, pitching the learning activities at the right level can be problematic. However, on this occasion, we felt positive that we had made a difference and seeded some new ideas that were doable at this school. The head teacher Andrew, who was also a participant, painted the big picture, noting that in the future, his students will "know what computers do, and they will be able to use it without hesitation and make it a part of their learning". He also added that he saw computers as "a tool that they will use in their lives". He felt grateful and buoyed by the fact that his school might be the only one in the western islands to have a roomful of computers for students and teachers.

We were once again very honoured when the school hosted a dinner for us at a local hotel in Mount Hagen. At the end of the second day, there was a convoy of four-wheel drives that took us all to the hotel. It was a simple dinner, but we thoroughly enjoyed ourselves. There's an indescribable magic to being in the company of nice people. We joked and shared stories of our work as another day ended in this lovely part of the world.

FIGURE 7.1 Teachers tinkering with the *Scratch* program

3 Two Years Later

Paul Ogil had made a few trips over the following two years at his own expense to visit the school and we were quite pleased that the school was making steady progress under the leadership of Andrew. One remarkable change that was already occurring was the building of a two-storey block that would house the new computer lab and the library. What an achievement? On one of Paul's visits, he was elated to see the excitement in students as they lined up for their computer class. "They could not wait to get their fingers on the keyboard". The joy in them was obvious and it was a scene that had become etched in his memory. He had a dream and hoped that one day in the future these children would look back and say, "these computers made a difference to us". Paul's commitment to his school and his community has been praiseworthy. Through his hard work, we shipped another twenty-five computers each to two other schools in Mount Hagen. As with the first shipment, Kelly Kerua and Peter Mughkerhegl came to our rescue by meeting the cost of shipping the computers to Holi Trinity Demonstration School and Koibunga Primary School. Like us, they were emotionally attached to their schools. Peter attended Koibunga Primary while Kelly was a student at the Holi Trinity Demonstration School.

We knew that there was a need for ongoing professional development and began working towards a strategy on how we could achieve this by working with teachers from all three schools. After some consultations with the schools, we agreed on a two-day workshop that would be hosted by Saint Theresia Kuruk Primary School in August 2018. We were very grateful to Christa Miyoni who agreed to deliver the workshop activities. Christa was one of our former QUT students who had participated in the outreach project in Somosomo District School in Fiji. After graduation, Christa started working as a primary school teacher. What was even more thrilling was that her school, Trinity Lutheran College on the Gold Coast gave her four days of paid leave to participate in this activity. We were very grateful to the school principal and her school for supporting this activity. It was the first time such support was given to the SEE Project. We were also very grateful to Peter Mughkerhegl who funded Christa's travel and accommodation expenses. Paul and his wife Helena also travelled at their own expense to support Christa with the delivery of the workshop.

Christa spent part of the first day asking teachers from the three schools questions about computers to establish their prior-knowledge. This gave her a good indication of where to start. She quickly realised that there was "a large spread of expertise". For example, one of the participating teachers who was also the school typist at one of the schools, knew a lot about how to operate computers and use programs such as *LibreOffice Writer*. On the other end of the spectrum, Christa found that there was a teacher who found it difficult to hold a computer mouse. While she found this range of abilities quite daunting; "the natural curiosity and enthusiasm of the teachers to learn new computer skills was heart-warming". According to Christa, this attitude of the teachers "definitely pushed" her "passion to serve this community, in the best way" she could.

After gathering their prior-knowledge, Christa wanted to work with the teachers to find out what they wanted to achieve from this two-day basic computer skill workshop. The key phrase that popped up was "everything about computers". She found this "funny" and responded by pointing out that "as their teacher she didn't know everything". Her initial activity focussed on reinforcing basic functions on the computer such as, using the mouse, opening and closing programs, and creating folders. The next activity explored *LibreOffice Impress*. After introducing them to some of the basics of this technology, "like adding text boxes, changing font and creating new slides" Christa challenged them to create a slide show about themselves. As we found two years earlier, some teachers found it really difficult to type on the keyboard. Some of the teachers particularly from Holi Trinity Demonstration School and Koibunga

Primary School were relatively new users of computers and their challenges with the keyboard was understandable. For them, Christa introduced *Tux Typing* to develop their keyboard skills. "The teachers loved this program – it was fun and interactive!"

On the second day, Christa showed the teachers a digital storybook about life in an Australian school that her students had created with her guidance. She deconstructed this task and demonstrated how digital storybooks can be created. The teachers were then guided to create a sample book that they could adopt as a classroom activity. All teachers grasped the idea and they were challenged to implement this as a task in their classrooms. It was pleasing that some of teachers took this idea on board. They shared the digital storybooks that their students had created with us.

To develop a closer bond with the teachers, Christa shared some personal information about her own background and heritage. The teachers were thrilled to hear that while she was born in Australia, her father was born in Milne Bay, a coastal town in PNG. She told the teachers, that although she felt connected to PNG, she lacked knowledge and understanding of many of the cultural traditions and practices. She was very interested to learn more about them and the teachers obliged. They shared and wrote about marriage ceremonies and in particular "bride price practices". In some parts of PNG, the family of the groom compensates the family of the bride by making payments in the form of money, property, livestock, or other commodities. In my view, this practice is the reverse of the dowry system in India.

The workshop provided a unique opportunity for the teachers at the three schools to learn about computers and some of their classroom applications. It was delivered by a highly competent classroom teacher. But this was also a true learning opportunity for Christa. She reflected on her experiences as follows:

> I personally believe that there should be more opportunities for teachers to help each other, particularly in developing countries. We have so much knowledge, information and experiences to share with the wider world and its upsetting to know that countries that lack these opportunities are falling even further behind. I hope my two-day workshop has provided these teachers with some skills that they can use to teach their students.

4   Lesson Learnt – Yes, We Can Make a Difference

Our work in PNG was truly gratifying. It was amazing that just by joining hands, we were able to not only provide the tools but also the skills that teachers needed to use effectively in the classrooms. In some respects, it mirrored the work of my ancestors who collaborated with the community, the head teacher, and teachers to deliver outcomes at my primary school in Fiji (see Chapter 2). There were no buckets of money to dip into. All that was needed was the will of a few good men and women! At Saint Theresia Kuruk Primary School, the building of a computer lab and library was an eye-opener in terms what good ideas can achieve (Figure 7.2).

The computer lab and library building started with Paul Ogil's dream of getting computers to his primary school. It was done in the hope of giving children in his village opportunities for a better education and a brighter future as a consequence. These were the opportunities that he was deprived of when he was a student here. As the head teacher, Andrew Collin played a critical leadership role in not only embracing Paul's idea but also proactively taking steps to transform it into reality. A new building together with a new generator were some of his initiatives to get the infrastructure readied for the technologies. But all this would have been futile if he was not able to support his teachers in their professional learning. As members of the community, Kelly Kerua and Peter Mughkerhegl's support to offset transportation expenses was praiseworthy. As a team in Australia we played our part

FIGURE 7.2   Inside the new computer lap (under-construction at the time of writing)

to support key players on the ground. Collectively we became cogs in a system which connected together to deliver productive outcomes that benefitted the school community. To tackle the social issue at hand, our thoughts and actions fuelled each other and almost in tandem – this is at the heart of critical pedagogy (Barbules & Berk, 1999). Our work in PNG could be a model that others can emulate because it demonstrates that "Yes, we can make a difference"!

CHAPTER 8

So, What Was the Impact?

> In the process of the ongoing education of teachers, the essential moment
> is that of critical reflection on one's practice.
>
> PAULO FREIRE

 The video accompanying this chapter is freely available online
at https://doi.org/10.6084/m9.figshare.10305314

"Where is the library?" I have been perplexed at where this simple question has
taken me at a personal and a professional level. It is the question that I asked
the head teacher at Naidovi Primary School in 2009 which started this enthral-
ling journey of knowledge sharing, learning, and deep reflection. Through the
experiences thus far, I have learnt so much about education in the developing
world. I would have never gained this knowledge if I had not ventured from my
comfort zone. Without doubt, the quality of learning that occurs by experiencing the world *in situ* cannot be rivalled by any of the existing teaching strategies and technologies. The privilege of working with some like-minded men
and women added to the quality of my experiences. Collectively, we were able
to create opportunities and, in the process, seed some new ideas for teaching
and learning in rural and remote schools. Who knows where the beneficiaries
will be in the future and how they will reflect on these opportunities? In my
view the real test of an educator is what he or she can do to change the world.
One way forward is to be a critical educator by example and in the process
raise the "ambitions, desires, and real hope for those who wish to take seriously the issue of educational struggle and social justice" (Giroux, 1988, p. 177).
Such a pathway may be a ray of sunshine in the "market-driven logic of neo-
liberal capitalism" (Bessell, 2009, p. 715) that appears to drive the education

© KONINKLIJKE BRILL NV, LEIDEN, 2020 | DOI:10.1163/9789004406872_008

agenda in higher institutions. Of note, the rising tide of negative attitudes and actions of some in power towards the underprivileged and marginalised is alarming.

In hindsight, our civic engagement in rural and remote schools began with a local problem or issue as a result of its impact on our critical consciousness (Giroux, 2010). The framework of our engagement followed a two-phase process with a series of stages and key questions (Table 8.1). In the exploration phase, we unpacked the problems and issues at a contextual level to develop a deeper understanding of why they existed and what had been done to deal with them. This was followed by critical and creative thinking on what we could do to support the schools as a consequence. The resulting ideas were communicated to the schools. Through further collaboration and communication, the most feasible option was implemented.

Action, evaluation and reflection underpinned the implementation phase. Our approaches strongly paralleled the cyclical processes that are adopted to solving problems of a technological or engineering nature (Duncan-Andrade & Morrell, 2008; Fantz, De Miranda, & Siller, 2011). Here too, each stage was guided by some key questions. However, how the stages played out in context varied and so did the questions. Each implementation taught us something new and equipped us with knowledge that impacted on the initiatives that followed. The SEE Project served as the conduit to connect one project to the next. We are confident that over the years, such an approach enabled us to make a positive contribution towards supporting the United Nations goal on Quality Education (UN, n.d.).

Perhaps the most significant aspect of our civic engagement was the impact it had on the participants. For each participant, there was a level of transformation at both a personal and professional level. Two of my university colleagues reflected on their Fijian outreach experiences as follows:

> The mild-mannered perseverance I observed is laudable in the face of often contradictory competitive funding limitations for an international outreach project with sustained and evidenced impact, engagement, and success. Likewise, the odd challenges of working with a chieftain-based culture reflect a quite different way of life. The fact that anything at all was achieved in Fiji is a testament to Vinesh's deeply held conviction to do right by the Fijian people. (Dr Richard Medland)

> I believe projects like these are life-changing experiences for everyone involved. There are so many tangible and intangible reciprocal benefits for our students and the communities they are immersed in. I wish

TABLE 8.1   An overview of the stages of civic engagement

Stages	Some critical questions
Phase 1: Critical thinking	
Issue identification	What is the issue?
	Why is it important to me/us?
	How can I/we make a difference?
Contextual understanding	Why does the issue exist in this context?
	Why does it need to be addressed?
	What has been done to address the issue in the past?
Issue exploration	What research has been done on the issue and what were the findings?
	What strategies have been applied elsewhere to deal with a similar issue?
	What are some feasible options for tackling it?
	What is the most feasible option and how can it be implemented?
	Can the issue be solved using the available human and physical resources and within the identified constraints?
	Is the proposed solution acceptable to all stakeholders?
	How will it benefit the stakeholders?
Phase 2: Implementation	
Action	How will the initiative be managed and what is the timeline?
	What will be the role of the participants?
	How can the resources (e.g. human, physical, financial) be used to optimise the outcomes?
	What criteria would be used to measure the outcomes?
	What measures will be put in place to make the initiative sustainable?
Evaluation	Does the solution address the identified issue?
	What aspects of the initiative worked?
	What were some of the challenges and barriers and how did they impact on the initiative?
	How can the challenges and barriers be overcome?
	What was impact of the initiative on the stakeholders?
	What changed as a consequence?
Reflection	What lessons were learnt from the initiative?
	What would be done differently next time?

that more students (and staff!) had the opportunity to engage in such experiences. I would jump at the chance to be involved in similar projects in the future. (Dr Carly Lassig)

Without doubt, the contributions of my colleagues like Richard and Carly had a significant impact on what we were able to achieve in schools in developing countries and as a consequence make a positive contribution to the quality of education agenda. The following sections outline the three types of engagement that I have been actively involved with over the past eight years: the school resources program, the university students outreach projects, and the professional development activities for enhancing teacher capacity. Each section highlights how it impacted on some of the participants.

1   School Resources Program

We achieved a lot through the SEE Project. The donation of resources was our core business and it proved to be a crucial first step for developing a partnership and goodwill with schools in developing countries. Without expecting anything in return, this gesture demonstrated to the recipients that we were genuinely motivated to support the quality of education in their schools. It opened new doors for further collaboration, especially in terms of university outreach projects. We have always been grateful for the assistance of QUT for donation of resources which eventuated through the support of the Deans of Faculties together with the Heads of Schools and Departments. Some of our university colleagues – Mal Van Nek, Jason Frew and Johnny Giang (Learning Environments & Technology Services), Sabrina Menezes and Senka Henderson (Education), Kate Harbison (Library), and Kelvin Modderman (Science and Engineering Faculty) – have gone out of their way to make our work possible. While we had no say in what resources we were given, we were able to find a new home for most of the items. With the digital products, we were pleased that we transformed e-waste to e-opportunity by recycling 'retired' university assets and in the process extended the shelf life of some of the resources that were used to build the technologies. Through all this effort, the SEE Project has, to date, donated more than a thousand individual digital technologies that have included laptops, desktops, cameras, digital projectors, and brand-new robotic and other teaching kits. In addition, we have donated more than two thousand library books. Whilst the value of the second-hand resources would be almost negligible in Australia because of limited demand, in developing countries they do retain some of their value. On the basis of the feedback received from some of the recipient schools about replacement value costs of the donated items, we estimate that the total value of our support would be in the vicinity of 500,000 (USD). This figure does not take into account the many hours spent in teacher professional development and support provided in other ways. In all, more than 60 schools in eight countries have directly benefitted from these donations. We also believe that between 15 to 20,000 students and their teachers in Fiji, Papua New Guinea, Malaysia, South Sudan, Bhutan, Solomon Islands, Vietnam, and Kenya have been the real beneficiaries. We believe that for a project with no funding other than in kind support from QUT, this has been a remarkable achievement. People from more than 100 countries have visited the project website (theseeproject.org) to read about our work. This is further evidence to the value of the work that we are doing. The following are accounts of how the donations impacted on a principal, a head teacher, and a classroom teacher.

1.1   *Segran Pillay (High School Principal, Suva, Fiji)*

In 2011, I delivered a presentation on ICT in schools for principals and head teachers at Naidovi Primary School (see Chapter 3). This presentation was prepared at the request of the Ministry of Education when Ramila and I undertook our first outreach project at this school. Segran Pillay (see Chapters 4 & 5) was an attendee and he was "extremely impressed" by my presentation because like me, he too had a deep interest in using technologies in education. In addition, Segran was buoyed to see the "achievements of the students" and what they were able to do with the laptops and robotic kits that were donated to Naidovi Primary School. The presentation reaffirmed Segran's belief "that ICT could make learning exciting, easier and engaging".

In 2013, Segran was transferred as the principal of Balata High School. For many students in the community, Balata was not their first choice for high school because of its location and reputation in terms of students' academic outcomes. His initial challenge was to change the image of this rural school and make it more appealing and marketable. He had to think of something that would give his school the edge. At the back of his mind he kept thinking of what he had witnessed at Naidovi Primary. "I was also thinking of the projects that high school students could achieve in Fiji if they had access to technologies". Working alongside the board of Balata High School, he formulated a shared vision to make the school smart, unique, and tech-savvy as part of a three-year development plan. The board was supportive of this vision but with limited financial resources, he could not afford the quantity of technologies that were needed to make classroom activities viable. Segran felt quite elated when he realised that the "SEE Project had been founded. It had its own website [that] shared a number of success stories of its engagement with other schools". Segran approached me and I can still remember the telephone conversation. I was extremely happy because I was talking to a school principal who was switched on and had a very good knowledge of technology. As a consequence, our journey began with Segran in 2013 with an initial donation of ten laptops and a data projector, and a lot more resources that followed. In a nutshell, Segran's vision and knowledge about teaching with technologies facilitated an educational transformation for his staff, students, and the school community. In 2016, Segran was promoted and transferred to a much larger school in the city. However, the partnership between Balata High School and the SEE project had been a significant part of his journey in teaching. He recalled some of the moments as follows:

> As more technologies rolled in, all teachers had access to research tools to prepare and deliver great lessons. The lesson notes, activities, past year exam papers, videos, and remedial questions were placed on the free and open source server built on Ubuntu. In 2014, all Year 13 students (23) were provided with laptops which they could take home for learning and for interacting with resources uploaded by teachers. These senior students were given a taste of tertiary education through lectures in school and activities uploaded in the class share folder. Within a few months, most of the Year 13 students had advanced significantly, especially in terms of their digital fluency.
>
> Teachers found it easier to present videos, animations, and graphical demonstrations of concepts that would have been boring and meaningless looking at a photocopied black and white image pasted in the notebook from a text book. It was during lesson observations that I saw how interested the students were during one of the lessons on "Plate Tectonics", a Year 13 Geography concept where the teacher showed different types of plate movements and its resultant landforms. This was way better than diagrams drawn on the board during my days as a student and worse from those teachers who tried demonstrating plate movements with their hands only. In another lesson, I was amazed to see how the English Teacher incorporated traditional Kenyan music in her presentation when she introduced the setting from the novel "A River Between". One of the Science Teachers got the students to play online simulation games to develop their conceptual understandings. Similarly, online videos opened a new world for the Home Economics teacher and her students. The staff of Balata High School were slowly adopting 21st century teaching strategies and tools to make lessons more meaningful. They were learning and at the same time assisting each other in the staffroom to learn contemporary methods of teaching and communication.

Further donation of desktop computers was placed in a Media Room that became a busy heart of the school. Teachers would take students for research, presentations, video editing, writing, and sharing ideas that focussed on real world projects. A few eye-catching projects that emerged from student research were further planned as school projects for 2016. These included the making of seats from old tyres, innovative backyard vegetable farming techniques, and a water fountain that was to be built from an extremely old water tank lying around. I observed that students were always keen to practice what they researched. It always gave a sense of satisfaction when the students came with ideas and would eagerly want to start projects. Students of Balata High School found a new meaning to education and loved coming to school as they could research and bring life to their ideas.

The computers that were setup in the library led to an increase in the number of student visits. While many were there to research and complete projects on the desktops placed in the library, others were taking a keen interest in reading free "Gutenberg" books saved on the SEE *Box* donated by the SEE Project. A group of students began watching short mathematics videos on *Khan Academy* (preloaded on the SEE *Box*). This interest from a talented group of students and teachers took them one step further and they went on to win the Year 9 Mathematics National Competition. I also attended this event. In a conversation, I asked a Mathematics teacher from an affluent city school if he was using *Khan Academy* for teaching. I was quite surprised when he answered, "Sir, what is *Khan Academy*?" I realised how lucky my students back at Balata were to have been introduced to technology-based learning through the SEE Project.

The students of Balata had always surprised us with their achievements. I still recall how the Year 10 students worked with the teachers and me to format school computers, delete viruses, and crimp cables for networking. The crimping of cables happened by accident when one of the desktops would not get connected to the network because of a loose "RJ45" fitting. I had the crimping tool but had never used it. So, the students used demonstration videos from YouTube to join a new RJ45 connector and soon were changing all loose connections. The academic achievements had gone to another level. Students at this school hardly scored an aggregate of 300 out of a total of 400 marks in the Fiji Year 13 Exams. Now some are excelling and achieving totals that exceed 350 in this critical examination. In 2015, one of the students scored the highest mark in Hindi in Fiji while the school received the Minister for Education's Award for the Best Results in External Exams in the ED3C category.

The three-year relationship that we shared between the SEE Project, QUT and Balata has been perhaps the best part of my leadership career. I do not recall any dull moments. The SEE Project Team will forever be remembered by the many students and teachers of Balata High School for paving new pathways that pushed them to another level. Though, I have been promoted to a school with four times the population of Balata, I miss the technology aspect of Balata and the achievements of students. I commend Dr Chandra for not forgetting his roots and giving back to Fiji in a big way – especially in the field of education. The input of the "SEE Family" who joined hands with him has meant so much to those who had so little!

1.2   *Dorthi Reddy (Primary School Teacher, Lautoka, Fiji)*

Ramila and I started working with Dorthi Reddy in 2011 on our first trip to Naidovi Primary School (see Chapter 3). We found her to be highly motivated, energetic, and someone who went out of her way to enrich the quality of her students' learning experiences. As an individual, she would easily fit in Rogers (2003) innovators and early adopters category for embracing technologies in her teaching and learning. A few years ago, she was transferred to Sabeto Sangam School that is situated in a rural area about 20 kilometres from the City of Lautoka. At Sabeto Sangam, Dorthi taught students in Class 8 and once she took up duty, she realised that her school was in need of resources, especially library books and computers. Based on her experiences at Naidovi, she believed that these resources could add value to the quality of classroom activities. A request was sent to us from the school head teacher Muniappa Reddy and we shipped 30 desktop computers, 300 library books and an assortment of items for the library (e.g. bookends and stickers for cataloguing). Their request clearly summarised how the resources would benefit the 300 students who were enrolled at this school. As per previous donations, the school met the cost of freight and other on-the-ground expenses. The feedback that I received from Dorthi reflects the impact that such donations can have on some teachers:

> I feel that the use of technology has eased my work so much that I am now more confident as a teacher. With technology my preparations for lessons have become more constructive, effective and interesting. It helps me with my research as well. I also use video presentations for some of my lesson delivery which makes teaching much more effective.

In the Fijian system, external exams still play a significant role. According to Dorthi, she felt that her teaching had improved over the years and this was reflected in the students' results:

I can proudly say that I was able to achieve a 78% pass rate in Year 8 final exams. This was in a class which had pass rates of 33% and 46% in Years 6 and 7 in previous years respectively. In 2018, two of my students achieved an average of more than 90% overall in their external exams. This is now a benchmark for current students in Year 8. I strongly believe that with the use of technology I am better equipped with the challenges as a teacher. I have seen that I have become more patient as a teacher and am able to achieve my set targets each year with improved results.

Dorthi pointed out that the computers have enabled her students to do research in school. Consequently, they do not have to pay and use online resources at internet cafes in town, creating learning opportunities for students who could not afford to travel to these cafes and pay for accessing this service. The computers impacted positively on the quality of their work, overall confidence with school work, and their engagement in lessons through more active participation. Dorthi also believed that their "work completion rate was faster".

Much of the change reported by Dorthi could be attributed to the leadership and vision of the head teacher, Muniappa Reddy. Leaders can make or break innovative changes in any organisation. It was the manner in which the computers were deployed in the school that made a significant difference. Of the 30 computers, 16 were set up in the computer lab (Figure 8.1), one in each one of the ten classrooms, two in the school office, one in the library, and one was installed in the kindergarten. In addition to some access in the classrooms, each class was also timetabled for forty-five to sixty minutes of computer use on a weekly basis. In this way the whole school had access to computers on a regular basis. Of significance was that the lower primary students used it for tasks such as learning phonics, blending sounds, rhymes, and jingles. Learning had become lessons that were also "quite interesting and structured. There is music and creativity so yes learning is much fun too". The teachers also reported that by having computers in their classrooms, their workloads had eased to a certain extent.

The library books that we had donated also had a positive impact on the students, such as their results in the Literacy and Numeracy Assessment (LANA) which is administered externally by the Ministry of Education in Fiji. Dorthi was instrumental in setting up the library in much the same way as we set up the library with other teachers at Naidovi Primary School. She also introduced a similar reading program where all classes at the school were scheduled to go to the library on a regular basis. Dorthi elaborated on the reading program:

There was no doubt that the library books have become an important tool which helps teachers in tackling literacy problems. Sabeto Sangam

FIGURE 8.1   The school computer lab at Sabeto Sangam School

has noted improved literacy rates and this is clearly seen in our LANA Assessment results. Children are taking interest in reading. We see them reading books during breaks and at other opportune moments throughout the day. The quality of books has motivated the children and they have more interest in going to the library. Even if I forget or overlook the scheduled time slot, students would remind me that we have to go to the library. My class borrows a book for two weeks. After reading they have to complete a summary sheet and file which shows the number of books they have read. A library record file is also kept in the class to show the borrowing and return of books.

1.3   *Andrew Collin (Head Teacher, Mount Hagen, Papua New Guinea)*
Our work at Saint Theresia Kuruk Primary School (see Chapter 7) in the Central Highlands of Papua New Guinea was one of a kind. While the task of getting the 30 desktop computers to the school was a remarkable achievement, what has happened since is praiseworthy. Much of the credit goes to the head teacher, Andrew Colin, and his team of dedicated staff. Andrew's knowledge of computers was minimal until they arrived at his school. This was also the case with many of his staff. In the workshops that Christa, Matthew, and I conducted at two different times, it was evident that many teachers were struggling with this new technology. The donation of the computers gave many teachers and

their students an opportunity to put their fingers on the keyboard for the first time, previously deprived because they could not afford to buy a computer. According to Andrew, to his knowledge "nearly all elementary and primary schools in Papua New Guinea" have not had access to computers despite all the technological advances that have been made in the past few decades.

It was Andrew's vision of enabling his students to step into the computer age that convinced him to embrace this radical change with technologies at his school. His leadership was critical, especially when his own knowledge of this technology and how it can be used in teaching and learning was so negligible. I was amazed at how he planned the strategies and then drew upon his financial resources to transform his ideas to reality. Of the countries that we have worked in, Papua New Guinea would have to be one in which funding for schools is among the lowest. From the numerous discussions that I had with Andrew, one quality that has shone through is his money management skills. In my view this is one aspect that is overlooked when school head teachers and principals are appointed in developing countries. But managing a school is no different to managing a small business. Without these skills, some of the capital works that were undertaken at the Saint Theresia Kuruk Primary School would have never eventuated. Andrew's first priority was to purchase a diesel generator to power the desktops because the local electricity supply was unreliable. His other significant achievement was "the building of a computer and library building at a value of more than K100, 000" (30,000USD) in 2017. From my observations, such transformations have only occurred in schools with strong and visionary head teachers and principals.

Andrew's initiatives did not stop at just the capital works that were triggered by the arrival of the computers. The professional development activities that we conducted together with the initiatives of his own staff have led to inclusion of lessons on the "Basics of Computers" in the school's regular timetable even though "it is not part of the curriculum in PNG". Each of the 22 classes from grades three to eight have been timetabled for 40 minutes each week in the computer lab, and teachers have a mandatory 90-minute time slot on Friday afternoons which enables them to develop knowledge and create activities for their students. The school deputy has developed a plan for this year with a series of graduated topics with supporting resources. The focus in term 1 is on topics such as 'manners, procedures and rules' and 'introduction to computers'. In term 2, students understand the basics of using computers such as turning it on and off and using the mouse. In term 3, the emphasis is on exploring the icons and programs on the desktop, and then in term 4, students will target programs such as *Tux Maths, Tux Typing* and *Tux Paint*. Some of the classes will work towards creating digital storybooks.

The impact of our initiatives on Segran, Dorthi and Andrew highlight the pathways and possibilities that access to library books and digital technologies can deliver when they are in the hands of competent principals, head teachers and classroom teachers. Quality resources can empower motivated teachers in a way that can deliver immense benefits to their students. There are other stories from schools that echo the benefits of our initiatives. It reinforces the importance of access to resources that have the potential to change the chalk and talk teacher-centred activities that dominate the classroom landscape in many developing countries. As a child, I hated school for this reason. But it is also likely that my teachers did not have access to resources to make the lessons more engaging. I am pleased that at least for some teachers and their students, our school resources program has made a small difference and seeded some changes for the better!

2   University Students Outreach Projects

The design and implementation of the students' outreach projects was unique. A distinctive feature of their engagement was that students with disciplinary backgrounds in Education, Information Technology, Engineering, Film and TV, Business, Health, and Science engaged in transdisciplinary teams towards a common goal. It was the first time I had the opportunity to interact with students from such diverse backgrounds. Whilst universities promote transdisciplinary engagement, transforming such an approach into reality is another matter. The real challenge is in finding a project with a common thread. Our focus on teaching with technologies was an ideal goal that all participants could relate to. Grants from the university and the Australian Government enabled us to undertake five outreach projects in Fiji and Malaysia. In many instances, the grants covered most of the students' expenses. All they had to do in return was to give up their time. From my point of view, I thought this funding support was a very good deal for the students. However, I was quite fascinated by how the students responded in my classes each time I publicised the opportunity for them to go on an outreach project in a developing country. On average there would be about ten percent who would show an interest in participating, but then I would ask them to complete and submit an expression of interest form which usually had four to five specific questions, and this would halve the number of interested students. In each one of the outreach projects, nearly all the students rated their experiences very highly. Without any reservations, many stated that it was a life-changing experience. They acknowledged that the work done by the SEE Project was highly significant and relevant towards creating a fairer and more just world. They all expressed an interest in making a difference in underprivileged communities. However, the high levels of adrenalin in many of the participating students dissipated quickly as they readjusted into their daily routines in Australia. What is probably most significant is that two to three students from each of the outreach projects have remained connected with the SEE Project. The statistics here supports my belief that 1% of the world's population cares about the developing world and they will actually get their hands dirty to do something about it. The sections which follow highlight the initiatives of some of these individuals and the paths that they followed afterwards.

2.1   *Ratu Epeneri Korovakaturaga (Architectural Assistant, Suva, Fiji)*
Ratu Epeneri Korovakaturaga was a student who was studying architecture at QUT. He was a Fijian Citizen and also the recipient of an AusAID scholarship. Epeneri was a participant and also the cultural ambassador on our outreach projects to Sabeto and Somosomo Schools in Fiji (see Chapter 5). Even though he had lived in Fiji for most of his life, both these projects enabled him to engage with schools and understand education in a way that he had not done previously. He was deeply concerned by the quality of education in rural and remote areas. Perhaps the most worrying aspect was the difference that he noticed in the schools that were run and managed by Indians as opposed to those schools that had Fijian leadership. He noticed that schools that were managed by Fijians were culturally rich but academically poor whereas he observed the reverse in schools that were managed by the Indians. While I never had the privilege to teach Epeneri at university, the outreach projects paved a path where both of us had a common interest. Epeneri and I often reflected on these differences and brainstormed strategies on what he could do to lift the quality of education after his return to Fiji. Perhaps at a personal level the most significant aspect of our engagement in the outreach projects was the bond of kinship that developed as a consequence. In keeping with our Fijian and Indian customs, he adopted me as an uncle and in return he was my honorary nephew. Epeneri is quite tall and whenever he spotted me on campus, he would yell "uncle", much to the confusion of the pedestrians who were around me at the time.

Epeneri returned to Fiji in 2016 after successfully completing his bachelor's degree in Design. He was one of our students who wholly participated in university life. He had a very balanced outlook and did well in not only his studies but led the South-East Queensland Fiji Students Association by example. On his return he gained employment in an architectural firm in Fiji. Epeneri reflected on his experiences as follows:

Being a part of the SEE Project was not only an eye opener but also a very humbling experience. My involvement really highlighted the importance of educating the students who are the future of Fiji. It was very upsetting to see that the schools had few resources that they could utilise to enable their students to learn to their full potential. One moment I'll never forget, was when the students saw a computer for the very first time. Having been exposed to computers for as long as I could remember, it was overwhelming to see the excitement and joy of these students. I could see their thirst for knowledge and deep hunger to learn about computers and how they could be used.

As a citizen of Fiji, Epeneri felt privileged to be educated. The opportunity to engage with schools through the SEE Project was an inspiration for him and he wanted "to contribute something back to the local rural and remote communities". He felt fortunate to have had the opportunity to study abroad. With this background, he felt "duty bound" to step out in the real world as a role model "to inspire and motivate the younger generations in Fiji to aspire for a good education". He was clear on why this was necessary but the lingering question and uncertainty in his mind was "how could this be achieved?" Epeneri reasoned the best strategy would be to collaborate and brainstorm ideas with other Fijian students who had studied in Australia and had recently returned home after graduating with degrees in their respective fields:

I knew I couldn't do it on my own and needed the help of my fellow scholarship recipients who had returned home. After an Australia Awards alumni function, I approached a few of my colleagues to express my ideas about giving back to our communities. I was exceedingly pleased to have received many positive responses and we arranged to meet the following week. I was overwhelmed to see the number of my colleagues, from various disciplines. Their level of enthusiasm was very high, and they were more than willing to contribute in any way they could. There was a strong desire to setup an entity that would formally drive our agenda further. After a few formal and informal meetings, the SEE Foundation Fiji was established. Through the assistance and partnership of the SEE Project in Brisbane, we have been able to assist a few schools around Viti Levu with library books and computers. We are also expanding our reach through various forms of social media including Instagram, Facebook, and YouTube to help inform, inspire, and motivate people. We see ourselves as a small organization that is trying to make a difference in our own communities.

Epeneri's initiatives could be described as a novel approach to dealing with some of the issues that confront the underprivileged in Fiji. I have not come across any other organisation like the SEE Foundation Fiji, which is steered by a group of young, highly educated people who gained their qualifications in Australia through AusAID scholarships. It is a model that AusAID could promote in other countries. There is no doubt that by founding and affiliating with SEE Foundation Fiji, young people like Epeneri not only become more proactive in supporting meaningful agenda like enhancing the quality of education, but they also develop their professional and social networks. But for such organisations to materialise, universities need to immerse students in real-world contexts that facilitate "disorienting" experiences that create "disequilibrium" and in the process discard old ideas and habits to adapt to new ways of thinking and behaving (Trilokekar & Kukar, 2011). As Epeneri pointed out, the SEE Project was an eye-opener. Without his active participation in the project and more importantly in the Sabeto and Somosomo schools, the SEE Foundation Fiji may not have materialised. This model of engagement is a step in the right direction that will make a difference to the quality of education in developing countries.

2.2   *Geoff Polzin (Part-time Lecturer, Brisbane, Australia)*

Geoff Polzin graduated with a bachelor's degree in Information Technology with Honours from QUT. He was one of the participants in the outreach project to Balata High School (see Chapter 5). Currently he teaches and coordinates in a unit that focusses on Information Systems and hopes to enrol for doctoral studies in the future. Geoff's engagement in the outreach project has had a significant impact on him. According to Geoff:

> My experience teaching robotics at Balata was a big part of getting me to where I am today both personally and professionally. Working closely with the teachers and students at Balata opened my eyes to the joys of teaching and completely changed my mind about pursuing the computer programming career that I had been working towards for the better part of three years. It was also rewarding to step out of my comfort zone and see first-hand the differences (and similarities) in culture as well as the additional challenges associated with working in a developing region.

Upon his return from Fiji, Geoff wanted to continue exploring ways to support the quality education agenda in developing countries. He adopted the *SEE Box* project that was initially developed for our work at Somosomo District School. The capabilities and the need of this device in underprivileged communities inspired Geoff to pursue a research project that specifically investigated the usefulness of the *see Box* in a real-world setting. To get this project underway, Geoff constructed and shipped two *see Boxes* to two primary school teachers in Malaysia who were the research participants. Despite some challenges, Geoff was very pleased that both teachers used the devices in their classrooms repeatedly. "One teacher was integrating it into their daily routine which was an incredibly gratifying outcome". The see Project has never had any funding – let lone funding for research. I was equally thrilled by Geoff's investigation and his findings. It was quite pleasing to learn that the *see Box* did have a place in the classroom.

2.3   *Christa Miyoni (Primary School Teacher, Gold Coast, Australia)*

Christa graduated with a bachelor's degree in Education in 2015. Since her graduation she has been employed as a primary school teacher on the Gold Coast. She was one of the participants in the outreach project to Somosomo District School in 2014 (see Chapter 5). She was quite touched by this engagement. In her reflections after the trip, she highlighted the impact of the project on her at both a personal and professional level. "Although we were there to teach the students and teachers about technology, science, and literacy; I believe that they taught me more about learning". She was quite moved by "their devotion, laughter, simplicity, and love". Christa reflected on Mother Teresa's quote where she discusses the dichotomy that exists in people's behaviours in the east the west. According to her, people in the West are "profit oriented" and everything is measured in terms of the results that are generated (Burnsed, 2014, p. 98). On the other hand, the people in the east "are more content to just be". The emphasis on the results is minimal and, in the process, people learn some of the bigger lessons of life. Christa, was able to draw this parallel between the lives of people in Australia and those she encountered in Somosomo. Her experiences motivated her to remain connected with the see Project. In 2017, she led a workshop for teachers in three primary schools that were supported by the see Project in Mount Hagen, png.

> My engagement over the years within the see Project, has made a magnitude of life-changing reverberations throughout my career and personal life. These influential experiences have helped define my identity and supported my personal beliefs. Through the acts of providing service to others using my head, heart, and hands, I've been able to grow as a teacher. These experiences have also enabled me to provide unique and interesting perspectives to those who are around me and especially my students. In my classroom, I often highlight the privilege that my students have in terms of the educational resources that they have at their

disposal in comparison to what I have seen in Fiji and PNG. I'll mention to my students "Please take care of that book, I've been to schools who don't even have access to nice books like ours". I have found sharing my personal photographs and stories of my trips with my students, brings a rich and authentic awe and wonder to them about the world they live in and who they share it with. It hasn't been uncommon for them to remember my short story about a small school, with a new library and second-hand books. Even weeks later, you'll hear children spread the message "Take care of that book, remember Miss Miyoni said some schools don't have books like us". Although their thoughts are initially about taking care of the book, I can only hope these conversations evolve and the thought about others is a critical part of their lives. I hope these conversations seed ideas on who they are in the same way as these experiences have done to me.

2.4 *Andrew Iddles (Primary School Teacher, Mount Isa, Australia)*
Andrew graduated with a bachelor's degree in Education in 2015. Since graduation, he has been working in low SES schools in Queensland. After his engagement at the Somosomo District School (see Chapter 5), he began taking proactive steps to enhance the quality of education in Fiji. "After my experiences of teaching in Taveuni, I was very keen to go back to Fiji and engage in a similar project". Fortunately, Andrew was one of the two successful recipients of the Mary and Carl Leonard International Relations Award. This scholarship was available to QUT students, through the generosity of Mary and Carl Leonard, who had devoted their lives to working in developing countries. This award enabled Andrew to return to Fiji at the start of 2015 and provide his service for three weeks in three SEE Project schools – Naidovi Primary School, Balata High School, and Toko Primary School. Six months later he went back at his own expense and consolidated some of the work he had started in the schools previously. In his reflections, Andrew was buoyed by the "incredible experience", "the new friendships" and the manner in which he was "accepted into a wonderful family in a Fijian village". He befriended this Fijian family and stayed with them for a couple of weeks while he taught at one of the schools. He was "so grateful to have had all these opportunities" and everyone welcomed him with open arms and in a nutshell, "Fiji truly is my home away from home". He also developed a deep understanding of the work of the SEE Project and how it was impacting on the schools. According to Andrew:

> My experiences in Fiji have had significant impact on my life personally and professionally. I think the biggest eye-opener for me was how

materialistic my life had become – always wanting the latest and greatest of everything. The Fijian way of life is all about family and community and making the most of what you've got – it was a refreshing wake up call for what is truly important in my life. I became a teacher, like many other like-minded people, to make a significant difference on children's lives. After teaching in Fiji, this changed a little. I came back with an understanding that teachers can have an impact, not just on the children that they teach, but also the wider community. It was this shift in my beliefs that motivated me to return to Fiji to work in schools that had received support and resources from The SEE Project in the past; and engage with new communities and schools to help establish strategies for the effective use of ICT.

My experiences in Fiji motivated me to join the National Exceptional Teachers for Disadvantaged Schools program which focused on upskilling teachers who had a passion for teaching in schools in disadvantaged communities within Australia. Since completing my degree, I have taught in low SES schools in Brisbane and remote Queensland. Teaching and living in these school communities gives me the same life fulfilling satisfaction as teaching in disadvantage communities in Fiji – that my teaching is having a significant positive impact on my students, the school, and the wider community. After recently getting married to my amazing wife, who shares the same reasons for teaching as I do, we look forward to continuing our career in low SES schools in remote Queensland for the next 5 years at least; and I would jump at the opportunity to work with more schools and communities in developing countries in the future.

2.5   Matthew Brown (Business Analyst, Brisbane, Australia)
Matthew Brown graduated from QUT with a bachelor's degree in Information Technology with grade point average of 6.9 (out of 7). Thus, Matthew is very talented academically. But more importantly he also has a strong social justice agenda. Matthew joined us on the project to Somosomo Primary School (see Chapter 5). He teamed with one of his colleagues; Lachlan Lindsay to develop the initial version of the SEE Box. The Fiji trip had a significant impact on him. According to Matthew:

> I think the main aspect that affected me was the way I see family. Fijian families are very close, very different from my own. This has increased the engagement with my own family and no doubt with (hopefully) my family in the future. Since Fiji I have been more carefree in my life, something the Fijians seem to have perfected. I feel I also seek out opportunities to learn about other cultures and see how they live as well. Given the choice

of visiting a developed country versus a less developed country, I would choose the developing country.

Matthew has remained connected with the SEE Project and me. In 2016, he took time off and travelled with Paul Ogil and me to Mount Hagan to assist in the delivery of training to teachers at Saint Theresia Kuruk Primary School (see Chapter 7). He built an upgraded version of the *SEE Box* and donated it to the teachers. Matthew explained his reasoning for selecting this school in Mount Hagan as follows:

> The main reason was due to the experience I got from the trips to Fiji. I love seeing how other cultures differ from my own. For me the way of life, the family structure, how happy they are and how welcoming they always are would be some of my strongest reasons. Additionally, I love helping and teaching people use technology. The creative process of developing the *SEE Box* and potentially other solutions really interests me as well. Seeing the community first hand is really the only way to understand their needs.

Matthew reflected on his PNG experience as follows:

> The PNG experience was different to Fiji but equally rewarding. The format we took in teaching the teachers to use technology I think was really effective and I got to engage with the teachers more than I was able to in the past in the Fiji trips. I found the concerns of damaging the computers interesting and something that I had never imagined. The community was very different to Fiji. The barred four-wheel drive that we were driven around in was a new experience. The school and community seemed to be far more engaged than in Fiji and I found it very promising that they have continued to develop their school's computer literacy program and, in the process, improve their students' chances in school and beyond. Paul was an amazing role model to the village and a great way of engaging the school as well.

2.6 *Lauren Edmondson (Post-Graduate Student, Sydney, Australia)*

Lauren joined us on the trip to Somosomo Primary in 2014 (see Chapter 5). After her graduation, she began her career as a primary school teacher at a Queensland State School. During this time, she also joined the local Rotaract Club and shared some of her stories of the outreach project. Her dream was to find strategies to give more to the community. With the support of her fellow members and the community, she spearheaded the "Books for Somosomo" drive. To transform this initiative into reality, she organised a fund-raising dinner with the help of the Fijian Methodist Church in Brisbane. Some local schools donated books to help her cause and eventually she was able to ship a container load of books that were distributed to Somosomo Primary and some other schools on the island of Taveuni.

Twelve months later she resigned and has since taught in Fiji, Cambodia, and Greece. According to Lauren:

> My 2014 experience with the SEE Project in Taveuni has had a profound impact on my life both professionally and personally. Through the project I developed a passion for helping to improve the educational outcomes of students from disadvantaged backgrounds. As a pre-service teacher in Taveuni, I learnt new classroom strategies and tools that I have applied throughout my teaching career. However, the most crucial lesson I learnt was the importance of cultural understanding and communication between teachers and other members of school communities. Following the completion of the project, I have taught in many international settings including Fiji and Cambodia. I have volunteered teaching English to adults in a refugee camp in Greece and continue volunteering as a co-teacher for online story telling workshops in Palestine. My interest in teaching overseas and volunteering can definitely be attributed to my experience with the SEE Project. The SEE Project provided me with an invaluable experience as a pre-service teacher; something that I will always be thankful for.

The reflections of Epeneri, Geoff, Christa, Andrew, Matthew, and Lauren highlight the actions that they have undertaken which has the potential to bring about a change for those who are disenfranchised from social, economic, and political opportunities (Burbules & Berk, 1999). While their engagement in developing countries was the trigger, they took these initiatives of their own accord. This is how critical pedagogy should play out in the lives of students. If all university students graduate with such outlook, the world will tilt in favour of the marginalised and the underprivileged.

3 Enhancing Teacher Capacity

3.1 *Assignment at UNESCO*
Apart from the school resources program and the student outreach projects, I have also been very proactive in finding other ways to enhance teacher

capacity. After all, the quality of education and teacher capacity go hand in hand. Other than the work undertaken with teachers in Fiji, Papua New Guinea, and Malaysia I was very much interested in executing a new project within an organisation that was actively engaged in advancing the quality education agenda internationally. Since its inception in 1946, the United Nations Educational Scientific and Cultural Organisation (UNESCO) has been actively engaged in developing and implementing strategies to support teachers in delivering quality learning outcomes in classrooms across the world. I felt that I could make a positive contribution to UNESCO's Strategy on Teachers (2012–2015) (UNESCO, 2012) which was in place at the time. The primary objective of this strategy was to meet the changing needs of education globally by positively addressing three key issues – (1) teacher shortage, (2) enhancing teacher quality through professional development, and (3) conducting research to support teaching and teacher quality. The strategy also put significant emphasis on the use of digital technologies in classrooms and in teacher training. All these were in my line of work. I felt that I could add some value to this agenda.

I searched on the UNESCO website for possible contacts. Given the size of this organisation, finding the right information was neither easy nor intuitive. Eventually I found the relevant contact details, and after a series of email exchanges and phone conversations, I was on track to lodge my application for long professional development leave through QUT. This leave enables academic staff to participate in a program of activities that adds value to the university's teaching, research, community, and professional service goals. In this instance, the leave would allow me to undertake a project at UNESCO. My application for a three-month stint was approved by the university in November 2013. I was grateful to the university for this opportunity. While I also received a small grant for travel, I had to cover a significant part of my living expenses in Paris by myself. Through the grapevine, I learnt that there was only one other academic from another faculty at QUT who had travelled overseas to undertake such an activity in another international organisation. Getting my paperwork sorted and approved from the UNESCO end was another challenge. I found the approval process to be one the most cumbersome tasks to navigate through my career. The documentation for my final approval did not eventuate until a week before my travel. There were times when cancelling my proposed professional development leave also crossed my mind. While I can whinge and whine about some of the bureaucratic hurdles, I am a 'glass half full person'. Interestingly, at a meeting on United Nations (UN) reform, the newly appointed Secretary-General, Antonio Guterres, was asked about what kept him awake at night. He responded by saying, "My answer is simple: bureaucracy. Fragmented structures. Byzantine procedures. Endless red tape" (McGeough, 2017, para. 4). I was only beginning to experience what it takes to work in a large international organisation. But throughout my attachment, I incurred the opportunity to work with some very good people. Francesc Pedró, the Chief of Teacher Development and Education Policies Unit, was very supportive throughout my appointment. Whilst I was not going to work directly in his team, he was a great mentor and colleague. There was something very special about Francesc, he was always there to listen and assist.

I officially began my duties at UNESCO on 2 September 2014 with a meeting scheduled between my supervisor Fengchun Miao and Hendrix Kapaipi, First Secretary for Education at the Zambian Embassy. By the time the meeting was over I had for the first time acquired some ideas on what I was expected to do at UNESCO. Apparently, UNESCO was approached by the Zambian Embassy in 2013 for training of teachers for their new computer studies course for high school students that was going to be introduced the following year. There were very few teachers who were trained to teach this subject. As I understood it, they were told that an expert from Australia would be arriving soon – he would assist them with this challenge. Apparently, *I* was that expert, expected to train a group of Zambian educators as master trainers. Upon their return, these trainers would then train the teachers identified to teach the computer studies course. In addition, I would also have to liaise with officials in the Curriculum Development Centre in Zambia in the identification of the master trainers who would travel to Paris. UNESCO would bear the cost of their travel, accommodation, and living expenses.

To get the course development underway, I had hoped I would have some examples of programs with a similar focus that UNESCO had implemented in other countries. The introduction of computer studies courses in schools is not new. I felt that I could have benefitted by building on some of these programs to tailor-make a course for the Zambian context. But this was wishful thinking. As the challenge of the task sank in, I realised that I had to develop this course from scratch. I had a blank canvas to work from. While this challenge was daunting, it was also exciting. I was immensely glad that UNESCO had vested the responsibility in me of leading this training. I had to think outside the box fairly quickly and strategically because the timeframe for the development of this course was less than two months.

I began to unpack the problem: my first step was to understand the context and the curriculum. I had some big questions to grapple with. For me to proceed with this task, I had to develop an understanding of the country and its education system. To develop an effective course, I also needed to be well-grounded in terms of what was expected in the curriculum, the background of the master trainers, and the computer resources that were available to the teachers on the ground. I wanted this workshop to be very user-friendly and appropriate to the Zambian context. I was most impressed to see that Zambia had a reasonably well-structured Computer Studies curriculum for children in Grades 8 to 12. I analysed the documents to understand and determine the needs of the workshop participants. I developed a training guide that incorporated some of the ideas from the UNESCO ICT Competency Framework for Teachers (UNESCO, 2011). The four key areas identified in the UNESCO framework included; understanding ICT in Education, curriculum and assessment, pedagogy, and ICT – aligned with the sessions in this training guide. The framework of the individual tasks incorporated Kolb's Learning Cycle of experiential learning (Kolb, 1984). There was an emphasis to incorporate online resources from the Internet (e.g. YouTube videos, websites) in the tasks. A participant self-evaluation checklist was also added to enable the participants to reflect on each of the sessions (De Bono, 1999; Hampe, 2013). Throughout the workshop development process there was ongoing communication between Fengchun Miao, Raphael Banda who was the National ICT Coordinator in the Curriculum Development Centre in Zambia, and myself.

After two months of hard work, the workshop was delivered over four days at the UNESCO Headquarters in Paris. While I facilitated most of the activities, there was some input from UNESCO staff as well. Attendance each day was 100%. The training focused predominantly on hands-on tasks to demonstrate the pedagogy of 'working-with-technology' rather than 'telling-about-technology'. This kept the participants highly engaged. Group discussions enabled them to gain insights on the Theory of Multiple Intelligences (Gardner, 1985), the TPACK Framework (Mishra & Koehler, 2006), the SAMR Model (Puentedura, 2005), Bloom's Taxonomy (Krathwohl, 2002) and Project-based learning (Thomas, 2000). These theoretical perspectives gave them ideas on how classroom activities can be developed. The inclusion of a range of other topics aligned with ICT (including presentations by UNESCO staff) also created opportunities for the participants to think outside the box. Showcasing of the SEE Box, the device that was created by our IT students who had participated in the outreach project at Somosomo and Balata, enabled the participants to see how online resources can be accessed offline. They all agreed that such a device had the potential for enhancing the quality of teaching and learning in their context as well.

A survey was administered at the end of the workshop to gather qualitative feedback from the participants. They were asked to respond to questions which sought their opinions on the quality of the sessions and the suitability of the training guide. In addition, they were also asked to express their thoughts on their confidence levels for the delivery of the workshop in Zambia and the challenges and issues they perceived that they would face in undertaking this task. All the participants believed that the sessions were very well designed and aligned with the requirements of the curriculum. In the words of one of the participants – the "content was highly relevant to the syllabus". Another participant pointed out that he was now "well equipped with the skills and knowledge" that he needed to "interpret the syllabus appropriately". The sessions were valuable because they were "easy to follow", "practical", "well illustrated", "catered for different abilities", and "well sequenced with increasing levels of complexity, but not beyond the capabilities of the teachers on the ground". The "activities were simplified to the levels that would not scare people without too many skills". The sessions also presented new ideas that enabled the participants to think creatively about their teaching. The incorporation of theoretical perspectives was beneficial because "the training not only provided the background content but also introduced us to various pedagogical approaches to teaching with ICT". The majority of the master trainers rated their overall learning experiences as either "excellent" or "very good".

All the participants also believed that all the facilitators were competent and confident in their presentations. The materials in the training module were "well organised, elaborate, and easy to follow" and there was "flexibility" in how the facilitator presented them. This enabled the participants to follow the facilitator's instructions and discussions with ease. A point that echoed in many of the participants' feedback was that the sessions were hands-on, and they were given multiple opportunities to apply their knowledge. As a consequence, the "master trainers were highly involved during the sessions" and the "practical experiences were enlightening". Another point raised was that "even though the participants had different skills and varying strengths, the sessions included everyone and at the end of the day no one felt left out". One of the participants felt that there "was room for everyone to share their ideas and talents and there was more emphasis on the strengths of each opinion that was expressed". This also gave the master trainers ideas and practical strategies so that they could present their classroom activities in their own contexts. While most of the participants could not identify any aspects of the workshop that needed to be changed or amended, a few felt that more time should have been allocated to some of the tasks. They all believed that it was well designed and highly relevant to the training of computer studies teachers in Zambia. They believed that they "were trained" and "very confident and looking forward to delivering the training ... competently and professionally". All in all, it was a very successful program. There was even a write-up about it on the UNESCO (2014) website.

The delivery of the program concluded my engagement with UNESCO and I returned home to Australia. One of the real tests of a master trainer training program is how it unfolds on the ground and in the context. I created a closed group on Facebook with the participating master trainers. This proved to be one of the more effective ways of keeping in touch with some of the participants and other teachers in their networks. There was some feedback from Raphael Banda from time to time. I was thrilled to read in one of the emails less than a year after the training that 2,675 teachers had been trained. There were plans to reach a further 3,000 teachers. According to R. Banda:

> We have adopted the resource materials developed in Paris with the help of Dr. Chandra. We have just included some materials that were not covered in Paris. Otherwise Dr. Chandra did a good job and we are very grateful indeed and were highly inspired by his work. (Personal communication, 16 September 2015)

While the Zambian Government, the master trainers, UNESCO, schools, and other agencies played a significant role in advancing the computer studies agenda on the ground, I was quite pleased that I had played a key role in getting the wheels in motion. Through Facebook posts and emails from the Zambian participants, I was kept in the loop. The efforts and the determination of some of the master-trainers was highly commendable. From what I could garner, they believed in the digital technologies agenda and the benefits it could deliver in Zambian classrooms. For these reasons, despite some very unique contextual issues, they kept moving forward.

3.2   Issac Katete (*High School Teacher, Kabwe, Zambia*)

I was buoyed to read about the hard work that Issac Katete one of the master-trainers from Paris was putting into the training of his fellow teachers. In total he trained 600 teachers in various centres throughout the country. The three-day local training programs were well-designed and monitored by the Ministry of General Education in Zambia. According to Issac, "the Paris training assisted me in developing the action plan for local trainings". Through creative thinking, the master trainers were able to overcome some challenges. For example, where they did not have access to data projectors, they used "flip charts" to deliver learner-centred activities. In places where electricity was an issue, innovative solutions were implemented such as powering laptops with car batteries. The master trainers even had to use their own laptops to deliver the training. Even though there were many contextual issues and many still linger on, Issac has remained focused, largely because of his attitudes towards Information and Communication Technology.

According to Issac, "the Paris training completely changed my career direction". At the time he was studying for a bachelor's degree in Education and majoring in Geography and Religious Education. "Even though I was in my final year, my majors did not make much sense". Issac was convinced that when he graduated, his degree would be no more than just a framed document that would recognise him as a graduate "just for the sake of it". For Issac, his special moment in Paris was when he received his "Master-trainers certificate at the UNESCO HQ. It was unbelievable, and I felt great!" After the Paris training, Issac "won a scholarship to pursue a bachelor's in Education degree majoring in ICT". He is now convinced that these technologies put the world at his "finger tips" and enjoys topics such as computer programming, artificial intelligence, information security, hacking, and cyberlaw. He has also been acknowledged for his hard work and interest in pursuing the digital technologies agenda in Zambia. Amongst his many accolades after the Paris training were his selection to participate in professional activities such as the Microsoft Innovative expert training in Hungary, and British council-sponsored International ICT Training for Teachers in the Republic of South Africa. Issac has also been hand-picked by the ministry to offer his services as a part-time writer for the development of Open Education Resources (OERs). He offers his services in other related area as well.

Supporting teachers like Issac can go a long way towards enhancing the quality of education in developing countries. We need to find ways to support our teachers like Issac who are the innovators and early adopters (Rogers, 2003) because they have the potential to transform the education landscape. All they need are opportunities and the support of those who have the power to facilitate a change.

4 Lesson Learnt – All This Is Worth Doing

One of the most significant lessons of this journey has been that even in the twentieth century, many are still deprived of quality education. The lack of resources and the ongoing professional development of teachers is seriously hampering the delivery of educational services. As a consequence, educational practices that I encountered "in my travels" were still very 'old school'. Other than chalk and talk, other opportunities for rich, quality learning were minimal. As I have said in different places in the book, children will learn, no matter where they are born, as long as teachers deliver interesting and engaging activities that are contextually relevant.

Of all the work that I have undertaken to lift the quality of education in developing countries, it was the experiences of one of my past pre-service teachers that has touched me the most. It was a university outreach project that was run by my colleagues in another school within our faculty. The focus of this service-learning program was to promote the benefits of inclusive education. All I did was to load some programs and hand six laptops that could be donated to the school in Bhutan where this project was based.

Stewart Duff graduated in 2014 with a bachelor's degree in Education and is employed as a teacher in Brisbane. He considered himself quite fortunate to have been given the opportunity to be a part of this group. According to Stewart, the laptops gave the Bhutanese teachers a way to use this relatively new technology to enhance inclusive practices. The QUT team worked alongside the Special Education teachers, to showcase the capabilities and potentials of the laptops particularly with students with learning difficulties and disabilities to communicate their understanding of content at hand. Stewart shared one his special moments as follows:

> One of the most emotional and touching moments occurred on the second day of working in the school. Our Service-Learning supervisor and another QUT student had been working with a young girl who was in a self-contained class. This student had extremely limited modes of communication.
>
> After observing the student on the first day, my supervisor decided to place a laptop computer in front of her and proceeded to read out some simple words. To everyone's astonishment, the girl started to type on the keyboard the words that were read out to her, with high accuracy and fluency. The teachers present in that room were absolutely stunned and overcome with emotion as they had just experienced something that was life-changing.
>
> Throughout the day the student continued to write and solve mathematical problems via the laptop computer. Although unable to express herself through traditional means of communication, she was able to show her knowledge and express herself through an alternative medium. A life in emotional and communicative isolation was over – a new chapter had begun. It was amazing to witness the transformation that technology can bring in a person's life (The SEE Project, 2014, para. 3, 4, & 5).

In a single day, this one child's whole life was changed. In the morning she was incapable of communication in her setting, with no understanding from her educators and carers of what she might know. By the afternoon, for the first time, she was showing what she knew, what she could do, all because a laptop had been placed before her. A door had been opened. In this instance, Stewart and the members of his team did all the hard work. My input was minimal, yet I feel that my little effort, just a few laptops freely given, provided some impetus to opening the world for this one child. What a small cost at my end for such a life-altering result halfway across the globe. For me personally, the impact that technology, and focused generosity, had on this one child makes my many years of work worthwhile. In an email, Stewart wrote "Thank you once again Vinesh. The laptops you donated will have far reaching benefits. Sometimes the impact of one's actions can be felt on the other side of the world". How many other children will access new learning, new opportunities, new pathways into their futures, thanks to those laptops, or those new computer studies teachers in Zambia? What impact will the inspired former outreach students continue to have in their own classrooms or in the professions they are now pursing, and what about the teachers those students upskilled in remote and rural schools? What doors will be opened by that once-barren library in Naidovi Primary, where this started for me way back in my own childhood education?

In every setting, in every institution, there are learners eager to learn and ready to have their world blown open with possibilities. For such learners, I will do this work over and over again – this is how a critical educator should function in the 21st century! We need real world strategies and the courage to step out of our comfort zones. By sharing and engaging with the disenfranchised, new knowledge is seeded both ways and, in the process, we all become more educated through our experiences. Consequently, this paves the way for a better world. As humans, we should leave some good footprints that future generations can not only follow but connect with and carve their own paths in unique and unseen ways.

References

ACARA. (2016). *National Report on Schooling in Australia 2013*. Retrieved from http://www.acara.edu.au/reporting/national-report-on-schooling-in-australia-2013/funding-australia-s-schools/an-overview-of-government-funding-of-schools

ACARA. (2017). *Key ideas*. Retrieved from https://www.australiancurriculum.edu.au/f-10-curriculum/technologies/key-ideas/

Albrechtsen, J. (2013, November 6). Handout mentality corrupts sense of responsibility. *The Australian*. Retrieved from https://gateway.library.qut.edu.au/login?url=https://search-proquest-com.ezp01.library.qut.edu.au/docview/1448398605?accountid=13380

AusAID. (2012). *Millennium development goals*. Retrieved from http://www.ausaid.gov.au/aidissues/mdg/Pages/home.aspx

Australian Government. (2014). *Australia's STEM workforce: A survey of employers*. Retrieved from http://www.chiefscientist.gov.au/wp-content/uploads/DAE_OCS-Australias-STEM-Workforce_FINAL-REPORT.pdf

Australian Government. (2016). *Papua New Guinea*. Retrieved from http://smartraveller.gov.au/Countries/pacific/Pages/papua_new_guinea.aspx

Australian National University. (n.d.). *CSR company in Fiji*. Retrieved from http://archives.anu.edu.au/exhibitions/csr-company-limited-fiji

Baker-Boosamra, M. (2006). From service to solidarity: Evaluation and recommendations for international service learning. *SPNA Review, 2*(1), Article 2. https://doi.org/10.1080/15236803.2006.12001452

Balogh, S. (2017). *Australian students among worst behaved in the developed world*. Retrieved from https://www.theaustralian.com.au/national-affairs/education/australian-students-among-worst-behaved-in-the-developed-world/news-story/73a493b8f105feb672482eb0d17b1b5f

Barr, K. J. (2012). *The socio-economic surveys of squatter and informal settlements*. Paper for Pacific Community Network housing project. Suva.

Batik & Bubbles. (2016). *A night at the museum – Pahang style*. Retrieved from http://batikandbubbles.com/blog/2016/10/9/an-inter-cultural-exchange

Berryman, S. E. (n.d.). *Designing effective learning environments: Cognitive apprenticeship models*. Retrieved from http://www.ilt.columbia.edu/ilt/papers/berry1.html

Bessell, S. (2009). Strengthening Fiji's education system: A view from key stakeholders. *Pacific Economic Bulletin, 24*(3), 58–70. Retrieved from https://openresearch-repository.anu.edu.au/handle/1885/18367

Birdwell, J. (2011). *This is the big society without borders-Service international* (Report). London: DEMOS. Retrieved from http://www.demos.co.uk/files/Service_International-web.pdf?1311850342

Bourdieu, P. (1973). *Cultural reproduction and social reproduction.* London: Tavistock.

Brodkin, E. (1972). The struggle for succession: Rebels and loyalists in the Indian mutiny of 1857. *Modern Asian Studies, 6*(3), 277–290. https://doi.org/10.1017/S0026749X00004133

Brown, L., Lei, J., & Strydom, M. (2017). Comparing international approaches to safeguarding children: Global lesson learning. *Child Abuse Review, 26*(4), 247–251. https://doi.org/10.1002/car.2486

Burbules, N. C., & Berk, R. (1999). Critical thinking and critical pedagogy: Relations, differences, and limits. In T. S. Popkewitz & L. Fender (Eds.), *Critical theories in education: Changing terrains of knowledge and politics* (pp. 45–65). New York, NY: Routledge.

Burnsed, K. W. (2014). *Beating the clock: Managing time God's way* (Information Bulletin. No 3, June 1971, p. 71). Bloomington, IN: WestBow Press. Retrieved from http://www.theaustralian.com.au/national-affairs/education/australian-students-among-worst-behaved-in-the-developed-world/news-story/73a493b8f105feb67248 2eb0d17b1b5f

Bybee, R. (2010). Advancing STEM education: A 2020 vision. *Technology and Engineering Teacher, 70*(1), 30–35. Retrieved from https://search.proquest.com/openview/75 bbe8b13bf3f54ebd755333ffd8621e/1?pq-origsite=gscholar&cbl=34845

Chandra, V. (2016). Understanding the role of a school principal in setting the context for technology integration: A TPACK perspective. In M. C. Herring, M. J. Koehler, & P. Mishra (Eds.), *Handbook of technological pedagogical content knowledge (TPACK) for educators* (2nd ed., pp. 235–247). New York: Routledge.

Chandra, V., & Briskey, J. (2012). ICT driven pedagogies and its impact on learning outcomes in high school mathematics. *International Journal of Pedagogies and Learning, 7*(1), 73–83. https://doi.org/10.5172/ijpl.2012.7.1.73

Chandra, V., Chandra, R., & Nutchey, D. (2014). Implementing ICT in schools in a developing country: A Fijian experience. In *ICTs and the millennium development goals: A United Nations perspective* (pp. 139–159). New York, NY: Springer US. https://doi.org/10.1007/978-1-4899-7439-6-9

Chandra, V., & Fisher, D. (2009). Students' perceptions of a blended web-based learning environment. *Learning Environments Research, 12*(1), 31–44. https://doi.org/10.1007/s10984-008-9051-6

Chandra, V., & Lloyd, M. M. (2008). The methodological nettle: ICT and student achievement. *British Journal of Educational Technology, 39*(6), 1087–1098. https://doi.org/10.1111/j.1467-8535.2007.00790.x

Chandra, V., & Mills, K. A. (2014). Transforming the core business of teaching and learning in classrooms through ICT. *Technology, Pedagogy and Education, 24*(3), 285–301. https://doi.org/10.1080/1475939X.2014.975737

Chandra, V., & Tangen, D. J. (2018). Demonstration of 21st century skills through an ICT teaching problem: Experiences of preservice teachers in a Fijian classroom. In

T. Gray, T. Downey, & M. Singh, (Eds.), *The Globalisation of higher education – Developing internationalised education in research and practice* (pp. 183–195). Sydney: Palgrave McMillan.

Chandra, V., & Watters, J. J. (2012). Re-thinking physics teaching with web-based learning. *Computers and Education, 58*(1), 631–640. https://doi.org/10.1016/j.compedu.2011.09.010

Clarke, E. (1987). *Assessment in Queensland secondary schools: Two decades of change 1964–1983*. North Quay: Department of Education, Queensland.

Collins, A., Brown, J. S., & Newman, S. E. (1989). Cognitive apprenticeship: Teaching the craft of reading, writing and mathematics. In L. B. Resnick (Ed.), *Knowing, learning and instruction: Essays in honor of Robert Glaser* (pp. 453–494). Hillsdale, NJ: Erlbaum.

Cook, L., & Friend, M. (1995). Co-teaching: Guidelines for creating effective practices. *Focus on exceptional children, 28*(3), 1–16. Retrieved from https://eric.ed.gov/?id=EJ545936

Dawson, V., & Venville, G. (2006). An overview and comparison of Australian and Territory K-10 science curriculum documents. *Teaching Science, 52*(2), 17–22. Retrieved from https://web.a.ebscohost.com/abstract?

De Bono, E. (1991). *Six thinking hats for schools: resource book for adult educators*. Logan, LA: Perfection learning.

De Bono, E. (1999). *Six thinking hats*. New York, NY: Little Brown and Co.

Delgado, A. J., Wardlow, L., McKnight, K., & O'Malley, K. (2015). Educational technology: A review of the integration, resources, and effectiveness of technology in K-12 classrooms. *Journal of Information Technology Education: Research, 14*, 397–416. https://doi.org/10.28945/2298

Deshpande, M. S. (2010). *History of the Indian caste system and its impact on India today*. Retrieved from http://digitalcommons.calpoly.edu/cgi/viewcontent.cgi?article=1043&context=socssp

Donnelly, K. (2007). Australia's adoption of outcomes based education: A critique. *Issues in Educational Research, 17*(2), 183. Retrieved from https://search.informit.com.au/documentSummary;dn=200801716;res=IELAPA;type=pdf

Dornan, M., & Pryke, J. (2017). Foreign aid to the Pacific: Trends and developments in the twenty-first century. Asia & the *Pacific Policy Studies, 4*(3), 386–404. https://doi.org/10.1002/app5.185

Duncan-Andrade, J. M. R., & Morrell, E. (2008). *The art of critical pedagogy: Possibilities for moving from theory to practice in urban schools* (Vol. 285). New York, NY: Peter Lang.

Eisenchlas, S. A., & Trevaskes, S. (2007). Developing intercultural communication skills through intergroup interaction. *Intercultural Education, 18*(5), 413–425. https://doi.org/10.1080/14675980701685271

Engineers Without Borders. (2011). *Water filtration*. Retrieved from https://www.ewb.org.au/resources/download/1905P2011-08-02_00:11:44

Fantz, T. D., De Miranda, M. A., & Siller, T. J. (2011). Knowing what engineering and technology teachers need to know: An analysis of pre-service teachers engineering design problems. *International Journal of Technology and Design Education, 21*(3), 307–320. https://doi.org/10.1007/s10798-010-9121-9

Fiji Bureau of Statistics. (2015). *2013–14 Household income and expenditure survey.* Retrieved from 2013-14_Household_Income_and_Expenditure_Survey.pdf

Fiji Times. (1874). *Past papers.* Retrieved from https://paperspast.natlib.govt.nz/newspapers/EP18741102.2.12

Freire, P. (1983). The importance of the act of reading. *Journal of Education, 165*(1), 5–11. https://doi.org/10.1177/002205748316500103

Freire, P. (2000). *Pedagogy of the oppressed* (30th anniversary ed.). New York, NY: Continuum.

Freire, P. (2001). *Pedagogy of freedom: Ethics, democracy, and civic courage.* Lanham, MD: Rowman & Littlefield.

Freire, P., & Macedo, D. (2005). *Literacy: Reading the word and the world.* South Hadley, MA: Bergin & Garvey Publishers.

Gardner, H. (1985). *Frames of mind: The theory of multiple intelligences.* New York, NY: Basic books.

Gillespie, D. (2014). *Free schools: How to get a great education for your kids without spending a fortune.* Sydney: MacMillan.

Gillion, K. L. (1958). *A history of Indian immigration and settlement in Fiji.* Retrieved from https://openresearch-repository.anu.edu.au/handle/1885/16380

Gillion, K. L. (1962). *Fiji's Indian migrants: a history to the end of indenture in 1920.* Melbourne: Oxford University Press.

Giroux, H. A. (1988). *Teachers as intellectuals: Toward a critical pedagogy of learning.* Granby, MA: Bergin & Garvey.

Giroux, H. A. (1992). *Border crossings.* New York, NY: Routledge.

Giroux, H. A. (2001). *Theory and resistance in education: Towards a pedagogy for the opposition.* Thousand Oaks, CA: Greenwood Publishing Group.

Giroux, H. A. (2010). Rethinking education as the practice of freedom: Paulo Freire and the promise of critical pedagogy. *Policy Futures in Education, 8*(6), 715–721. https://doi.org/10.2304/pfie.2010.8.6.715

Giroux, H. A. (2011). *On critical pedagogy* (1st ed.). New York, NY: Bloomsbury Publishing.

Giroux, H. A., & Giroux, S. (2004). *Take back higher education: Race, youth, and the crisis of democracy in the Post-Civil Rights Era.* New York, NY: Palgrave Macmillan.

Global Issues. (2013). *Poverty facts and stats.* Retrieved from http://www.globalissues.org/article/26/poverty-facts-and-stats

Goodhart, D. (2017). *The road to somewhere: The populist revolt and the future of politics.* London: Hurst Publishers.

Gounder, F. (2011). *Restorying indenture: The first Fiji Hindi speakers narrate Girmit.* Retrieved from http://mro.massey.ac.nz/handle/10179/2659

Government of Fiji. (1926). *Report of the education commission.* Suva, Fiji: Government Printer.

Hampe, N. (2013). *Reflective practice and writing: A guide to getting started.* Retrieved from http://www.alia.org.au/sites/default/files/documents/ Reflective.Practice.Writing.Guide20130409JB.pdf

Hattie, J. (2008). *Visible learning: A synthesis of meta-analyses relating to achievement.* New York, NY: Routledge.

Hayasaka, E. (2005). *Donating technology or trash?* Retrieved from https://www.bu.edu/sjmag/scimag2005/opinion/donatingcomputers.htm

Hays, J. (2008). *Rubber in Malaysia.* Retrieved from http://factsanddetails.com/ southeast-asia/Malaysia/sub5_4e/entry-3702.html

Hew, K. F., & Brush, T. (2007). Integrating technology into K-12 teaching and learning: Current knowledge gaps and recommendations for future research. *Educational Technology Research and Development, 55*(3), 223–252. https://doi.org/10.1007/ s11423-006-9022-5

Hill, I. (2012). Evolution of education for international mindedness. *Journal of Research in International Education, 11*(3), 245–261. https://doi.org/10.1177/1475240912461990

Hite, M. T. (2006). *Traditional book donation to Sub-Saharan Africa: An inquiry into policy, practice and appropriate information provision.* Retrieved from https://cdr.lib.unc.edu/indexablecontent/uuid:b0733540-c360-4eb2-965a-0bb41cef58c8

Hogan, J., & Down, B. (2015). A STEAM School using the Big Picture Education (BPE) design for learning and school – What an innovative STEM Education might look like. *International Journal of Innovation in Science and Mathematics Education, 23*(3), 47–60. Retrieved from https://openjournals.library.sydney.edu.au/index.php/ CAL/article/viewFile/10333/10262

Hollows, D. (2010). *Evaluating ICT for education in Africa.* Retrieved from http://pure.rhul.ac.uk/portal/files/1773319/DavidHollowThesisFinalCopy.pdf

Holmes, O. (2015). *Forest fires in Indonesia choke much of South-East Asia.* Retrieved from https://www.theguardian.com/environment/2015/oct/05/forest-fires-in-indonesia-choke-much-of-south-east-asia

Hwa, Y. Y. (2011). *Lessons from English-Medium Science and Mathematics Education in Malaysia (PPSMI)* (Doctoral dissertation). Williams College, Williamstown, MA.

International Labour Organisation. (2016). *Centralizing decent work in the response to tropical Cyclone Winston.* Retrieved from http://www.ilo.org/wcmsp5/groups/ public/---asia/---ro-bangkok/---ilo-suva/documents/publication/wcms_465248.pdf

Kincheloe, J. L. (2008). *Critical pedagogy primer.* New York, NY: Peter Lang.

King, J. T. (2004). Service-learning as a site for critical pedagogy: A case for collaboration,caring, and defamiliarisation across borders. *Journal of Experiential Education, 26*(3), 121–137. https://doi.org/10.1177/105382590402600304

Kivunja, C. (2015). Exploring the pedagogical meaning and implications of the 4Cs "super skills" for the 21st century through Bruner's 5E lenses of knowledge construction to improve pedagogies of the new learning paradigm. *Creative Education, 6*(2), 224–239. https://doi.org/10.4236/ce.2015.62021

Koehler, M (2012). *TPACK explained*. Retrieved from http://matt-koehler.com/tpack2/tpack-explained/

Kolb, D. (1984). *Experiential learning as the science of learning and development*. Englewood Cliffs, NJ: Prentice-Hall.

Krathwohl, D. R. (2002). A revision of Bloom's taxonomy: An overview. *Theory into practice, 41*(4), 212–218. https://doi.org/10.1207/s15430421tip4104_2

Kumar, K. K. (2017). Reading for pleasure and academic success: A preliminary note. *Pacific Journal of Education, 1*(1), 113–124.

Lal, B. V. (1992). *Broken waves: A history of the Fiji Islands in the twentieth century* (Vol. 11). Honolulu, HI: University of Hawaii Press.

Lal, B. V. (1998). *Crossing the Kala Pani: a documentary history of Indian indenture in Fiji*. Suva: Fiji Museum.

Lal, B. V. (2000). *Chalo Jahaji: On a journey through indenture in Fiji*. Canberra: ANU E Press.

Lingam, G. I., & Lingam, N. (2013). Making learning and teaching a richer experience: A challenge for rural Fijian primary schools. *Educational Research and Reviews, 8*(21), 2160. Retrieved from http://citeseerx.ist.psu.edu/viewdoc/download?doi=10.1.1.679.8681&rep=rep1&type=pdf

Lough, B. J. (2009). Principles of effective practice in international social work field placements. *Journal of Social Work Education, 45*(3), 467–480. https://doi.org/10.5175/JSWE.2009.200800083

Maida, C. A. (2011). Project-based learning: A critical pedagogy for the twenty-first century. *Policy Futures in Education, 9*(6), 759–768. https://doi.org/10.2304/pfie.2011.9.6.759

Marginson, S., Tytler, R., Freeman, B., & Roberts, K. (2013). *STEM: Country comparisons: International comparisons of Science, Technology, Engineering and Mathematics (STEM) education*. Retrieved from https://dro.deakin.edu.au/eserv/DU:30059041/tytler-stemcountry-2013.pdf

Marshall, P. M. (2017). *British India and the 'Great Rebellion'*. Retrieved from http://www.bbc.co.uk/history/british/victorians/indian_rebellion_01.shtml

Matthews, A. (2017). *In 2017, corporal punishment still legal in QLD non-government schools*. Retrieved from http://www.abc.net.au/triplej/programs/hack/corporal-punishment-qld/8310160

Matthey, J. (2015). *Calls to scrap live broadcasts of State of Origin matches in Papua New Guinea*. Retrieved from http://www.news.com.au/sport/sports-life/calls-to-scrap-live-broadcasts-of-state-of-origin-matches-in-papua-new-guinea/news-story/f959c952ed67283278c122d9f19da6c8

McGeough, P. (2017). *On United Nations' drift, Antonio Guterres beats Donald Trump to the punch*. Retrieved from https://www.smh.com.au/world/on-united-nations-drift-antnio-guterres-beats-donald-trump-to-the-punch-20170919-gyk4ds.html

McLean, M. (2006). *Pedagogy and the University: Critical Theory and Practice*. London: Continuum.

McNamara, K. E. (2013). A state of emergency: How local businesses experienced the 2012 flood in Fiji. *Australian Journal of Emergency Management, 28*(3), 17–23. Retrieved from https://search.informit.com.au/documentSummary;dn=512148404017761;res=IELAPA

Ministry of Education, National Heritage, Culture and Arts. (2012). *Annual report 2012*. Retrieved from http://www.education.gov.fj/images/AnnualReports/Annual%20Report%202012.pdf

Ministry of Education, National Heritage, Culture and Arts. (2013). *Annual report 2013*. Retrieved from http://www.education.gov.fj/images/images/AnnualReports/Annual%20Report_2013.pdf

Ministry of Education, National Heritage, Culture and Arts. (2015). *Annual report 2015*. Retrieved from http://www.education.gov.fj/images/2015_Ministry_of_Education_Annual_Report.pdf

Mishra, P., & Koehler, M. (2006). Technological pedagogical content knowledge: A framework for teacher knowledge. *Teachers College Records, 108*(6), 1017–1054. https://doi.org/10.1111/j.1467-9620.2006.00684.x

Mohan, P. P., Lingam, G. I., & Chand, D. D. (2017). Teachers' perceptions of the impact of professional development on learning and teaching in a developing nation. *Australian Journal of Teacher Education, 42*(11), 2. https://doi.org/10.14221/ajte.2017v42n11.2

Moyo, D. (2009). *Dead aid: Why aid is not working and how there is a better way for Africa* (1st American ed.). New York, NY: Farrar, Straus and Giroux.

Naidu, V., & Reddy, M. (2002, June). *ALTA and expiring land leases: Fijian farmers' perceptions of their future*. A Ford Foundation Funded Project Report. University of the South Pacific (USP) and Pacific Migration Research Network (PacMRN).

Narayan, N. A. (2014). The reforms to improve the internal assessment system: Teachers' perceptions. *International Journal of Education and Research, 2*(10), 105–112. Retrieved from https://www.researchgate.net/profile/Nilesh_Narayan/publication/317905080_The_reforms_to_improve_the_internal_assessment_system_Teachers%27_perceptions/links/59516266of7e9b329234cb8f/The-reforms-to-improve-the-internal-assessment-system-Teachers-perceptions.pdf

National Archives. (n.d.). *Britain and the slave trade*. Retrieved from http://www.nationalarchives.gov.uk/slavery/pdf/britain-and-the-trade.pdf

Nor, N. M., Leong, K. E., & Salleh, U. K. M. (2017). Changes in the Malaysian School Curriculum from the pre-independence years until the New Millennium. In M. Samuel, M. Tee, & L. Symaco (Eds.), *Education in Malaysia* (pp. 101–118). Singapore: Springer.

OECD. (2014). *Teachers love their job but feel undervalued, unsupported and unrecognised*. Retrieved from http://www.oecd.org/education/teachers-love-their-job-but-feel-undervalued-unsupported-and-unrecognised.htm

Olken, B. A., & Pande, R. (2012). Corruption in developing countries. *Annual Review of Economics, 4*(1), 479–509. https://doi.org/10.1146/annurev-economics-080511-110917

One Nation. (2014). *Cut foreign aid*. Retrieved from http://www.onenation.com.au/current_affairs/cut-foreign-aid

Oxfam. (2017). *You and Oxfam, tackling poverty together*. Retrieved from https://www.oxfam.org.au/what-we-do/aid-and-development/campaign-for-australian-aid/australias-aid-effort/

Pennington, B., Ireland, N., & Narsey, W. (2010). *Fiji education sector program*. AidWorks Number: INF528, Independent Completion Report, 4.

Provost, C. (2013). *Researchers find one-fifth of foreign aid never leaves donor countries*. Retrieved from https://www.theguardian.com/global-development/2013/sep/24/foreign-aid-never-reaches-intended-recipients

Puentedura, R. R. (2012). *The SAMR model: Background and exemplars*. Retrieved from http://www.hippasus.com/rrpweblog/archives/2012/08/23/SAMR_BackgroundExemplars.pdf

QUT. (2017). *Real world learning 2020 vision*. Retrieved from https://www.qut.edu.au/about/strategic-ambitions/real-world-learning-2020-vision

RACHEL PI. (2014). Retrieved from http://worldpossible.org/pi/

Republic of Fiji. (n.d.). *Constitution of the Republic of Fiji*. Retrieved from http://www.paclii.org/fj/Fiji-Constitution-English-2013.pdf

Ricci, C. (2015). *More than 100 million children worldwide do not attend school. Why?* Retrieved from https://www.theage.com.au/education/more-than-100-million-children-worldwide-do-not-attend-school-why-20150212-13cf1q.html

Richardson, J. T., Best, J., & Bromley, D. G. (Eds.). (1991). *The satanism scare*. London: Routledge.

Roberts, D. (2017). *Sweet Brexit: What sugar tells us about Britain's future outside the EU*. Retrieved from https://www.theguardian.com/business/2017/mar/27/brexit-sugar-beet-cane-tate-lyle-british-sugar

Rogers, E. M. (2003). *Diffusion of innovations* (5th ed.). New York, NY: Free Press.

Russell, M. A. (1976). Low-tar medium-nicotine cigarettes: A new approach to safer smoking. *British Medical Journal, 1*(6023), 1430–1433. https://doi.org/10.1136/bmj.1.6023.1430

Sadler, D. R. (1989). Formative assessment and the design of instructional systems. *Instructional science, 18*(2), 119–144. https://doi.org/10.1007/BF00117714

Sahib, S. A. (1963). *Educational reorganisation in the colony of Fiji*. Retrieved from http://shodhganga.inflibnet.ac.in//handle/10603/58925

Samuel, M., Tee, M. Y., & Symaco, L. P. (2017). The educational landscape of Malaysia. In M. Samuel, M. Tee, & L. Symaco (Eds.), *Education in Malaysia. Education in the Asia-Pacific Region: Issues, concerns and prospects* (pp. 1–16). Singapore: Springer.

Sanadhya, T. (1914/1991). *My 21 years in the Fiji Islands* (J. D. Kelly & U. K. Singh, Trans.). Suva, Fiji: Fiji Museum. (Original work published in 1914)

Sharma, S. K. (2017). *Danger of dredging – What are our options?* Retrieved from http://www.fijitimes.com/story.aspx?id=384928

Snow, D. (2014). *The birth of Empire: The East India company*. Retrieved from https://www.bbc.co.uk/programmes/b042w0xt

Spiegler, T., & Bednarek, A. (2013). First-generation students: What we ask, what we know and what it means: An international review of the state of research. *International Studies in Sociology of Education, 23*(4), 318–337. https://doi.org/10.1080/0962 0214.2013.815441

Tavola, H. G. (1990). *Secondary education in Fiji: An investigation into school effectiveness in a changing society*. Retrieved from http://etheses.lse.ac.uk/1199/

Tee, M. Y., & Samuel, M. (2017). Teachers and teaching in Malaysia. In M. Samuel, M. Tee, & L. Symaco (Eds.), *Education in Malaysia. Education in the Asia-Pacific Region: Issues, concerns and prospects.* Singapore: Springer.

The SEE Project (2014). *Stewart's experiences in Bhutan*. Retrieved from https://theseeproject.org/2014/11/19/stewarts-experiences-in-bhutan/

The SEE Project. (2015). *Dr Siti's reflections on making the inaugural collaboration between QUT and UPM a reality*. Retrieved from https://theseeproject.org/2015/ 10/21/dr-sitis-reflections-on-making-the-inaugural-collaboration-between-qut-and-upm-a-real-possibility/

Tharoor, S. (2017). *Inglorious Empire: what the British did to India*. London: Hurst. Retrieved from http://etheses.lse.ac.uk/1199/

The White House. (2015). *Remarks by the president at the GLACIER Conference*. Anchorage, AK. Retrieved from https://obamawhitehouse.archives.gov/the-press-office/2015/09/01/remarks-president-glacier-conference-anchorage-ak

Thomas, J. W. (2000). *A review of research on project-based learning*. Retrieved from http://www.bie.org/images/uploads/general/9d06758fd346969cb63653d00dca 55c0.pdf

Thompson, D., & Arora, T. (1991). Why do children bully? An evaluation of the long-term effectiveness of a whole-school policy to minimize bullying. *Pastoral Care in Education, 9*(4), 8–12. https://doi.org/10.1080/02643949109470762

Thomson, S., De Bortoli, L., & Underwood, C. (2017). *PISA 2015: Reporting Australia's results*. Retrieved from https://research.acer.edu.au/cgi/viewcontent.cgi?referer=https://scholar.google.com.au/&httpsredir=1&article=1023&context=ozpisa

Trilokekar, R., & Kukar, P. (2011). Disorienting experiences during study abroad: Reflections of pre-service teacher candidates. *Teaching and Teacher Education, 27*(7), 1141–1150. https://doi.org/10.1016/j.tate.2011.06.002

UN. (n.d.). *Sustainable development goals*. Retrieved from https://www.un.org/sustainabledevelopment/sustainable-development-goals/

UNESCO. (2011). Competency framework for teachers. Version 2.0. *United Nations Educational, Scientific and Cultural Organization*.

UNESCO. (2012). *UNESCO strategy on teacher (2012–2015)*. Retrieved from http://unesdoc.unesco.org/images/0021/002177/217775E.pdf

UNESCO. (2014). *Zambian teachers trained on using new technology*. Retrieved from https://en.unesco.org/news/zambian-teachers-trained-using-new-technology-o

Underwood, J., & Dillon, G. (2011). Chasing dreams and recognising realities: Teachers' responses to ICT. *Technology, Pedagogy and Education, 20*(3), 317–330. https://doi.org/10.1080/1475939X.2011.610932

UNDP. (2016). *Human development reports*. Retrieved from http://hdr.undp.org/en/content/human-development-index-hdi

Vasek, L. (2012). *Labor a major recipient of own foreign aid, says Julie Bishop*. Retrieved from http://www.theaustralian.com.au/national-affairs/foreign-affairs/carrs-aid-shift-a-cut-bishop/newsstory/cb772648d1fd1629cce39913e1fd1a96?sv=fb47dbc75e491b07395f6bf7e6738a67

Vygotsky, L. S. (1978). *Mind in society: The development of higher psychological processes*. Cambridge, MA: Harvard University Press.

Wall, S. (2008). Easier said than done: Writing an autoethnography. *International Journal of Qualitative Methods, 7*(1), 38–53. https://doi.org/10.1177/160940690800700103

Werner, L., Denner, J., & Campe, S. (2014). Children programming games: A strategy for measuring computational learning. *ACM Transactions on Computing Education (TOCE), 14*(4), 24. https://doi.org/10.1145/2677091

Wessel, N. (2007). Integrating service learning into the study abroad program: US sociology students in Mexico. *Journal of Studies in International Education, 11*(1), 73–89. https://doi.org/10.1177/1028315305283306

Western Australian Department of Education Services. (2001). *Investing in government schools: Putting children first*. Perth: Department of Education Services. Western Australia.

White, C. M. (2001). Affirmative action and education in Fiji: Legitimation, contestation, and colonial discourse. *Harvard Educational Review, 71*(2), 240–268. https://doi.org/10.17763/haer.71.2.p1057320407582to

World Bank. (2017). *Access to electricity.* Retrieved from https://data.worldbank.org/
indicator/EG.ELC.ACCS.RU.ZS?locations=F

Worthington, B. (2018). *Live exports: Maritime officials block shipment of 65,000 sheep
to the Middle East.* Retrieved from http://www.abc.net.au/news/2018-04-08/
maritime-officials-block-live-export-65000-sheep-to-middle-east/9631602

Zell, H. M., & Thierry, R. (2015). Book donation programmes for Africa: Time for a
reappraisal? Two perspectives. *African Research & Documentation. Journal of
SCOLMA (the UK Libraries and Archives Group on Africa), 127,* 3–137. Retrieved from
https://s3.amazonaws.com/academia.edu.documents/49345348/Book_donation_
programmes_for_Africa__part_1__final

Index

Printed in the United States
By Bookmasters